Lincoln in His Own Time

WRITERS IN THEIR OWN TIME

Joel Myerson, *series editor*

LINCOLN

in His Own Time

A Biographical
Chronicle of His Life,
Drawn from Recollections,
Interviews, and
Memoirs by Family,
Friends, and
Associates

EDITED BY

Harold K. Bush, Jr.

University of Iowa Press,
Iowa City

University of Iowa Press, Iowa City 52242
Copyright © 2011 by the University of Iowa Press
www.uiowapress.org
Printed in the United States of America

The University of Iowa Press is a member of Green Press Initiative
and is committed to preserving natural resources.

Printed on acid-free paper

Library of Congress Cataloging-in-Publication Data
Lincoln in his own time: a biographical chronicle of his life,
drawn from recollections, interviews, and memoirs by family,
friends, and associates / edited by Harold K. Bush, Jr.
    p.   cm. — (Writers in their own time)
Includes bibliographical references and index.
ISBN-13: 978-1-60938-044-1 (pbk.)
ISBN-10: 1-60938-044-4 (pbk.)
ISBN-13: 978-1-60938-045-8 (e-book)
ISBN-10: 1-60938-045-2 (e-book)
1. Lincoln, Abraham, 1809–1865.
2. Lincoln, Abraham, 1809–1865 — Friends and associates.
3. Lincoln, Abraham, 1809–1865 — Family.
4. Presidents — United States — Biography.
I. Bush, Harold K. (Harold Karl), 1956–
E457.2. L8325 2011
973.7092 — dc22   2011013908

Contents

Contents

Introduction: Remembering Lincoln

IN THE MIDSUMMER of 2004, on the very weekend that I was strolling around Washington, D.C., among the many monuments and historic sites that direct a citizen's attention to the meaning of our nation, I marveled at the newly opened World War II Memorial, smack dab in the center of the Mall. It was hot and sunny, and yet tens of thousands of tourists and I were struck by the sheer scale of the memorial and by our mutual bonds with the dead. Less than a mile away, in a sense witnessing the throngs of tourists, was the most famous monument in America, the Lincoln Memorial. Etched into its marble walls are some of Lincoln's most enduring words: "It is for us the living, rather, to be dedicated here to the unfinished work which they who fought here have thus far so nobly advanced. It is rather for us to be here dedicated to the great task remaining before us . . . that from these honored dead we take increased devotion to that cause for which they gave the last full measure of devotion." The solemn tone of that Independence Day weekend compared well with an anecdote told by John Steinbeck about his own visit to the Lincoln Memorial with his son. After they both stood for some time in the shadow of the great president, Steinbeck's son blurted out in awe, "Oh! Lord! We had better be great."[1]

"That cause," Lincoln called it—perhaps a cause that seemed to most of his listeners, in 1863, rather obvious, a commonplace. Indeed, Lincoln's way with words has shaped our national idea of ourselves more than those of any other American before or since. As Garry Wills has argued, Lincoln wrought an American mythical ideology that remains resonant for many Americans today. Wills memorably dubbed Lincoln a "great artist of America's Romantic period" who accomplished, virtually singlehandedly, the "recontracting of our society on the basis of the Declaration as our fundamental charter."[2] A century and a half later, one must wonder how common such a view of America has remained; and yet, there seems little doubt that among all Americans from his time onward, Abraham Lincoln is the

Fletcher C. Ransom, "Lincoln, the Student," 1935. Courtesy of the Abraham Lincoln Presidential Library and Museum.

figure who is most associated with the idea of an American creed, a "cause" that is somehow both knowable and doable.

Later that same afternoon, I saw on the newsstand the latest issue of *U.S. News*: an American flag at its center, with the words "Special Issue: Defining America: Why the U.S. Is Unique" (June 28–July 5, 2004). It was further evidence of the Lincoln legacy: the great Emancipator who attempted to craft a fresh, new definition of America in those brilliant engraved sentences that have captivated us for so long. The issue of *U.S. News* redounded with the phrases of American mythos: "a national legacy," "the American Dream," "the meaning and purpose of our nation." Delicious sounding words, to be sure. And presumably, those crowds in Washington come here in part because the National Mall is symbolic of certain massive abstractions, the monuments and museums being mystic containers of all the various values and beliefs to which every American supposedly subscribes.

The concept of an American mission and identity goes back way before Lincoln was born in 1809, of course—roughly 200 years before his birth,

Abraham Lincoln while a traveling lawyer, taken in Danville, Illinois, 1857. Library of Congress.

Leopold Grozelier, "Hon. Abraham Lincoln, Republican Candidate for the Presidency," 1860. Library of Congress.

in fact. Even prior to there being an "America," people believed that something special was in the offing for the "virgin" landmass that came to be denoted simply as America—a designation that has become somewhat controversial. Poets throughout American history have sung the praises of that American "something," often with bravado and sometimes with obsession. To whatever extent, the American idea sprang from this powerful sensibility of an inherent American drivenness, or "entelechy" as Myra Jehlen once memorably called it—a sensibility that is largely castigated these days as "American exceptionalism" or as a remnant of an American "empire" of conquest and pillage.[3] But the American tradition of our nation as having a special mission has been highlighted by the likes of Tom Paine, John Adams, and Thomas Jefferson in the eighteenth century; Ralph Waldo Emerson, Walt Whitman, and Robert Ingersoll in the nineteenth century; John F. Kennedy, Martin Luther King Jr. and Ronald Reagan in the twentieth; and now perhaps best reincarnated in Barack Obama, self-aware acolyte of this grand tradition, in the twenty-first. Yet none of these spokespersons has surpassed the magic of the master American poet him-

Samuel G. Alshuler, "Abraham Lincoln, President-elect," 1860. Library of Congress.

self, Abraham Lincoln, in illuminating the nature of America's sublime object of desire, a creed he considered to be embodied especially in the Declaration of Independence: "I have often inquired of myself, what great principle or idea it was that kept this confederacy so long together. It was . . . something in that Declaration giving liberty, not alone to the people of this country, but hope to the world for all future times."[4]

The American hope, for Lincoln, is somehow subordinate to a greater hope, a cosmic hope in which the American version is perhaps the great exemplar in human society. And this cosmic hope transcends language's ability to contain it. Even for Lincoln, the object of American hope is, and to some extent must remain, by definition, impossible: impossible to name, impossible to define, and impossible to embody completely. It's not implausible to claim that it is the same mysterious object of hope that *U.S. News* was trumpeting to the world on its cover that week before Independence Day, 2004: the meaning and *telos* of America.

This basic American creed, containing a set of common ideas, values, and beliefs, constitutes what might be called the metaphysics of America, the civil religion by which we attempt to order our communal enterprise. Over this domain of belief, Lincoln has presided for a very long time.

"A Job for the New Cabinet Maker," *Frank Leslie's Illustrated Newspaper*, February 2, 1861. Collection of Harold K. Bush, Jr.

Drawing upon G. K. Chesterton's famous quote, we might even suggest that America remains even at this late date a "nation with the soul of a church"—a phrase that became the title of Sidney Mead's influential volume detailing what he called the religion of the republic.[5] Catherine Albanese builds on this idea, asserting that "the American Revolution was *in itself* a religious experience, a hierophany collectively manifested and received, which provided the fundamental basis for American civil religion as we know it."[6]

The religious character of Abraham Lincoln is most visibly expressed in the temple-like compound constructed on the Mall in remembrance of him and in the sacred treatment of his most famous words, which are etched into the stone of the shrine itself.[7] But significantly, recognition of his godlike attributes and public veneration for his sacred qualities were not the commonplace experiences of Lincoln's lifetime; in fact, a fascinating part of the story is the extent to which he was actively disliked and even vilified by many Americans for the vast majority of his national career. Such extreme satire and ridicule of the "ape-like" president are seen in some of the cartoons reprinted in this introduction, for example. This hostility has long historical roots, and even today a minor subgroup of commentators continues to malign Lincoln as an instigator of racist policies and war crimes. What's worse—and perhaps predictably—many of these writers have libertarian and even latent pro-Confederacy tendencies that motivate their rancorous critiques.[8] And sometimes Lincoln's legacy has been manipulated by Confederate sympathizers trying to make Lincoln out to be one of their kind. As John Hope Franklin notes, the racist preacher Thomas Dixon tried to sketch Lincoln "as a Southerner fully in sympathy with the Lost Cause. . . . For Dixon, it was not Lincoln's humanitarianism or humility or belief in democracy that elevated him to greatness. Rather . . . it was the racism [he and others] thought they saw in Lincoln that ennobled him and made him a Southerner."[9]

Thus, it should be immediately stated, there never really has been unanimous consent about the meaning of Lincoln and his legacy, and there is still no national consensus about this most mysterious and elusive Proto-American chieftain. Despite widespread adulation, harsh depictions must still be factored into our accounts of Lincoln. And yet in most of the selections in this book, one senses (though in much more restrained terms than the effusive poet) the devotion expressed in its rawest form by the

"Jeff Davis's November Nightmare," *Frank Leslie's Illustrated Newspaper*, December 3, 1864. Collection of Harold K. Bush, Jr.

starstruck Walt Whitman, circa October 1863: "Saw Mr. Lincoln standing, talking with a gentleman, apparently a dear friend. His face & manner have an expression & are inexpressibly sweet—one hand on his friend's shoulder, the other holds his hand. I love the President personally."[10]

The tale of Lincoln's early life and political emergence is scripted better than any Hollywood blockbuster. Something of his backwoods, out-of-nowhere legend is caught in the opening lines of his good friend Joshua Speed's *Reminiscences of Abraham Lincoln* (1884)[†]: "In the spring of 1836 I first saw Abraham Lincoln. He had been a laborer, a flatboatman, a deputy surveyor, and for one term a member of the legislature. I heard him spoken of by those who knew him as a wonderful character. They boasted that he could outwrestle any man in the county, and that he could beat any lawyer in Springfield speaking." Here was a man of the regular folks, who could wrestle with flesh and with words and wasn't afraid of rolling up his sleeves and getting down to serious work. Meanwhile he was an avid reader and a precocious thinker, with a nearly miraculous gift for language the most surprising detail of all, given his prairie circumstances.[11] These elements all became standard fare in Lincoln reminiscence and art, especially his noted proficiency with an axe and as a raftsman on the mighty rivers of the American hinterlands.

Lincoln's entry into national politics, with his election to the U.S. Congress in 1846, coincided with what David M. Potter famously dubbed "the impending crisis" of America: beginning roughly in 1848, escalating through the 1850s, and culminating with the election of Lincoln as president of a Union on the verge of rapidly falling apart.[12] Into this national crisis stepped the backwoodsman from the Middle West, swinging his broad axe and speaking in a Bible- and Shakespeare-studded Hoosier vernacular. And after the choppiest waters of the War had been navigated, despite unimaginable terror and violence, the Union was saved—at the cost, sadly, of the chieftain's own life it seemed. A heavy price it was, but the mythic elements suggest a three-hanky film that has yet to be made (although Steven Spielberg is now developing a biopic of the martyred president based on a Tony Kushner screenplay, and Robert Redford's film *The Conspirator*, based on the assassination and subsequent conspiracy, was released in the spring of 2011.

The president-elect's official entry into national leadership has attained a legendary status. On February 11, 1861, Abraham Lincoln boarded a train from his home of many years, Springfield, Illinois, to what would become his new home, the White House in Washington, D.C. Lincoln's inauguration as the sixteenth president would take place less than a month later, on March 4. By this time, however, the state of the Union had declined significantly since Lincoln's election in November 1860. Already a total of seven states had declared their intention to leave the Union, beginning with South Carolina's radical "ordinance" dissolving its union with the other states, adopted on December 20, 1860. South Carolina was followed, in rapid order, by the other prominent Deep South states, all of which proceeded

A. I. Keller, "Lincoln Delivering the Gettysburg Address," *Harper's Weekly* (February 10, 1900). Courtesy of the Abraham Lincoln Presidential Library and Museum.

to seize federal properties and assets within their state borders, including forts, arsenals, mints, post offices, customhouses, and port facilities.[13]

Although it is true that Lincoln had "arrived" on the national scene a number of years earlier, first as a one-term U.S. congressman from his home district in Illinois but then most notably during his unsuccessful senatorial campaign of 1858 against Stephen Douglas, highlighted by the legendary debates, it is clear that he felt as though he were an instrument on a special mission as he set out for the capital that cold winter day. But the mission was one that was also to be undertaken by the people: "It is with you, the people, to advance the great cause of the Union and the constitution, and not with any one man."[14] The journey to Washington was planned as an important rhetorical and symbolic event. It was Lincoln's attempt to instill dedication and commitment to the cause of the Union. According to Stephen Oates, the trip was "all Seward's idea," the purpose being to "expose [Lincoln] to the public and to rally Union morale."[15]

Lincoln's uncanny rhetorical brilliance is noticeable in many of his sundry letters and speeches and other writings. But by almost all accounts, this reputation is based primarily upon a very small number of documents: the "House Divided" speech (1858), the Cooper Union Address (1860), the two inaugural addresses (1861, 1865), and the Gettysburg Address (1863), generally considered to be his masterpiece (although recently some critics have argued that the Second Inaugural in fact outshines the address at Gettysburg[16]). The scholarship and analysis on Lincoln's words are of course extensive, but surely one of the most important aspects of his legacy was his great gift as a writer of some of the great American words, a gift that contemporaries often noted. Noah Brooks, for example, waxes eloquent over Lincoln's power and illustrates this power in another of his great sentences[†]: "In some of the loftier flights of his eloquence may be found traces of a strong poetic fancy—an imagination fired by love of country, and inspired by the contemplation of the stirring events that have marked its history. No more striking example of this can be found anywhere than in the memorable words which closed his First Inaugural Address: 'The mystic chords of memory, stretching from every battle-field and patriot grave to every living heart and hearth-stone, all over this broad land, will yet swell the chorus of the Union, when again touched, as surely they will be, by the better angels of our nature.'" Given this power, it is not surprising that some of Lincoln's utterances have been called "the words that remade America," and it almost goes without saying that he is "the best of all presidential speechwriters."[17] As one veteran Lincoln scholar unapologetically claims in a recent volume, the Gettysburg Address is nothing less than a sort of gospel, one suggesting "spiritual rebirth": "When Lincoln's words are best understood, they bring that potential to Americans, indeed to people everywhere."[18] Powerful words, indeed.

But it may be that it was his saintly departure, and not his arrival, that has loomed most significant with regard to our cultural memory—the fact that he was murdered on Good Friday of 1865, as the war drew to its close. The traumatic effect was heightened by the retrospective claims that Lincoln's death was somehow "necessary": fated by God, a circumstance of American destiny. This determinist view was bolstered by Lincoln's premonitions of his untimely demise. A few months before the war's conclusion, he told his friend Owen Lovejoy that he might die even before peace

Fletcher C. Ransom, "Lincoln at Gettysburg," lithograph of the painting, circa 1920. Courtesy of the Abraham Lincoln Presidential Library and Museum.

came: "This war is eating my life out; I have a strong impression that I shall not live to see the end."[19]

The sudden loss of the redeemer president shocked a nation that thought it had already seen it all, but utter despair even outdid itself as Lincoln returned to Illinois in a coffin. Indeed, the solemn funeral train procession that deposited the slain president back in Springfield in 1865 reflected and fostered an enormous increase in the mythic quality of Lincoln as redeemer and emancipator, a status that attained unimaginable heights in the days and weeks after his death. Almost immediately, a massive effort to refigure the work and accomplishment of Lincoln began, as preachers, poets, journalists, and artists all undertook the task of mythologizing a man to such an extent that revisionist historians have done little since to undermine or challenge it.

Historical investigations of the weeks following Lincoln's death have revealed the huge outpouring of emotion by Americans throughout the

J. L. Magee, "Satan Tempting Booth to the Murder of the President,"
1865. Library of Congress.

North. The train journey westward, departing on April 21, took twelve days and allowed mourners in a number of major cities to pay their respects and pass by the open coffin. New York saw at least 60,000 turn out; 120,000 came and went in Chicago; and on May 3 and 4, over 75,000 silently passed by the bier in Springfield. It is no exaggeration to claim that the "redefinition of Lincoln's place in American thought, his swift transcendence from history into folklore, was one of the more remarkable cultural phenomena of our history. . . . Lincoln the man was swallowed by the myth."[20]

Three themes marked the immediate mythologization of Lincoln in the aftermath of his death. First was the comparison with Moses. In *America's Prophet: Moses and the American Story*, Bruce Feiler documents the many ways that the Exodus story has served the needs of Americans: the story arises again and again because it tells of "the courage to escape oppression and seek the Promised Land."[21] Oppressed slaves were particularly drawn to Exodus, as in the famous jubilees and gospel songs of the South, and so very naturally Lincoln became figured as the Moses whose inspiration and leadership were central to the slaves' ability to break free from that oppression against all odds and make their way through the resulting wilderness.

The comparison with the biblical exodus has long been a commonplace of Lincoln scholarship. For example, Henry Ward Beecher, speaking in Brooklyn on April 23, compared Lincoln to Moses, both of whom could only approach the promised land without actually entering it. Among African Americans the comparison was even more strongly assumed, as selections in this volume demonstrate[†]: Uncle Ben stated that in America, "God needed more than a Moses of the Israelite kind, and needed one of a type unknown before," and so "God created Lincoln as the rough person needed for this great task" (see John E. Washington). And Charles J. Stewart's detailed analysis of 372 sermons delivered by Northern preachers in the weeks following the murder showed that Uncle Ben's and Beecher's Old Testament allusions were normative: "nearly half of the sermons" compared Lincoln directly to Moses.[22]

The second theme was directly related to Lincoln being wounded on Good Friday: the comparison with Jesus. Most importantly, besides his fulfilling the office of the prophet, Jesus gave his life as a ransom for many (Matthew 20:28). Similarly, the speeches, eulogies, sermons, and iconography about the fallen president commonly referred to his death as a kind of ransom for the Union: a sacrifice made necessary by the very great evils of the nation. Lincoln's death, in other words, was figured as a substitutionary sacrifice for the ongoing work of the nation. Many prominent American politicians, authors, and ministers spoke in glowing terms about the deceased leader. Ralph Waldo Emerson[†], for example, speaking at the Unitarian church in Concord on April 19, explained that "Serene Providence" is able to create "its own instruments" and suggested rather prophetically that Lincoln "may serve his country even more by his death than by his life." In Philadelphia on April 23 (the same day on which the corpse rested in Independence Hall, scene of Lincoln's most memorable speech on the train journey to Washington in 1861), Philips Brooks[†], like many preachers from Maine to Illinois, claimed that Lincoln's death was "no accident, no arbitrary decree of Providence." Something in his "character," said Brooks, "produced the catastrophe of his cruel death." Lincoln was, in fact, the "type-man" of the country, and his character was "the character of an American under the discipline of freedom." He was "the anointed and supreme embodiment" of "the American truths." Brooks enjoined his listeners to "thank God forever for his life and death," suggesting like so many others that Lincoln's death was in fact God's Providence and will. Again, Stewart's sermon analysis indicates that Brooks's central appeal was a commonplace: 92 percent of the sermons "stated that God had allowed the assassination."[23]

Atonement, or at-one-ment, is of central importance in the rhetoric of Lincoln: his desire to bring all Americans together into one big happy family. Lincoln's fundamental faith in a form of national sympathy and solidarity is a primary feature of the American romanticism that dominated his rise and political career. Further, this feature can be readily identified with the similar philosophies of other key Civil War–era writers such as Walt Whitman, Frederick Douglass, and Harriet Beecher Stowe, all of whom worried that the grand Union was quickly falling apart. Lincoln became, in essence, the spotless Passover lamb given for the new American project, the redeemer whose death might atone for the sins of a nation. In the public imagination, Father Abraham died for his country. More than any other American in our national history, Lincoln's death was, like that of Jesus, ordained by God; it was all part of God's providential plan for America's unique role in world history — at least, in the common perception.

The upshot is that, for many writers, politicians, and ministers, a correct interpretation of Lincoln's death could be found in the profound suffering

Lincoln's death mask, 1865.
Library of Congress.

and loss that would issue in what Lincoln himself hauntingly and perhaps prophetically described as a "new birth of freedom" in his most sacred of texts, delivered on the battlefield at Gettysburg. It was as if the Union had been sacramentally redeemed, sealed, and memorialized forever through the blood of the prophet, and that a "new nation" or even greater calling was now on the horizon. Philips Brooks[†] stated, "The new American nature will supplant the old. We must grow like our president, in his truth, his independence, his religion, and his wide humanity. Then the character by which he died shall be in us, and by it we shall live." Thus will Americans be imbued with the dead leader's very spirit, just as Christians are filled with the Holy Spirit: "If you abide in My word, then you are truly disciples of mine; and you shall know the truth, and the truth shall make you free"; "You know Him because He abides with you, and will be in you" (John 8:31–32; 14:17). In Brooks's formulation, Jesus and Lincoln become almost identical in spirit and in mission.

Moreover, Lincoln became mythically the direct link between the religious and the political realms of the Union. His cagey politics ensured the survival of the Union at a time when it was very much in doubt; he struck genius in his ability to pit his team of rivals one against the other, in search of the best strategies and tactics for maintaining the nation. His judicious and wise character, and perhaps most importantly his death, sealed his fate in public memory as the absolute embodiment of America's "civil religion." Not coincidentally, Lincoln's best public speeches exemplified this civil religion to a degree that has not yet, and perhaps never will be, surpassed. His words, diligently and expertly crafted, are among the most sublime ever penned by an American, and it is right that he should make an appearance in this series as one of our nation's quintessential authors. He has given Americans words and ideas that we try to enact and the most venerated and important creedal statements that we have.[24]

A third theme is the recognition of Lincoln's personal sadness and depression, traits that were somehow symbolic of the trials of the nation. Lincoln was often associated with both melancholy and grief, and was almost certainly afflicted by what we would call today a mood disorder (possibly clinical depression). He also may have suffered at various times from post-traumatic stress disorder.[25] Primarily this resulted most obviously from the deaths of two of his sons, Eddie in 1850 and then the favored son Willie in the White House in the winter of 1862. But a diagnosis would certainly consider the two alleged "breakdowns" earlier in life—the first in 1835, then again in 1840–41—events that are largely accepted by today's historians as evidence of long-term mental affliction. The debate regarding the reasons for these breakdowns continues, as does discussion over the extent to which Lincoln may have been on at least one occasion suicidal.[26] But Lincoln's deep melancholy and mournful appearance were a common feature of many firsthand accounts throughout his presidency, as in these comments by British writer Edward Dicey in 1862: "[I was struck by the] look of depression [which] . . . I am told by those who see him daily, was habitual to him, even before the then recent death of his child, whose loss he felt acutely. You cannot look upon his worn, bilious, anxious countenance, and believe it to be that of a happy man."[27] And yet Grace Greenwood† could fondly recall "that my eyes have gazed full into those sad, prophetic eyes, whose tired lids were pressed down at last by the long-prayed-for Angel of Peace." There seemed to be something angelic even in Lincoln's melancholy.

Perhaps counterintuitively, Lincoln's generative "habitual" grief would serve many useful ends throughout his career. Joshua Wolf Shenk goes so

S. J. Ferris, "Washington and Lincoln (Apotheosis)," 1865.
Library of Congress.

far as to provide an extensive account of the many "benefits" of Lincoln's
melancholy, including the fostering of such attributes as resolve, perseverance, vision, and even an ultimate sense of purpose: the survival of the
Union. In this regard, perhaps none of the benefits of Lincoln's sadness and
grief were so majestically illustrated as in the sentiments expressed at Gettysburg in November 1863, a speech saturated with grief and the invocation
of unending bonds with the dead. This uncanny notion of continuing bonds

"Lincoln Statue at the Lincoln Memorial," 1922. Library of Congress.

with the dead is eerily reminiscent of Lincoln's figure of the "mystic chords of memory": Lincoln seemed almost obsessed with the ways that the survivors must continue to be motivated by the better angels of the deceased. As he put it in the Gettysburg Address, "It is for us the living, rather, to be dedicated here to the unfinished work which they who fought here have thus far so nobly advanced." Lincoln's calling for the presence of the dead heroes alludes to biblical passages such as Hebrews 12, where we are asked to be mindful of the fact that we are forever "surrounded by a cloud of witnesses." Thus, the habitual sadness associated with Lincoln is another way of noting the continuing presence of the dead. This "cloud of witnesses" is a phenomenon that is not merely negative but also generative and highly motivating. As Hebrews puts it, these spirits allow us to "run the race with endurance."

More concretely, Lincoln is often depicted as a father bereaved by the deaths of his children, as here by Elizabeth Keckley[†]: "Great sobs choked his utterance. He buried his head in his hands, and his tall frame was convulsed with emotion. I stood at the foot of the bed, my eyes full of tears, looking at the man in silent, awe-stricken wonder. His grief unnerved him, and made him a weak, passive child. I did not dream that his rugged nature could be so moved. I shall never forget those solemn moments — genius and greatness weeping over love's idol lost. There is a grandeur as well as a simplicity about the picture that will never fade. With me it is immortal — I really believe that I shall carry it with me across the dark, mysterious river of death." Keckley notes a certain "grandeur" in Lincoln's traumatic bereavements, and her account is filled with words bespeaking a sort of spiritual mystery and awe regarding the extent of the great leader's humble despair in the face of death. As such, it captures perfectly the posthumous memory of the stricken president, whose parental grief somehow exemplified the far greater loss of sons brought about by the terrible war. Father Abraham wept for us all, it seemed, as did Jesus: "He saw the city, and wept over it" (Luke 19:41).

Consequently, given the combination of these mythic elements, Lincoln has been the most studied, most storied, and most well-documented American who has ever lived (by far, in fact). It is surprising to recall that as early as the year 1936, the great Lincoln scholar J. G. Randall could ask, in the pages of the prestigious *American Historical Review*, whether Lincoln studies already had completed their work. Randall, then the dean of the craft, seemed to suggest in the midst of the Great Depression that there was no longer anything new to say about the martyred president.[28] Evidently the answer turned out to be in the negative, and the Lincoln publishing industry, which celebrated the 200-year anniversary of his birth in 2009, continues steaming onward nearly fourscore years after Randall suggested all had been accomplished. Granted, much of the scholarship has not always been of a high quality; however, the output has included such magisterial achievements as Michael Burlingame's so-called "green monster": a massive two-volume, 2000-page biography that draws upon one man's lifetime of Lincoln scholarship (*Abraham Lincoln: A Life*). Scores of volumes, edited by Burlingame and other top scholars, many of them published by academic presses with very high standards of excellence, provide access to massive amounts of primary documents: interviews, letters, and newspaper files that earlier were available only to those seriously committed to dusty, far-flung archives. The entire collected works of Lincoln have been available on the web and searchable for over a decade.[29] In fact, the digital vaults on Lincoln have so superseded those of any other figure that the race isn't really even close. These accomplishments provide the standard for teams of scholars of other major figures. The history of Lincoln scholarship has even developed its own account of itself, as presented by several notable scholars in recent times.[30] In light of Randall's grandiose claims almost eighty years ago that there was nothing more to say, it is charming to hear Matthew Pinsker, one of the great Lincoln scholars of our time, admit the following: "Previous generations of Lincoln scholars have been like Ahab stalking his whale, engaged in a lonely, somewhat doomed endeavor. Their inability to fully traverse the vast oceans of data does not reflect poorly on those scholars but rather on the impossibility of their task."[31]

Even in the midst of numerous outstanding achievements, the goal of "knowing Lincoln" still seems to evade us. As such, the production here of another volume on Lincoln is not an easy assignment. Clearly we are in flush times as far as the vast amount of data is concerned, as we begin another project elaborating Mr. Lincoln, but it is daunting as well, to sift through dozens of candidates for this volume and wonder where to begin. Therefore, it seems altogether fitting and proper, as Lincoln might put it, for me to spell out some of my intentions here and the logic of some of the choices.

It seems to me, as a literature professor and as a practitioner of cultural studies and social analysis, that any depictions of Lincoln, both "in his own time" and in the early twenty-first century, need to begin with a few criteria. Given the sheer heft of the Lincoln bookshelf at this late date, it is clear that any account of Lincoln must sift through a very long list of books that have compiled all manner of tall tales, reminiscences, and anecdotes—and must do so with a fixed number of foci in mind. For this volume, I would like to state up front what I am trying to do—and also, what I am *not* trying to do here. Beginning with the latter, I am certainly not trying to supplant what has already been done, nor trying to give a comprehensive account of the man as seen either by eyewitnesses or by those who experienced the period of Lincoln's life or knew such witnesses firsthand. A select list of those sorts of volumes, filled to overflowing with anecdotes and reminiscences, are listed in the bibliography. Although I do utilize materials that occasionally speak to Lincoln's biographical realities—his upbringing, his family, his political adventures, his trial work, and so on—I have consciously decided that the biography of Lincoln has been exceptionally well documented over the years and this volume seeks to add very little to that sort of enterprise.

What this book does attempt, however, seems unique among all these assorted other volumes. Here I have pieced together many of the best reflections about Lincoln as a thinker, reader, writer, and rhetor. I am more interested in showing not only the development of a powerful mind, but perhaps even more crucially the *perception* of this Great American Mind, often by equally brilliant American minds of a decidedly literary and poetical bent. Additionally, I have tried to present some of the most significant contemporary meditations about the memory of Lincoln: the developing and ongoing discussion about his legacy and his long-term cultural significance. A particularly fascinating subtext of this discussion is the vast interest in Lincoln's religious beliefs and spirituality, an interest that began immediately after his demise and continues to this day. All told, I am trying to map what might be termed a genealogy of the cultural work and iconic status of Lincoln as quintessential scribe and prophet of the American project. And I have chosen to limit my choices to commentary by those whose lives intertwined with Lincoln's, or else those who had direct access to eyewitnesses, meaning that the selections end around the centennial of Lincoln's birth and the advent of the First World War a few years later.

Many of the selections here are rather well known, and their inclusion seems essential, especially insofar as they reveal the thoughts and analyses of a number of important writers who lived during the Lincoln era. Even so, the veteran Lincoln scholar will notice a variety of obvious omissions. Important contemporary commentators such as Francis B. Carpenter, Petroleum V. Nasby, Artemus Ward, John Hay, George Bancroft, John Nicolay, Ulysses S. Grant, and others are not included here. Moreover, the commemorative poetry has not been included though there are numerous excellent selections. Some like Whitman's are quite well known, while others such as those by Julia Ward Howe, Bayard Taylor, or William Cullen Bryant are not as widely remembered. Simply put, hard choices were made to allow for concision and variety. Most long entries were pared for brevity and focus: this technique allowed for the inclusion of what I took to be the heart of some of the most important memoirs and well-known anecdotes, many by famous contemporary authors such as Hawthorne, Douglass, Stowe, Howells, and Lowell. Many other selections included here are less well known or have been nearly lost to history, buried in dusty old books, journals, or newspapers. They are provided here because they add breadth and depth to the picture being sketched, and deserve wider circulation.

In effect this account covers much biographical ground, but focuses on several crucial themes. First, many of the excerpts consider Lincoln as an author who crafted some of the most memorable lines in our national vocabulary. This theme includes the abundant information presented by various authors about Lincoln's use of literature and other writings, and their influence upon him, from the Bible to Shakespeare to the southwest humorists. Surprisingly, English professors have largely ignored the work of Lincoln and his passionate participation in the literary culture of his day.[32] This collection aims at augmenting the view of Lincoln as a man of letters.

Second, many selections document the rise and emergence of a particular cultural memory of Lincoln—one might even say the mythologization of the martyred president, a phenomenon that commenced immediately upon his death. To be sure, elements of this are seen in depictions prior to his assassination, but the change upon his demise is one of the most striking elements of the historical memory of Lincoln. Third, and related to this, many of these accounts show the ways that Lincoln's contemporaries understood him as a religious thinker and sacred symbol. Many of these writers describe Lincoln as either devout Christian, radical freethinker, or even as atheist. Further, many depictions illustrate the deeply religious categories of thinking that exemplified American culture of that era.

In retrospect, one might be struck by the way that our contemporary understanding of Lincoln is in so many ways already implicit in the ways he was depicted during his final years in office and in the aftermath of the war itself. His untimely death seemed to accelerate this symbolic transformation. Abraham Lincoln (and, I would argue, his most cherished words) became forever the direct link between the religious and the political realms of the Union. His life, and perhaps most importantly his death, sealed his fate in public memory as the absolute embodiment of America's mythic "civil religion," one that his best public speeches exemplified to a degree that has not yet, and perhaps never will be, surpassed.

Of course, the myth continues unabated, even today. The vast crowds on the National Mall attest to his historical and philosophical heft as they visit Abe at his hallowed throne. The "clouds of witnesses" keep moving to and fro.

And our redeemer president still superintends the whole scene, clutching at the arms of his stony chair, as he did two score and ten years ago when a Baptist preacher from Georgia spoke in his shadow of a Dream.

Except for manuscript material that I have transcribed myself, almost all texts in this volume are taken from the first printed versions. In a few cases they are based on either the autograph manuscript or a later published version authorized by the author. For clarity, I have silently corrected obvious typographical and other errors to conform to current standard usage. Generally I have allowed nineteenth-century spellings to stand and have modernized the texts as little as possible. Titles of books and periodicals have been italicized throughout. In this introduction, a dagger (†) is used to indicate that the referenced text is reprinted in this volume. Complete bibliographical information for each text is provided in an unnumbered note following the entry, and the bibliography at the end of the volume contains all of the texts cited throughout the introduction and the rest of the collection.

The Lincoln scholarly community has been generous and willing to help in my work on this project. In particular, I would like to mention the help of Michael Burlingame, Douglas Wilson, Allen Guelzo, Richard Wightman Fox, Robert Bray, and Barry Schwartz—all of whom corresponded with me, evaluating my selections and suggesting others along the way. Their books have set the bar very high for all of us. I have also been aided by numerous librarians and curators. James Cornelius, curator at the Lincoln

Presidential Library in Springfield, was a gracious host and an encyclopedic resource, pointing me in several fruitful directions. Thanks to John Waide and his fine staff here at the St. Louis Room of the Pius XII Library of Saint Louis University. Thanks also to Penelope Lonergan, curator of the Bernard H. Hall Abraham Lincoln Collection of the Sisters of Charity of Leavenworth at the University of Saint Mary in Leavenworth, Kansas.

The list of biographical and critical works on Lincoln that have informed and inspired me over the years is immense indeed, and I have tried to include in the bibliography what I consider to be the most important. Here I would like to mention those Lincoln scholars whose work has been of crucial value in my thinking. Besides the names already mentioned, I and all scholars of Lincoln are indebted to books and articles written or edited by Roy Basler, Merrill Peterson, Garry Wills, Andrew Delbanco, Gabor Boritt, Harold Holzer, Ronald White, Doris Kearns Goodwin, David Zarefsky, Mark Noll, David H. Donald, and Mark Neely — and really so many more that I find it hard to create a short list. Thanks for those thousands of hours, all devoted to a single life!

My own personal debt is just as wide-ranging. My wife, Hiroko, inspires me through her persistent spirit and her promise not to go away; and she insists that I take my time to do my best, and then to bow and give even more thanks. We both continue to be inspired by our son Daniel, and thank him for those continuing bonds. Our many friends are the reason we have made it this far; I simply cannot name them all here, but will give very special mention to the Frankos, the Johnsons, the Leiboviches, the Penicks, the Victors, and the Middekes, and more general recognition to all our beloved New City folk. Professionally, I owe much to my colleagues at Saint Louis University as well as to the excellent research assistants who helped me get this project done: Kyle Crews, Jonathan Lux, and Matthew Miller. Thanks to my many colleagues elsewhere, sprinkled throughout the nation and world, made much closer these days through the Web. A special tip of the hat goes to the Twain scholarly family and all the folks at the Conference on Christianity and Literature. Joel Myerson has been the original motivation for taking on this project and I thank him for extending to me the offer to create this volume. I applaud the staff at the University of Iowa Press; they have been a joy to work with. Special thanks go to Holly Carver, Charlotte Wright, and Karen Copp in particular.

Notes

1. Quoted in James A. Percoco, *Summers with Lincoln: Looking for the Man in the Monuments* (New York: Fordham UP, 2008), 175.

2. See Garry Wills, *Inventing America: Jefferson's Declaration of Independence* (Garden City, NY: Doubleday, 1978), xiv. Wills reaffirms and develops this general interpretation of Lincoln's powerful words in *Lincoln at Gettysburg: The Words That Remade America* (New York: Simon and Schuster, 1992). Other important works on the Declaration include Carl Becker, *The Declaration of Independence: A Study in the History of Political Ideas* (New York: Vintage, 1958); Stephen E. Lucas, "Justifying America: The Declaration of Independence as a Rhetorical Document," in Thomas W. Benson, ed., *American Rhetoric: Context and Criticism* (Carbondale: Southern Illinois UP, 1989), 67–103; Pauline Maier, *American Scripture: Making the Declaration of Independence* (New York: Knopf, 1997); and Harold K. Bush, *American Declarations: Rebellion and Repentance in American Cultural History* (Urbana: U of Illinois P, 1999).

3. See Myra Jehlen, *American Incarnation: The Individual, the Nation, and the Continent* (Cambridge, MA: Harvard UP, 1986), 3–25. The literature on American exceptionalism and the building of a national ideology is quite extensive; good volumes to begin with include Ernest Tuveson, *Redeemer Nation* (Chicago: U of Chicago P, 1968); Catherine L. Albanese, *Sons of the Fathers: The Civil Religion of the American Revolution* (Philadelphia: Temple UP, 1976); Nathan Hatch, *Sacred Cause of Liberty* (New Haven: Yale UP, 1977); Sacvan Bercovitch, *American Jeremiad* (Madison: U of Wisconsin P, 1978); Ruth Bloch, *Visionary Republic* (Cambridge: Cambridge UP, 1985); Andrew Delbanco, *The Real American Dream: A Meditation on Hope* (Cambridge, MA: Harvard UP, 1999). Likewise, the literature on American empire and conquest is huge and growing. See for example three critical studies: Patricia Limerick, *Legacy of Conquest: The Unbroken Past of the American West* (New York: Norton, 1988); Andrew J. Bacevich, *American Empire: The Realities and Consequences of U.S. Diplomacy* (Cambridge, MA: Harvard UP, 2002); and Eric J. Sundquist, *Empire and Slavery in American Literature, 1820–1865* (Jackson: UP of Mississippi, 2006).

4. Don E. Fehrenbacher, ed., *Abraham Lincoln: Speeches and Writings, 1859–1865* (New York: Library of America, 1989), 213.

5. Sidney Mead, *The Nation with the Soul of a Church* (New York: Harper and Row, 1975).

6. Catherine L. Albanese, *Sons of the Fathers: The Civil Religion of the American Revolution*, 6.

7. On the cultural weight of the Memorial and its status as symbol for the grandeur of American metaphysical beliefs, see Christopher Thomas, *The Lincoln Memorial and American Life* (Princeton: Princeton UP, 2002). On wandering the Mall more generally, see James A. Percoco, *Summers with Lincoln*.

8. See two volumes by Thomas J. DiLorenzo: *The Real Lincoln: A New Look at Abraham Lincoln, His Agenda, and an Unnecessary War* (New York: Three Rivers, 2003) and

Lincoln Unmasked: What You're Not Supposed to Know about Dishonest Abe (New York: Three Rivers, 2006). On Lincoln as white racist see Lerone Bennett Jr., *Forced into Glory: Abraham Lincoln's White Dream* (Chicago: Johnson, 2000). For a discussion of the racist preacher Thomas Dixon's version of Lincoln (which in certain ways complicates the common understanding of Dixon), see Brook Thomas, "Thomas Dixon's *A Man of the People*: How Lincoln Saved the Union by Cracking Down on Civil Liberties," *Law and Literature* 20.1 (2008), 21–46.

9. See John Hope Franklin, "The Use and Misuse of the Lincoln Legacy," *Chicago Tribune*, February 12, 1930, 32–33.

10. Walt Whitman, *Notebooks and Unpublished Prose Manuscripts*, ed. Edward F. Grier (New York: New York UP, 1984), 2:539.

11. See Robert Bray's excellent report, "What Abraham Lincoln Read—An Evaluative and Annotated List," *Journal of the Abraham Lincoln Association* 28.2 (Summer 2007), 28–81.

12. See David M. Potter, *The Impending Crisis: 1848–1861* (New York: Harper and Row, 1976), as well as William Freehling, *The Road to Disunion: Volume II: Secessionists Triumphant 1854–1861* (Oxford: Oxford UP, 2007).

13. On these matters, see James McPherson, *Battle Cry of Freedom: The Civil War Era* (Oxford: Oxford UP, 1988), especially 235, 262.

14. Roy P. Basler, ed., *The Collected Works of Abraham Lincoln* (New Brunswick, NJ: Rutgers UP, 1953), 4:215. These words were spoken in Cleveland on February 15, 1861.

15. Stephen B. Oates, *With Malice toward None: A Life of Abraham Lincoln* (New York: Harper Perennial, 1994), 223, 225.

16. See Ronald C. White, Jr., *Lincoln's Greatest Speech: The Second Inaugural* (New York: Simon and Schuster, 2002), as well as Garry Wills, "Lincoln's Greatest Speech?" in *Atlantic Monthly*, September 1999, 60–70.

17. The first quote is the subtitle of Garry Wills's *Lincoln at Gettysburg: The Words That Remade America*; the second is from Theodore C. Sorenson, "Abraham Lincoln: A Man of His Words," *Smithsonian* 39.7 (October 2008).

18. Gabor Boritt, *The Gettysburg Gospel: The Lincoln Speech That Nobody Knows* (New York: Simon and Schuster, 2006), 3.

19. Francis B. Carpenter, *The Inner Life of Abraham Lincoln: Six Months at the White House* (New York: Hurd and Houghton, 1867), 17.

20. Harold Holzer, Gabor S. Boritt, and Mark E. Neely, Jr., *The Lincoln Image: Abraham Lincoln and the Popular Print* (Urbana: U of Illinois P, 2001), 149.

21. Bruce Feiler, *America's Prophet: Moses and the American Story* (New York: Morrow, 2009), 298.

22. Charles J. Stewart, "The Pulpit and the Assassination of Lincoln," *Quarterly Journal of Speech* 50.3 (1964), 299–300.

23. Ibid., 302.

24. The term "civil religion" derives from Robert Bellah's classic essay. The scholarship on Lincoln's important place in the construction of an American civil religion is a heady batch, perhaps best characterized by the following titles: Allen C. Guelzo, *Abraham*

Lincoln: Redeemer President (Grand Rapids: Eerdmans, 2003); Lucas E. Morel, *Lincoln's Sacred Effort: Defining Religion's Role in American Self-Government* (Lanham, MD: Lexington Books, 2000); Joseph R. Fornieri, *Abraham Lincoln's Political Faith* (DeKalb: Northern Illinois UP, 2003); and Richard Carwardine, *Lincoln: A Life of Purpose and Power* (New York: Knopf, 2008).

25. See Joshua Wolf Shenk, *Lincoln's Melancholy: How Depression Challenged a President and Fueled His Greatness* (Boston: Houghton Mifflin, 2005), 62–65.

26. See Joshua Wolf Shenk, "Eureka Dept.: The Suicide Poem," *New Yorker*, June 14, 2004.

27. Quoted in Shenk, *Lincoln's Melancholy*, 178.

28. J. G. Randall, "Has the Lincoln Theme Been Exhausted?" *American Historical Review* 41.2 (1936), 270–94.

29. Available at the University of Michigan website: < quod.lib.umich.edu/l/lincoln/>

30. See Matthew Pinsker, "Lincoln Theme 2.0," *Journal of American History* 96.2 (2009), 417–40.

31. Ibid., 438.

32. Important recent exceptions include studies such as Andrew Delbanco, *The Real American Dream*; Douglas L. Wilson, *Lincoln's Sword: The Presidency and the Power of Words* (New York: Knopf, 2006); Fred Kaplan, *Lincoln: The Biography of a Writer* (New York: Harper, 2008); Michael T. Gilmore's *The War on Words: Slavery, Race, and Free Speech in American Literature* (Chicago: U of Chicago P, 2010); John Stauffer, *Giants: The Parallel Lives of Frederick Douglass and Abraham Lincoln* (New York: Twelve Books, 2008); and Daniel Mark Epstein, *Lincoln and Whitman: Parallel Lives in Civil War Washington* (New York: Ballantine, 2004). Also included are two special issues of major literary journals in 2009: *College English* 72.2, which covered "Reflections on Lincoln and English Studies"; and *American Literary History* 21.4, covering "Lincoln and Cultural Value: A Forum." I discuss aspects of Lincoln in relation to Mark Twain and religion in my book *Mark Twain and the Spiritual Crisis of His Age* (Tuscaloosa: U of Alabama P, 2007), and in relation to American cultural traditions of protest and repentance in *American Declarations*.

Chronology

1778	January	Thomas Lincoln (Abraham's father) is born in Virginia
1782		Thomas and family relocate to northern Kentucky
1806	12 June	Thomas marries Nancy Hanks
1807	10 February	Thomas and Nancy's daughter, Sarah, is born
1808		Thomas purchases Sinking Spring, a farm outside of Hodgenville, Kentucky
1809	12 February	In a log cabin in Kentucky, Abraham Lincoln is born
1811		Lincoln family moves to a large farm on Knob Creek
1812		Thomas, the brother of Lincoln, is born and dies shortly thereafter
1816		Lincoln family crosses the Ohio River and settles in the backwoods of southern Indiana
1817		Abraham, age 7, shoots a wild turkey but immediately is overwhelmed by sadness — and never hunts game again
1818	5 October	Abraham's mother, Nancy Hanks Lincoln, dies of "milk sickness"
1819	2 December	Abraham's father marries a widow, Sarah Bush Johnston, becoming stepfather to her three children

1828	20 January	Lincoln's married sister Sarah dies while giving birth
	April	Lincoln and Allen Gentry take a flatboat to New Orleans, where Lincoln observes a slave auction
1830	March	Lincoln and his family move to Illinois where they settle on forested land on the Sangamon River, outside of Decatur
1831		Lincoln makes a second flatboat trip to New Orleans and later settles in New Salem, Illinois, working as a clerk in the village store
1832		Runs for Illinois General Assembly; the Black Hawk War begins
	April	Lincoln enlists in the military, becoming captain of his rifle company and serving a total of three months, never fighting in a battle
	August	Loses the election; with a partner, William Berry, buys another village store in New Salem
1833		Lincoln's store goes bust, leaving him deeply in debt
		Appointed postmaster of New Salem, and later appointed deputy county surveyor
1834	August	Lincoln is elected to the Illinois General Assembly and begins to study law
	December	Meets Stephen A. Douglas, 21, a Democrat
1835	25 August	Ann Rutledge, Lincoln's love interest, dies from fever at age 22 and he enters a sustained period of grief and depression
1836		Reelected to the Illinois assembly
	September	Receives his law license; begins courtship of Mary Owens, but has another episode of depression in December

1837		Lincoln is a key influence in having the Illinois state capital moved from Vandalia to Springfield
	April	Leaves New Salem to settle in Springfield, where he becomes a law partner of John T. Stuart
		His proposal of marriage to Mary Owens is turned down and the courtship ends
1838		Successfully defends Henry Truett in a famous murder case; reelected to Illinois assembly, becoming Whig floor leader
1839		Travels extensively in Illinois as a lawyer on the Eighth Judicial Circuit
	December	Admitted to practice in U.S. Circuit Court
		Meets Mary Todd, 21, at a dance
1840		Presents his first case before the Illinois Supreme Court
		Reelected to the Illinois Assembly, after which he becomes engaged to Mary Todd
1841		Breaks off engagement with Mary Todd on New Year's Day; experiences further episodes of depression
	March	Forms new law partnership with Stephen T. Logan
	August	On a trip by steamboat to Kentucky, he witnesses twelve slaves chained together
1842		Resumes courtship with Mary Todd; accepts a challenge to a duel by Democratic state auditor James Shields over published letters making fun of Shields
	22 September	Duel is averted by an explanation of letters
	4 November	Marries Mary Todd in Springfield

1843		Tries but fails in his attempt to garner the Whig nomination for U.S. Congress
	1 August	His first son, Robert Todd Lincoln, is born
1844		Lincoln family purchases and moves into a house in Springfield
		Speaks in support of Henry Clay, one of his great heroes, in the presidential election
		Dissolves the law partnership with Logan in favor of setting up his own practice
1846	10 March	A second son, Edward Baker Lincoln ("Eddie"), is born
		Nominated to be the Whig candidate for U.S. Congress
	3 August	Elected to House of Representatives
1847		Moves into a boardinghouse in Washington, D.C., with his wife and sons
	6 December	Takes his seat when Thirtieth Congress convenes; presents resolutions criticizing the Polk administration's hostilities toward Mexico
1848	22 January	Speaks on the House floor against President Polk's war policy with Mexico
		Supports Whig candidate General Zachary Taylor as the nominee for president, campaigning for him in Maryland, Massachusetts, and Illinois
1849		Returns to Springfield and leaves politics to practice law
	22 May	Granted U.S. Patent No. 6,469 (the only president ever granted a patent) for a hydraulic device for lifting ships
1850	1 February	His son Edward dies after a two-month illness
		Lincoln resumes his travels in the Eighth Judicial Circuit covering over 400 miles in

		fourteen counties in Illinois; "Honest Abe" gains reputation as an outstanding lawyer
	21 December	His third son, William Wallace Lincoln ("Willie"), is born
1851	17 January	Lincoln's father, Thomas, dies
1853	4 April	His fourth son, Thomas ("Tad"), is born
1854		Lincoln reenters politics as he is outraged at the Kansas-Nebraska Act
	November	Elected to Illinois legislature but turns down the seat so that he can attempt (unsuccessfully) to become U.S. senator
1856		Lincoln is a key leader in the organization of the new Republican party of Illinois
	19 June	Gets 110 votes for the vice-presidential nomination of the Republican convention, which garners national attention
		Campaigns in Illinois for Republican presidential candidate, John C. Frémont
1857		Criticizes the U.S. Supreme Court's decision in the case of Dred Scott, which denied the citizenship of slaves or even their descendants
1858	16 June	Nominated to be the Republican candidate for U.S. Senate from Illinois, opposing Democrat Stephen A. Douglas; delivers the "House Divided" speech at the state convention in Springfield
	21 August	First in a series of widely disseminated debates with his opponent Douglas, delivered to big audiences and extensively covered in the national press, making Lincoln a well-known figure throughout the North
		Writes first autobiographical statement

	2 November	Douglas is chosen for the U.S. Senate over Lincoln by a vote of 54 to 46 in the Illinois House
1859	December	Writes the second of three short autobiographical statements
1860	18 May	Nominated to be the Republican candidate for president of the United States, opposing Northern Democrat Stephen A. Douglas and Southern Democrat John C. Breckinridge
	June	Composes the third of the autobiographical statements
	6 November	Elected sixteenth U.S. president and the first Republican; receives 180 of 303 electoral votes and roughly 40 percent of the popular vote
	20 December	South Carolina is first state to secede from the Union, followed in short order by Mississippi, Florida, Alabama, Georgia, Louisiana, and Texas
1861	11 February	Delivers his famous farewell to friends and supporters at Springfield train station as he leaves for Washington
	4 March	Delivers his First Inaugural Address and is sworn in as the sixteenth president
	12 April	Fort Sumter in Charleston harbor is attacked by Confederate troops and the Civil War begins
	April–May	Virginia secedes from the Union, followed shortly by North Carolina, Tennessee, and Arkansas, thus forming the eleven-state Confederacy
	3 June	Political rival Stephen A. Douglas dies unexpectedly
	21 July	The Union suffers a surprising defeat at Bull Run in northern Virginia

	11 September	Revokes General John C. Frémont's unauthorized proclamation of emancipation in Missouri
1862	20 February	Son Willie dies in the White House at age 11; Mary Todd Lincoln is emotionally traumatized and never fully recovers
	6 April	Confederate attack on Grant's troops at Shiloh leaves 13,000 Union troops killed or wounded
	16 April	Signs the District of Columbia Emancipation Bill
	30 August	Union defeated in the second battle at Bull Run; Lincoln relieves Union commander General John Pope
	17 September	General Robert E. Lee and the Confederate troops are stopped at Antietam in Maryland, the bloodiest day in U.S. military history
	22 September	Issues a preliminary Emancipation Proclamation freeing the slaves
	5 November	Names Ambrose E. Burnside as commander of the Army of the Potomac, replacing General George B. McClellan
	13 December	Army of the Potomac defeated at Fredericksburg in Virginia
1863	1 January	Issues the final Emancipation Proclamation freeing all slaves in Confederate territory
	25 January	Appoints Joseph ("Fighting Joe") Hooker as commander of the Army of the Potomac, replacing Burnside
	29 January	General Ulysses S. Grant is placed in command of the Army of the West and ordered to take Vicksburg
	2–4 May	Union defeat at Chancellorsville in Virginia; Confederate General Stonewall Jackson is mortally wounded and Hooker retreats

	28 June	Appoints George G. Meade as commander of the Army of the Potomac, replacing Hooker
	1–3 July	Confederate defeat at the Battle of Gettysburg
	4 July	Vicksburg is captured by General Grant
	13–16 July	Draft riots in New York City
	10 August	Meets with abolitionist Frederick Douglass regarding full equality for black Union troops
	19–20 September	Union defeat at Chickamauga in Georgia; Lincoln appoints General Grant to command all operations in the western theater
	3 October	Issues Proclamation of Thanksgiving
	19 November	Delivers the Gettysburg Address at a ceremony dedicating the grounds of the battle as a national cemetery
1864	10 March	Appoints Grant general-in-chief for all Federal armies; William T. Sherman succeeds Grant as commander in the West
	3 June	7,000 Union casualties in twenty minutes at Cold Harbor, Virginia
	8 June	Nominated for president by National Union convention, a coalition of Republicans and others
	2 September	Atlanta is captured by Sherman's army
	8 November	Reelected president, defeating Democrat George B. McClellan with 212 of 233 electoral votes and 55 percent of the popular vote
1865	4 March	Delivers Second Inaugural Address
	9 April	General Lee surrenders to General Grant at Appomattox Courthouse in Virginia
	11 April	Lincoln's last public speech, which focused on the problems of reconstruction, and the United

	States flag is raised over Fort Sumter in South Carolina
14 April	Lincoln and wife Mary see the play "Our American Cousin" at Ford's Theater; during the third act of the play, John Wilkes Booth bursts into the president's box and shoots the president in the head
	Doctors attend to the president in the theater then move him to a house across the street; Lincoln never regains consciousness
15 April	President Lincoln dies at 7:22 A.M.
26 April	John Wilkes Booth is shot and killed in a barn in Virginia
4 May	Lincoln is laid to rest in Oak Ridge Cemetery, outside Springfield, Illinois
6 December	The Thirteenth Amendment to the U.S. Constitution is ratified and slavery is abolished

[Autobiographical Statement, 1858]

ABRAHAM LINCOLN

> Abraham Lincoln wrote three autobiographies in a two-year period, from 1858 to 1860. This first, terse effort was prepared at the request of Charles Lanman, who was compiling the *Dictionary of Congress*.

JUNE [15?] 1858

Born, February 12, 1809, in Hardin County, Kentucky.

Education defective.

Profession, a lawyer.

Have been a captain of volunteers in Black Hawk war.

Postmaster at a very small office.

Four times a member of the Illinois legislature, and was a member of the lower house of Congress. Yours, etc.,

A. Lincoln

Roy P. Basler, ed., *The Collected Works of Abraham Lincoln* (New Brunswick, NJ: Rutgers UP, 1953), 2:459.

[Statement to William Herndon, after 1865?]

John Hanks

John Hanks (1802–1889) was Lincoln's mother's cousin. Lincoln met Hanks in 1822 when Hanks moved from Kentucky to southern Indiana, where he lived in the Lincoln household. Abraham and John hired out for a time splitting fence rails. Denton Offut, a frontier merchant, later hired them to take a flatboat to New Orleans. Hanks would claim later that the sight of the horrors of slavery in New Orleans set Lincoln on the path to his later anti-slavery convictions. Despite his earlier Democratic leanings, Hanks became the banner carrier for Lincoln's "Rail Splitter" candidacy in 1860 and voted Republican that year. Throughout the Civil War, Hanks was singular amongst the Hanks/Lincoln clan in his unwavering loyalty to Lincoln, serving in the Twenty-first Illinois Volunteer Infantry from 1861 to 1864.[1] He also attended Lincoln's funeral in Springfield.

I WAS BORN IN Kentucky on the ninth day of February 1802 in Nelson County four miles of Beardstown. My father moved to Hardin County in 1806. I knew Abraham Lincoln in Kentucky. Abraham was known among the boys as a bashful, somewhat dull, but peaceable boy; he was not a brilliant boy, but *worked* his way by toil; to learn was hard for him, but he walked slowly, but surely. He went to school to a man by the name of Hazel; the school was but a short distance. Lincoln lived on the bank of Knob Creek, about a half-mile above the Rolling Fork, which empties into Salt River, which empties into Ohio River. Abraham Lincoln's mother and I were cousins. Abraham and I are second cousins. I knew Mrs. Nancy Lincoln or Nancy Sparrow before marriage. She was a tall slender woman, dark-skinned, black hair and eyes, her face was sharp and angular, forehead big. She was beyond all doubts an intellectual woman, rather extraordinary if anything. She was born in Mercer County, Kentucky, about 1780; her nature was kindness, mildness, tenderness, obedience to her husband. Abraham was like his mother very much. She was a Baptist by profession.

[2]

My recollection — in fact Abraham's father told me so — that his great-grandfather was an Englishman, came from England and settled in Virginia. This is the family reputation. When I was in Kentucky in 1864, I was shown a house in Mercer County which was said to be the house that Abraham's grandfather had built. I doubt the house, but I don't the farm, about ten miles from the mouth of Kubick River, about ten or twelve miles from Harrisburg, southeast from Harrodsburg.

I knew Thomas Lincoln in Kentucky, knew him well. He was cabinet and house carpenter, farmed after he got married, still working at his trade. He was a man about five feet ten inches high, weighed about 180, eyes dark gray, hair black, a little stoop-shouldered, a good-humored man, a strong brave man, a very stout man, loved fun, jokes, and equaled Abe in telling stories. Happiness was the end of life with him. He, Thomas, was older than his wife, say about five years, being born about 1775. Thomas was born in Virginia; so was his wife. Thomas was six years of age when he came to Kentucky. His father was killed by the Indians, as Dennis Hanks has said. The Indian story of Dennis Hanks is generally correct as told you by Dennis, so is Chapman's story generally correct. Thomas told me so. My father and Lincoln's were born in old Virginia in what I called the Rappahannock River. We knew each other in Virginia; that is, the founders did. Abraham's mother was my first cousin. Abraham's grandmother was my father's sister. Abraham's grandfather and mother on his mother's side lived Mercer County, Kentucky, about twenty miles south of Abraham's grandfather on his father's side, the one killed by the Indians. Dennis Hanks and I are cousins. Mr. Sparrow and Mrs. Sparrow never came to Illinois. They lived in Kentucky in Mercer County. Sparrow married my father's sister. Henry Sparrow was his name, lived and died in Mercer County, never came to Indiana. They came from old Virginia. All these families came from about the same county, can't say what county.

Thomas Lincoln moved to Indiana in 1818, probably 1816, and settled in Spencer County, near what is now called Gentryville, Indiana. I stayed in Kentucky, did not come out when Dennis Hanks did. Dennis Hanks came out in about 1818. Mrs. Lincoln died, say in 1818, I think, and lies buried southeast of the Lincoln farm about a half-mile in a rise, knoll, or knob. She was buried by the side of Mr. Hall and his wife, as I understand it. I came out to Indiana in 1822 after Thomas Lincoln had married his second wife, and stayed in Indiana near to and with Thomas Lincoln for four years. I remember Abraham well in Indiana. He was then ten years of age, and fourteen years when I left Indiana and went back to Kentucky. I was, in 1822, twenty years.

Abraham was farming when I got there and when I left and went to Kentucky, he went to school but little. He went to school to Dorsey or Swaney, I can't now say which. Old man Lincoln's house was a rough, rough log one, not a hewed one; his second one was sorter hewed, but is gone — never standing in 1860. The third one was hewed logs — that one was never occupied by Lincoln; it was up but not inhabited; the house stood east and west and faced the south, chimney on east end. It was, is, about four miles to Gentryville from the Lincoln farm, west of east a little. The house stood on a round hill, knoll or knob. Lincoln's farm was on the forks of Big Pigeon and Little Pigeon. The Big Pigeon is north and the little one south.

When Lincoln, Abe, and I returned to the house from work, he would go to the cupboard, snatch a piece of corn bread, take down a book, sit down in a chair, cock his legs up as high as his head and read. He and I worked bare-footed, grubbed it, plowed, mowed, and cradled together, plowed corn, gathered it, and shucked corn. Abraham read constantly when he had an opportunity; no newspapers then; had monthly meetings at church, sometimes at private houses. Abe went to church generally — not always. I know he read Weem's Washington when I was there, got it wet — it was on a kind of bookshelf close to the window — the bookshelf was made by two pins in the wall and a clapboard on them, books on that. Lincoln got it of Crawford, told Crawford and paid it in pulling fodder by two or three days' work. He frequently read the Bible. He read *Robinson Crusoe*, Bunyan's *Pilgrim's Progress*. Lincoln devoured all the books he could get or lay hands on; he was a constant and voracious reader. I never could get him in company with woman; he was not a timid man in this particular, but did not seek such company. He was always full of his stories, as much so in Indiana as Illinois. He would go out in the woods and gather hickory bark, bring it home, and keep a light by it and read by it, when no lamp was to be had — grease lamp — handle to it which stuck in the crack of the wall. Tallow was scarce. Abraham was a good hearty eater, loved good eating. His own mother and stepmother were good cooks for their day and time. In the summer he wore tan linen pants and flax shirt and in the winter he wore linsey-woolsely, that is, during the time I was there. I have seen

[4]

Lincoln—Abraham—make speeches to his stepbrothers, stepsisters, and youngsters that would come to see the family.

I moved from Kentucky to Illinois in the fall of 1828 and settled where I now live—four miles northwest of Decatur—and built the first house in Decatur. I wrote to Thomas Lincoln what kind of a country it was; he came to this State the first day of March 1830—to my house. He then built ten miles west of Decatur, and about a hundred steps from the N.F. of Sangamon River and on the north side of it on a kind of bluff. The house, the logs of it, I cut myself in 1829 and gave them to old man Lincoln. The house set east and west, fronted south, chimney to west end, the same house which was shown in Chicago. Lincoln broke up fifteen acres of land. Abraham and myself split the rails; he owned four yoke of oxen; broke prairie for others. Two yoke belonged to Thomas Lincoln and two to my brother. Dennis Hanks came out at the summer time. Mr. and Mrs. Hall—Dennis Hanks married Abraham's stepsister, so did Hall. Abraham during the winter of 1830–31 walked three miles and made a thousand rails for Major Warnick.

I knew Abraham's own sister Sarah; she was a short-built woman, eyes dark gray, haired dark brown; she was a good woman, kind, tender, and good-natured, and is said to have been a smart woman. That is my opinion.

After Abraham got to Decatur, rather to Mercer, my county—a man by the name of Posey came into our neighborhood and made a speech; it was a bad one, and I said Abe could beat it. I turned a box or keg, and Abe made his speech. The other man was a candidate; Abe wasn't. Abe beat him to death, his subject being the navigation of the Sangamon River. The man after the speech was through, took Abe aside and asked him where he had learned so much and what he did so well. Abe explained, stating his manner and method of reading and what he had read; the man encouraged Lincoln to persevere.

Offutt came to my house in February 1831 and wanted to hire me to run a flatboat for him, saying that he had heard that I was quite a flatboat man in Kentucky; he wanted me to go badly. I went and saw Abe and John Johnston, Abe's stepbrother; introduced Offutt to them. We made an engagement with Offutt at 50¢ per day and $60 to make the trip to New Orleans. Abe and I came down the Sangamon River in a canoe on March 1831, landed at what is now called and known as Jamestown—five miles east of Springfield — once called Judy's Ferry. We left our canoe in charge of Mr. Mann, walked afoot to Springfield, and found Offutt. He was at a tavern in Oldtown, probably Elliott's; it was Elliott's. He, Offutt, expected to find his boat according to contract at the mouth of Spring Creek, five miles north of Springfield, got disappointed. Abe, Johnston, and myself went down to the mouth of Spring Creek and there cut the timbers to make the boat; we were about two weeks cutting our timber — suppose it was on Congress land. Abe walked afoot to Springfield, thence to Judy's Ferry, got the canoe, and floated it down to the mouth of Spring Creek, where the timber was cut; we then rafted the logs down to Sangamon River to what is called Sangamontown, seven miles northwest of Spring Creek, walked one mile, eat two meals a day. When we got to Sangamontown we made a shanty, shed. Abe was elected cook. We sawed our lumber at Kirkpatrick's mill on Prairie Creek about one and a half miles southwest of Sangamontown. We hewed and sawed the timber at the mouth of Spring Creek. We finished making and launching the boat in about four weeks. We loaded the boat with barrel pork, corn, and live hogs and left Sangamontown. I remember a juggler's show at Sangamontown. Abe went to it. Abe was full of jokes during all this time, kept us all alive. Offutt was a Whig, so was Lincoln, but he could not hear Jackson wrongfully abused — especially where a lie and malice did the abuse. I can say that Abe never was a Democrat; he was always a Whig; so was his father before him.

We landed at the New Salem mill about April 19 and got fast on Rutledge's mill dam, now called Bill's mill dam. We unloaded the boat, that is, we changed goods from one boat to a borrowed one, rolled the barrels forward, bored a hole in the end of the boat over the dam — water ran out and thus we got over; on the dam part of a day and one night. We then went on down to the Yellow Bank or the Blue Banks on the Sangamon River near Squire Godby's about one mile above the mouth of Salt Creek. We purchased some hogs of, I think, Squire Godby — am not sure — tried to drive them, couldn't, ran them back in the pen, caught them, Abe held the head of them, I the tail and Offutt sewed up their eyes, wouldn't drive, couldn't put them in a cart, carried them to the boat about one mile to the river. Abe received the hogs, cut open them. Johnston and I hauled them to Abe. We then proceeded, Offutt, John Johnston, Abe Lincoln, and myself, down the Sangamon River, thence into Illinois. We kept our victuals and in fact slept down in the boat, at one end; went down in the boat, at one end; went down by a kind of ladder through a scatter hole. We used plank as sails and cloth, sometimes, rushed through Beardstown in a hurry—people came out and laughed at us—passed Alton, Cairo, and stopped at Memphis, Vicksburg, Natchez, etc. There is nothing worthy of being known going down the river.

I can say we soon—say in May—we landed in New Orleans. There it was we saw Negroes chained, maltreated, whipped, and scourged. Lincoln saw it, his heart bled, said nothing much, was silent from feeling, was sad, looked bad, felt bad, was thoughtful and abstracted. I can say knowingly that it was on this trip that he formed his opinions of slavery; it ran its iron in him then and there—May 1831. I have heard him say often and often. Offutt, Johnston, Abe, and myself left New Orleans in June 1831. We came to St. Louis on the steamboat together, walked to Edwardsville twenty-five miles northeast of St. Louis, Abe, Johnston, and myself. Abe and Johnston went to Coles County and I to Springfield, Sangamon County. Thomas Lincoln had moved to Coles County in 1831 in, say, June.

I came near forgetting some facts. I was in the Black Hawk War, was Sherman's defeat, which was on the fourteenth day of May 1832. Lincoln was out on that war. I went in March 1832; Lincoln started as captain of the New Salem company about the same time. Lincoln was at Dixon's Ferry at the time of Sherman's defeat. I did not go to the Battle of the Bad Axe. Lincoln, I think, was there, though not in the action, as I understand it. I was out about four or six months; so was Lincoln. Lincoln went with Major Henry, I know. I was discharged at Ottawa and Lincoln at Rock Island or near that; met at Dixon's Ferry, after the Sherman defeat. Lincoln went out with Henry. We were ordered to build a fort at Ottawa to protect the people. The Sherman defeat affair grew out of the drunkenness, folly, cowardice. The fight with Black Hawk was about sundown, one hour by sun at or near Sycamore Creek. About 700 Indians and about 200 whites.

Note

1. Mark Neely, *The Abraham Lincoln Encyclopedia* (New York: Da Capo, 1982), 187.

Emanuel Hertz, ed., *The Hidden Lincoln: From the Letters and Papers of William H. Herndon* (New York: Viking Press, 1938), 345-49.

"Conversation with
Hon. S. T. Logan at Springfield" (1875)

Stephen Trigg Logan

> Stephen Trigg Logan (1800–1880), lawyer and jurist, was born in Franklin County, Kentucky, and received his early education in Frankfort, Kentucky, serving at age thirteen as clerk in the office of the secretary of state. He was admitted to the Kentucky bar at age twenty. After relocating to Illinois, the Illinois legislature elected Logan judge of the First Judicial Circuit in 1835; he presided at the court from January 1835 until March 1837, when he resigned and returned to law practice. In 1841 Logan formed a partnership with Abraham Lincoln, whom he had met when Lincoln ran for the state legislature in 1832. In his reminiscences, Logan claimed a substantial role in Lincoln's legal education. "He made a very considerable impression on me," Logan later wrote. "Lincoln's knowledge of the law was very small when I took him in."[1] The two became partners not only in law but also in Whig politics. Logan and Lincoln dissolved their partnership by mutual agreement in 1844.
>
> President Lincoln appointed Logan in 1862 to a commission in Cairo, Illinois, charged with investigating claims against the government. It was Logan's last personal involvement with Lincoln.
>
> The following statement was recorded by John G. Nicolay (1832–1901), Lincoln's personal secretary in the White House and, later, his biographer.

I CAME TO Springfield on the 16th of May 1832 — was here during part of the excitement which attended the arrival of the "Talisman," though that excitement had by that time received something of a check, as the boat in going out of the river was nearly torn to pieces.

That was a very wet season — all the flat lands south of here were covered with water — I suppose I rode for a mile south of here with the water up to my horse's legs.

Then there came a great change in the weather. After the 16th of May I think there was but one shower until the 7th of September and that just only enough to wet the dust. I don't think I have seen so dry a season here since. That summer it was quite common to see the soil cracked open. I have seen it in places so that I could put my hand down into the crack.

Very soon after I came I began to get the symptoms of the chills and fever, and then I wished I had never left Kentucky. But then I couldn't get away; I would have left if I could have done so. In those days I have often seen ten wagons going back to where I saw one coming this way.

In those days we were bringing seed corn from Kentucky, and all our flour came from Cincinnati. Money was very scarce — I have paid $1 per bushel for corn to feed my horse.

That was the year of the Black Hawk war — the troops came through here, and the road from here to Sangamon river was all dust for one hundred yards wide, where there was low brush. The Sangamon river was so low that year that by laying a few rocks, one could cross it dry shod almost any where.

Many people doubted then whether this country could be inhabited at all. I would have gone right back to Kentucky if I could have had a railroad to go on.

I became acquainted with Lincoln that year. They were making a canvass for the legislature. I had very soon got acquainted with Stuart, because we were both Whigs. Stuart and Lincoln were the only two men who attracted my attention in that canvass. I never saw Lincoln until he came up here to make a speech. I saw Lincoln before he went up into the stand to make his speech. He was a very tall and gawky and rough looking fellow then — his pantaloons didn't meet his shoes by six inches. But after he began speaking I became very much interested in him. He made a very sensible speech. It was the time when Benton was running his theory of gold circulation. Lincoln was attacking Benton's theory and I thought did it very well.

It was a speech of perhaps half an hour long. All the candidates made speeches. The meeting was held at the old Court house where the present State House stands. This county was then very large. In addition to Sangamon it embraced all of Logan, Menard, part of Mason, and most of Christian. In addition to the speeches at the Court House they used to have a good many fights at the groceries. Two gangs of country bullies used to meet here and fight one another. One was from Lick Creek, and the other from Spring Creek. I had seen a good deal of that sort of thing in Kentucky, and was somewhat used to it, but a stranger would have considered this a pretty hard country, I suppose. All the candidates made speeches at the meetings in those times, but nobody else.

The manner of Mr. Lincoln's speech then was very much the same as his speeches in after life — that is the same peculiar characteristics were apparent then, though of course in after years he evinced both more knowledge and experience. But he had then the same novelty and the same peculiarity in presenting his ideas. He had the same individuality that he kept up through all his life.

I knew nothing then about his avocation or calling at New Salem. The impression that I had at the time was that he was a sort of loafer down there.

I think that about that time he had concluded to quit work as a common day laborer, and try to make his living in some other way. Up to that time I think he had been doing odd jobs of surveying, and one thing and another.

But one thing we very soon learned was that he was immensely popular, though we found that out more at the next election than then.

In 1832 while he got a very large vote in his own precinct of New Salem, they hadn't voted for him very well in other parts of the county. This made his friends down there very mad, and as they were mostly democratic, but were for Lincoln on personal grounds, in the next race (1834) they told their democratic brethren in the other parts of the county that they must help elect Lincoln, or else they wouldn't support the other democratic candidates. This they did purely out of their personal regard for him, and through that influence he was elected in 1834. That was the general understanding of the matter here at the time. In this he made no concession of principle whatever. He was as stiff as a man could be in his Whig doctrines. They did this for him simply because he was popular — because he was Lincoln.

He showed his superiority among them right away even yet while he was making rails. I believe he worked for a man named Kirkpatrick for a while.

He was always very independent and had generally a very good nature. Though he had at times, when he was roused, a very high temper. He controlled it then in a general way, though it would break out sometimes — and at those times it didn't take much to make him whip a man. He wanted to whip Judge Jesse Thomas here once in a canvass for an election. It was after he had been elected a time or two — perhaps in 1840. The court was sitting here at the time, and the crowd was in the Court House listening to the electioneering speeches.

In the election of 1832 he made very considerable impression upon me as well as upon other people.

In the campaign of 1834 he was much more known though I knew personally less about that canvass than in that of 1832. I was then practicing law and was attending to my work and studies. I was on the bench in 1836 — was elected in the spring of 1835, and remained until 1837.

He (L.) was at the head of the project to remove the seat of government here; it was entirely entrusted to him to manage. The members were all elected that session upon one ticket. But they all looked to Lincoln as the head.

I was in Vandalia that winter and had a talk with Lincoln there. I remember that I took him to task for voting for the Internal Improvement scheme. He seemed to acquiesce in the correctness of my views as I presented them to him. But he said he couldn't help himself — he had to vote for it in order to secure the removal here of the seat of government.

My partnership with him in the practice of law was formed in 1841. I had had Baker before that. But I soon found I could not trust him in money matters. He got me into some scrapes by collecting and using money though he made it all right afterwards. You know Baker was a perfectly reckless man in matters of money. Baker was a pretty good lawyer. When he would try he could manage his materials as well as most men. Lincoln's knowledge of law was very small when I took him in. There were no books out here in those days worth speaking of.

I don't think he studied very much. I think he learned his law more in the study of cases. He would work hard and learn all there was in a case he had in hand. He got to be a pretty good lawyer though his general knowledge of law was never very formidable. But he would study out his case and make about as much of it as anybody. After a while he began to pick up a considerable ambition in the law. He didn't have confidence enough at first.

He had been in partnership with Stuart, and Stuart never went much upon the law. Things have changed very much here since then. Lawyers must know very much more now than they needed to do in those times. Stuart was never a reader of law; he always depended more on the management of his case.

After Lincoln went in with me he turned in to try to know more and studied to learn how to prepare his cases.

I think he began reading perhaps a couple of years before he came up here. He used to come up here and borrow a book at a time and take it down there with him to read.

Note

1. Stephen T. Logan, *Memorials of the Life and Character of Stephen T. Logan* (Springfield, IL: H. W. Rokker, 1882), 3.

Michael Burlingame, ed., *An Oral History of Abraham Lincoln: John G. Nicolay's Interviews and Essays* (Carbondale: Southern Illinois UP, 1996), 34–37.

"My Childhood Home I See Again" (1846)

ABRAHAM LINCOLN

Lincoln was a deft and winning writer in a number of literary forms, including poetry, of which he was also an avid reader from his youth until his days in the White House. Written in two parts and sent in a letter of 1846 to another budding poet, Andrew Johnston, whom Lincoln had known in the Illinois legislature, "My Childhood Home I See Again" was published under Lincoln's name in the Quincy (Illinois) *Whig* in 1848. The poem was occasioned by Lincoln's return to his southern Indiana home in 1844, and in particular his visit to the graves of his mother and only sister who were both buried there. Although the poem might seem rather conventional in its usage of both pastoral and graveyard imagery, "My Childhood Home I See Again" is also a powerfully sentimental homage to his prairie youth, and is even more compelling given the strains and challenges of his struggles in Indiana.

My childhood-home I see again,
    And gladden with the view;
And still as mem'ries crowd my brain,
    There's sadness in it too.

O memory! thou mid-way world
    'Twixt Earth and Paradise,
Where things decayed, and loved ones lost
    In dreamy shadows rise.

And freed from all that's gross or vile,
    Seem hallowed, pure, and bright,
Like scenes in some enchanted isle,
    All bathed in liquid light.

As distant mountains please the eye,
    When twilight chases day —

As bugle-tones, that, passing by,
    In distance die away —

As leaving some grand water-fall
    We ling'ring, list its roar,
So memory will hallow all
    We've known, but know no more.

Now twenty years have passed away,
    Since here I bid farewell
To woods, and fields, and scenes of play
    And school-mates loved so well.

Where many were, how few remain
    Of old familiar things!
But seeing these to mind again
    The lost and absent brings.

The friends I left that parting day —
    How changed, as time has sped!
Young childhood grown, strong manhood grey,
    And half of all are dead.

I hear the lone survivors tell
    How nought from death could save,
Till every sound appears a knell,
    And every spot a grave.

I range the fields with pensive tread,
    And pace the hollow rooms;
And feel (companions of the dead)
    I'm living in the tombs.

A[nd] here's an object more of dread,
    Than ought the grave contains —
A human-form, with reason fled,
    While wretched life remains.

[14]

Poor Matthew! Once of genius bright, —
    A fortune-favored child —
Now locked for aye, in mental night,
    A haggard mad-man wild.

Poor Matthew! I have ne'er forgot
    When first with maddened will,
Yourself you maimed, your father fought,
    And mother strove to kill;

And terror spread, and neighbours ran,
    Your dang'rous strength to bind;
And soon a howling crazy man,
    Your limbs were fast confined.

How then you writhed and shrieked aloud,
    Your bones and sinnews bared;
And fiendish on the gaping crowd,
    With burning eye-balls glared.

And begged, and swore, and wept, and prayed,
    With maniac laughter joined —
How fearful are the signs displayed,
    By pangs that kill the mind!

And when at length, tho' drear and long,
    Time soothed your fiercer woes —
How plaintively your mournful song,
    Upon the still night rose.

I've heard it oft, as if I dreamed,
    Far-distant, sweet, and lone;
The funeral dirge it ever seemed
    Of reason dead and gone.

To drink its strains, I've stole away,
    All silently and still,

Ere yet the rising god of day
    Had streaked the Eastern hill.

Air held his breath; the trees all still
    Seemed sorr'wing angels round.
Their swelling tears in dew-drops fell
    Upon the list'ning ground.

But this is past, and nought remains
    That raised you o'er the brute.
Your mad'ning shrieks and soothing strains
    Are like forever mute.

Now fare thee well: more thou the cause
    Than subject now of woe.
All mental pangs, but time's kind laws,
    Hast lost the power to know.

And now away to seek some scene
    Less painful than the last —
With less of horror mingled in
    The present and the past.

The very spot where grew the bread
    That formed my bones, I see.
How strange, old field, on thee to tread,
    And feel I'm part of thee!

Basler, ed., *Collected Works*, 1:367–70.

From *Reminiscences of Abraham Lincoln* (1884)

JOSHUA F. SPEED

Joshua Fry Speed (1814–1882), like Lincoln, was a Kentuckian who lived much of his adult life in Springfield. He became a partner in a general store and met Lincoln on April 15, 1837, when the young lawyer arrived in Springfield seeking lodgings. Speed offered Lincoln his room above the store and for four years the men slept in the same bed. Joshua Fry Speed was, like Lincoln, a Whig.

Speed's return to Kentucky in 1841 coincided with the year in which Lincoln's engagement to Mary Todd was broken, and Lincoln's letters to Speed provide some of the most intimate glimpses into Lincoln's personality and personal life of all of his correspondence. Lincoln's severe depression during this time drove him to visit "Farmington," the Speed home near Louisville, several times.[1]

Speed served in the Kentucky legislature at the same time Lincoln was in the U.S. House of Representatives, but the two men grew apart politically as slavery became an increasingly important issue in American politics. With the outbreak of the Civil War, Speed remained loyal to the Union and was active in smuggling arms supplied by President Lincoln to Unionists in Kentucky. After the war, he wrote nine letters about Lincoln to William H. Herndon, and delivered an address containing his "Reminiscences of Abraham Lincoln."

IN THE SPRING OF 1836 I first saw Abraham Lincoln. He had been a laborer, a flatboatman, a deputy surveyor, and for one term a member of the legislature. I heard him spoken of by those who knew him as a wonderful character. They boasted that he could outwrestle any man in the county, and that he could beat any lawyer in Springfield speaking.

In 1836 he was a candidate for re-election, and I believe I heard the first speech he ever made at the county-seat.

At that time there were but two parties, Whig and Democrat. Lincoln was a Whig and the leading man upon the ticket. I was then fresh from Kentucky, and had heard many of her great orators. It seemed to me then, as it seems to me now, that I never heard a more effective speaker. He carried the crowd with him and swayed them as he pleased. So deep an impression did he make, that George Forquer, a man of much celebrity as a sarcastic speaker and great State reputation as an orator, rose and asked the people to hear *him*. He commenced his speech by saying that this young man would have to be taken down, and he was sorry that the task devolved upon him. He made what was called one of his slasher-gaff speeches, dealing much in ridicule and sarcasm. Lincoln stood near him with his arms folded, never interrupting him. When Forquer was done Lincoln walked to the stand, and replied so fully and completely that his friends bore him from the court-house on their shoulders.

So deep an impression did this first speech make upon me that I remember its conclusion now.

Said he, "The gentleman commenced his speech by saying that this young man will have to be taken down, and he was sorry that the task devolved upon him. I am not so young in years as I am in the tricks and trades of a politician; but, live long or die young, I would rather die now, than, like the gentleman, change my politics, and simultaneous with the change receive an office worth $3,000 per year, and then have to erect a lightning-rod over my house to protect a guilty conscience from an offended God." To understand the point of this, Forquer had been a Whig, but changed his politics, and had been appointed register of the land office, and over his house was the only lightning-rod in the town or county. Lincoln had seen it for the first time on the day before. Not understanding its properties, he made it a study that night by aid of a book, bought for the purpose, till he knew all about it.

The same quality of mind that made him look into and understand the use and properties of that lightning-rod made him study and understand all that he saw. No matter how ridiculous his ignorance upon any subject might make him appear, he was never ashamed to acknowledge it; but he immediately addressed himself to the task of being ignorant no longer.

The life of a great and good man is like the current of a great river. When you see its force and power, you at once think of its source, and what tributaries go to make the great river. England is expending vast sums now to discover the source of the Nile, and our own government at considerable expense sent an expedition to explore the Amazon and its valleys. So the student of history, when he hears of a great man who has attracted attention, desires to know whence it came, what was his origin, his habits of thought and study, and all the elements of his character.

Lincoln studied and appropriated to himself all that came within his observation. Every thing that he saw, read, or heard, added to the store of his information—because he thought upon it. No truth was too small to escape his observation, and no problem too intricate to escape a solution, if it was capable of being solved. Thought, hard, patient, laborious thought, these were the tributaries that made the bold, strong, irresistible current of his life. The great river gets its aliment from the water-shed that feeds it, and from the tributaries naturally flowing into it. Lincoln drew his supplies from the store-house of nature. Constant thought enabled him to use all his information at all times and upon all subjects with force, ease, and grace.

As far as he knew, and it was only by tradition, his ancestors came from England with Penn and settled in Pennsylvania. Thence they drifted down to Virginia; thence to Kentucky, where Lincoln was born on the 12th of February, 1809, on the banks of the Nolin, in what was then Hardin County, now Larue. He went from Kentucky to Indiana, where he lost, as he always called her, his "*angel mother*," at ten years of age. From Indiana, with his father and step-mother, he went to Illinois.

Leaving his father and step-mother in Macon County, he pushed on to Sangamon County, and stopped at New Salem, on the Sangamon River, where he became a boatman and made two trips to New Orleans. While a flatboatman he studied that subject, as he did everything else, and invented a machine for lightening flatboats over shoals, a model of which is in the Patent Office now.

He resided at New Salem about eight years. The society was rough, the young men were all wild, and full of fun and frolic. All the manly sports that pertained to a frontier life were in vogue there. Running, wrestling, jumping, gander-pulling, and horse-racing. In all the games and races, in which he was not engaged, he was always selected as one of the judges. From the justness of his decisions on all occasions he was called honest Abe. As he grew older, and until his death, his sobriquet was "Honest old Abe."

In the spring of 1837 he took his license as a lawyer. Then began with him the real battle of life. Leaving the field of his youthful sports, pleasures, and pains, where he was the leading man, he came to a bar then considered the best in the State, and perhaps as good as any in the West. He entered with diffidence upon his new career, coming in contact with Logan and Cyrus

Walker, older than he and men of renown, John J. Hardin, E. D. Baker, Douglas, and Browning, all near his own age. They were all educated men, in the ordinary acceptation of the word. They had read many books, and studied law, many of them with able lawyers. He had read but few books, but had studied those. They were such as he borrowed from his friend, John T. Stuart, with whom he formed a partnership. He studied them at his humble home on the banks of the Sangamon, without a preceptor or fellow student. With such preparation he came to bar. From this time forward he took a leading position in the State.

It was in the spring of 1837, and on the very day that he obtained his license, that our intimate acquaintance began. He had ridden into town on a borrowed horse, with no earthly property save a pair of saddle-bags containing a few clothes. I was a merchant at Springfield, and kept a large country store, embracing dry goods, groceries, hardware, books, medicines, bed-clothes, mattresses, in fact every thing that the country needed. Lincoln came into the store with his saddle-bags on his arm. He said he wanted to buy the furniture for a single bed. The mattress, blankets, sheets, coverlid, and pillow, according to the figures made by me, would cost seventeen dollars. He said that was perhaps cheap enough; but small as the sum was, he was unable to pay it. But if I would credit him till Christmas, and his experiment as a lawyer was a success, he would pay then, saying, in the saddest tone, "If I fail in this, I do not know that I can ever pay you." As I looked up at him I thought then, and think now, that I never saw a sadder face.

I said to him, "You seem to be so much pained at contracting so small a debt, I think I can suggest a plan by which you can avoid the debt and at the same time attain your end. I have a large room with a double bed up-stairs, which you are very welcome to share with me."

"Where is your room?" said he.

"Up-stairs," said I, pointing to a pair of winding stairs which led from the store to my room.

He took his saddle-bags on his arm, went up stairs, set them down on the floor, and came down with the most changed countenance. Beaming with pleasure he exclaimed, "Well, Speed, I am moved!"

Mr. Lincoln was then twenty-seven years old — a lawyer without a client, no money, all his earthly wealth consisting of the clothes he wore and the contents of his saddle-bags. For me to have seen him rise from this humble position, step by step, till he reached the Presidency — holding the reins of government in as trying times as any government ever had — accomplishing more during the four years of his administration than any man had ever done — keeping the peace with all foreign nations under most trying circumstances — putting down the most gigantic rebellion ever known — assassinated at fifty-eight years of age — borne to his final resting place in Illinois, amid the tears of the nation and of the civilized world, and even his former foes in arms acknowledging they had lost their best friend — seems more like fable than fact.

From the commencement of his political career he was the acknowledged standard-bearer of the Whig party in the State, and his supremacy was never questioned. As a lawyer, after his first year, he was acknowledged among the best in the State. His analytical powers were marvelous. He always resolved every question into its primary elements, and gave up every point on his own side that did not seem to him invulnerable. One would think, to hear him present his case in the court, he was giving the case away. He would concede point after point to his adversary until it would seem his case was conceded entirely away. But he always reserved a point upon which he claimed a decision in his favor, and his concession magnified the strength of his claim. He rarely failed in gaining his cases in court.

Mr. Lincoln was a social man, though he did not seek company; it sought him. After he made his home with me, on every winter's night at my store, by a big wood fire, no matter how inclement the weather, eight or ten choice spirits assembled, without distinction of party. It was a sort of social club without organization. They came there because they were sure to find Lincoln. His habit was to engage in conversation upon any and all subjects except politics.

One evening a political argument sprang up between Lincoln and Douglas, which for a time ran high. Douglas sprang to his feet and said, "Gentlemen, this is no place to talk politics; we will discuss the questions publicly with you."

A few days after the Whigs held a meeting, and challenged the Democrats to a joint debate. The challenge was accepted, and Douglas, Lamborn, Calhoun, and Jesse B. Thomas were selected by the Democrats, Logan, Baker, Browning, and Lincoln were selected by the Whigs. Such intellectual giants of course drew a crowded house. The debate took place in the Presbyterian church, and lasted for eight nights, each speaker taking one night. Like true knights they came to fight in intellectual armor clad. They all stood high, and each had his followers, adherents, and admirers. This was in January, 1840.

Lincoln's speech was published as a campaign document. The conclusion of that speech, as an evidence of his style at that early day is, I think, worth repeating here:

"If ever I feel the soul within me elevate and expand to those dimensions not wholly unworthy of its Divine Architect, it is when I contemplate the cause of my country, deserted by all the world beside, and I standing up boldly and alone, hurling defiance at her victorious oppressors. Here, without contemplating consequences, before heaven and in the face of the world, I swear eternal fealty to the just cause, as I deem it, of the land of my life, my liberty, and my love. And who, that thinks with me, will not fearlessly adopt the oath I take! Let none falter who thinks he is right, and we may succeed. But if, after all, we shall fail, be it so; we still have the proud consolation of saying to our consciences, and to the departed shade of our country's freedom, that the cause approved of our judgments and adored of our hearts we never faltered in defending."

Mr. Lincoln delivered this speech without manuscript or notes. It filled seven columns in the Sangamon Journal, and was pronounced by all who heard it as exactly what he had said. He had a wonderful faculty in that way. He might be writing an important document, be interrupted in the midst of a sentence, turn his attention to other matters entirely foreign to the subject on which he was engaged, and take up his pen and begin where he left off without reading the previous part of the sentence. He could grasp, exhaust, and quit any subject with more facility than any man I have ever seen or heard of.

Lincoln had the most tender heart for any one in distress, whether man, beast, or bird. Many of the gentle and touching sympathies of his nature, which flowered so frequently and beautifully in the humble citizen at home, fruited in the sunlight of the world when he had power and place. He carried from his home on the prairies to Washington the same gentleness of disposition and kindness of heart. Six gentlemen, I being one, Lincoln, Baker, Hardin, and others were riding along a country road. We were strung along the road two and two together. We were passing through a thicket of wild plum and crab-apple trees. A violent wind-storm had just occurred. Lincoln and Hardin were behind. There were two young birds by the roadside too young to fly. They had been blown from the nest by the storm. The old bird was fluttering about and wailing as a mother ever does for her babes. Lincoln stopped, hitched his horse, caught the birds, hunted the nest and placed them in it. The rest of us rode on to a creek, and while our horses were drinking Hardin rode up. "Where is Lincoln?" said one. "Oh, when I saw him last he had two little birds in his hand hunting for their nest." In perhaps an hour he came. They laughed at him. He said with much emphasis, "Gentlemen, you may laugh, but I could not have slept well to-night, if I had not saved those birds. Their cries would have rung in my ears." This is one of the flowers of his prairie life. Now for the fruit.

The last time I saw him was about two weeks before his assassination. He sent me word by my brother James, then in his Cabinet, that he desired to see me before I went home. I went into his office about eleven o'clock. He looked jaded and weary. I staid in the room until his hour for callers was over; he ordered the door closed, and looking over to where I was sitting, asked me draw up my chair. But instead of being alone, as he supposed, in the opposite direction from where I sat, and across the fire-place from him, sat two humble-looking women. Seeing them there seemed to provoke him, and he said, "Well, ladies, what can I do for you?" One was an old woman, the other young. They both commenced talking at once. The President soon comprehended them. "I suppose," said he, "that your son and your husband are in prison for resisting the draft in Western Pennsylvania. Where is your petition?" The old lady replied, "Mr. Lincoln, I've got no petition; I went to a lawyer to get one drawn, and I had not the money to pay him and come here too; so I thought I would just come and ask you to let me have my boy." "And it's your husband you want?" said he, turning to the young woman. "Yes," said she.

He rung his bell and called his servant, and bade him to go and tell Gen. Dana to bring him the list of prisoners for resisting the draft in Western Pennsylvania.

The General soon came, bringing a package of papers. The President opened it, and, counting the names, said, "General, there are twenty-seven of these men. Is there any difference in degree of their guilt?" "No," said the General. "It is a bad case, and a merciful finding." "Well," said the President, looking out of the window and seemingly talking to himself, "these poor fellows have, I think, suffered enough; they have been in prison fifteen months. I have been thinking so for some time, and have so said to Stanton, and he always threatened to resign if they are released. But he has said so about other matters, and never did. So now, while I have the paper in my hand, I will turn out the flock." So he wrote, "Let the prisoners named in the within paper be discharged," and signed it. The General made his bow and left. Then, turning to the ladies, he said, "Now ladies, you can go. Your son, madam, and your husband, madam, is free."

The young woman ran across to him and began to kneel. He took her by the elbow and said, impatiently, "Get up, get up; none of this." But the old woman walked to him, wiping her apron with the tears that were coursing down her cheeks. She gave him her hand, and looking into his face said, "Good-bye, Mr. Lincoln, we will never meet again till we meet in Heaven." A change came over his sad and weary face. He clasped her hand in both of his, and followed her to the door, saying as he went, "With all that I have to cross me here, I am afraid that I will never get there; but your wish that you will meet me there has fully paid for all I have done for you."

We were then alone. He drew his chair to the fire and said, "Speed, I am a little alarmed about myself; just feel my hand." It was cold and clammy.

He pulled off his boots, and, putting his feet to the fire, the heat made them steam. I said overwork was producing nervousness. "No," said he, "I am not tired." I said, "Such a scene as I have just witnessed is enough to make you nervous." "How much you are mistaken," said he; "I have made two people happy to-day; I have given a mother her son, and a wife her husband. That young woman is a counterfeit, but the old woman is a true mother."

This is the fruit of the flower we saw bloom in the incident of the birds.

Mr. Lincoln was a cool, brave man. His physical courage was never questioned. His moral courage was grand. He was cautious about expressing himself against public sentiment when it would do no good; but when it became necessary he did so with emphasis, earnestness, and force. . . .

Lincoln was fond of anecdotes, and told them well. It was a great mental relief to him. All great thinkers must have mental relaxation. He did not know one card from another, therefore could not play. He never drank, and hated low company. Fault has been found by some fastidious persons with his habit of story-telling — in other words, with his method of illustration by means of anecdote. It is said this was undignified. A fable, a parable, or an anecdote, is nothing more than illustrating a real case by an imaginary one. A positive statement embraces but one case, while a fable, a parable, or an anecdote may cover a whole class of cases.

Take, for instance, his conversation with W. C. Reeves, of Virginia, whom he greatly admired. Reeves came with other gentlemen from Richmond soon after his inauguration. A convention was in session in Richmond to decide whether Virginia would go out or stay in the Union. Mr. Reeves was a Union man, and proceeded to advise the President. His advice was, to surrender Forts Sumter and Pickens, and all the property of the Government in the Southern States. Mr. Lincoln asked him if he remembered the fable of the Lion and the Woodsman's Daughter. Mr. Reeves said that he did not. Aesop, said the President, reports that a lion was very much in love with a woodsman's daughter. The fair maid, afraid to say no, referred him to her father. The lion applied for the girl. The father replied, your teeth are too long. The lion went to a dentist and had them extracted. Returning, he asked for his bride. No, said the woodsman, your claws are too long. Going back to the Dentist, he had them drawn. Then, returning to claim his bride, the woodsman, seeing that he was disarmed, beat out his brains. "May it not be so," said Mr. Lincoln, "with me, if I give up all that is asked."

I have often been asked what were Mr. Lincoln's religious opinions. When I knew him, in early life, he was a skeptic. He had tried hard to be a believer, but his reason could not grasp and solve the great problem of redemption as taught. He was very cautious never to give expression to any thought or sentiment that would grate harshly upon a Christian's ear. For a sincere Christian he had great respect. He often said that the most ambitious man might live to see every hope fail; but, no Christian could live to see his fail, because fulfillment could only come when life ended. But this was a subject we never discussed. The only evidence I have of any change, was in the summer before he was killed. I was invited out to the Soldier's Home to spend the night. As I entered the room, near night, he was sitting near a window intently reading his Bible. Approaching him I said, "I am glad to see you so profitably engaged." "Yes," said he, "I am profitably engaged." "Well," said I, "if you have recovered from your skepticism, I am sorry to say that I have not." Looking me earnestly in the face, and placing his hand on my shoulder, he said, "You are wrong Speed, take all of this book upon reason that you can, and the balance on faith, and you will live and die a happier and better man."

I am indebted for the following to Judge Gillespie, one of Mr. Lincoln's most trusted and intimate friends, who occasionally went to Washington to see him. Wanting no office, he was always welcome. The Judge says, Mr. Lincoln once said to me that he could never reconcile the prescience of the Deity with the uncertainty of events. But he thought it would be profitless to teach his views.

The Judge adds, I asked him once what was to be done with the South after the rebellion was put down. He said some thought their heads ought to come off; but, said he, if it was left to me, I could not tell where to draw the line between those whose heads should come off, and those whose heads should stay on. He said that he had recently been reading the history of the rebellion of Absalom, and that he inclined to adopt the views of David. Said he, "When David was fleeing from Jerusalem Shimei cursed him. After the rebellion was put down Shimei craved pardon. Abishai, David's nephew, the son of Zeruiah, David's sister, said, 'This man ought not to be pardoned, because he cursed the Lord's anointed.' David said, 'what have I to do with you, ye sons of Zeruiah, that you should this day be adversaries unto me. Know ye that not a man shall be put to death in Israel.'"

This was like his anecdotes, and was illustrative of what he thought would come about. He would be pressed to put men to death because they had rebelled. But, like David, he intended to say, "know ye that not a man shall be put to death in Israel."

Mr. Lincoln's person was ungainly. He was six feet four inches in height; a little stooped in the shoulders; his legs and arms were long; his feet and hands large; his forehead was high. His head was over the average size. His eyes were gray. His face and forehead were wrinkled even in his youth. They deepened in age, "as streams their channels deeper wear." Generally he was a very sad man, and his countenance indicated it. But when he warmed up all sadness vanished, his face was radiant and glowing, and almost gave expression to his thoughts before his tongue could utter them. If I was asked what it was that threw such charm around him, I would say that it was his perfect naturalness. He could act no part but his own. He copied no one either in manner or style. His style was more florid in the published speeches of his early life than his later productions. . . .

Mr. Lincoln was a man of great common sense. He was a common man expanded into giant proportions; well acquainted with the people, he placed his hand on the beating pulse of the Nation, judged of its disease, and was ever ready with a remedy. He had an abiding faith in the good sense and intuitions of the people. Wendell Phillips aptly described him as the Indian hunter, who lays his ear to the ground and listens for the tramp of the coming millions.

I have often been asked where Lincoln got his style. His father had but few books. The Bible, Esop's Fables, Weems's Life of Washington, and Bunyan's Pilgrim's Progress. These he almost committed to memory. From these I suppose he got his style. His mind was not quick, but solid and retentive. It was like polished steel, a mark once made upon it was never erased. His memory of events, of facts, dates, faces, and names, surprised every one.

In the winter of 1841, a gloom came over him till his friends were alarmed for his life. Though a member of the legislature he rarely attended its sessions. In his deepest gloom, and when I told him he would die unless he rallied, he said, "I am not afraid and would be more than willing. But I have an irrepressible desire to live till I can be assured that the world is a little better for my having lived in it." A noble and commendable ambition. It is for posterity to say whether his ambition was gratified. Four millions of slaves were made freemen by his proclamation, and the principle engrafted in the Constitution of his country, that, for all time, men and women shall not be bought and sold. If it be permitted him to look back upon the land of his love, how gratified he must be to see that no party in this broad land opposes the great principles he advocated and established. Even now the mystic chords of memory, stretching from every battle-field and patriot grave to every living heart and hearthstone all over the land, is swelling the chorus of the Union, and all hearts are touched by the better angels of our nature.

In early summer of 1841, Mr. Lincoln came to Kentucky and spent several months at Farmington, the home of my mother, near this city. On his return to Illinois, thinking that some recognition of the kindness shown him was due, he wrote a letter to my sister, Miss Mary Speed, in which he gives among other things an account of his trip on a steamboat from Louisville to St. Louis, and though the letter has been published I will here give a portion of it.

The scene he describes bears so intimate a relation to his after-life, I think it probable that it may be considered as concentrating his opposition to slavery. He says, "A fine example was presented on board the boat for contemplating the effect of condition upon human happiness. A gentleman had purchased twelve negroes in different parts of Kentucky, and was taking them to a farm in the South. They were chained six and six together, a small iron clevis was around the left wrist of each, and this fastened to the main chain by a shorter at a convenient distance from the others, so that the negroes were strung together precisely like so many fish upon a trot-line. In this condition they were being separated forever from the scenes of their childhood, their friends, their fathers and mothers, and brothers and sisters, and many of them from their wives and children, and going into perpetual slavery, where the lash of the master is proverbially more ruthless than anywhere else; and yet amid all these distressing circumstances, as we would think them, they were the most cheerful and apparently happy people on board. One, whose offense for which he was sold was an over-fondness for his wife, played the fiddle almost continually, and others danced, sung, cracked jokes, and played various games with cards from day to day. How true it is that 'God tempers the wind to the shorn lamb,' or, in other words, that he renders the worst of human conditions tolerable, while he permits the best to be nothing better than tolerable."

Note

1. Mark Neely, *The Abraham Lincoln Encyclopedia*, 285.

Joshua F. Speed, *Reminiscences of Abraham Lincoln and Notes of a Visit to California: Two Lectures* (Louisville: John P. Morton, 1884), 16–41.

From *The Life of Abraham Lincoln* (1860)

WILLIAM DEAN HOWELLS

> William Dean Howells (1837–1920), who became arguably America's most
> famous and influential author and editor in the years after the Civil War, was
> born in Martin's Ferry, Ohio, the son of William Cooper Howells, a "country
> printer." His father's radical newspaper struggled to survive in pro-slavery
> southern Ohio, and Howells learned sympathy for liberty and social justice
> at home, sensibilities that became crucial to his art. Beginning to set type in
> childhood, he acquired habits of hard work that remained to his deathbed.
> *My Literary Passions* (1895) and *Years of My Youth* (1916) tell how this amaz-
> ing autodidact, schooled largely in the print shop, also mastered languages
> and literatures.
>
> Between 1860 and 1916 Howells published thirty-six novels, twelve books
> of travel, ten volumes of short stories and sketches, and many other col-
> lections of literary criticism, poetry, and drama. He also managed to com-
> pose two presidential campaign biographies, the first being his work during
> Lincoln's campaign of 1860. In 1861, Lincoln's secretaries John G. Nicolay
> and John Hay helped Howells win appointment as the U.S. consul in Venice.
> These excerpts suggest similarities between the frontier youths of Lincoln
> and his biographer Howells, a congruence that made Howells such an ex-
> cellent observer of Lincoln's own voracious appetite for both everyday hard
> work and the enchantments of the printed page.

. . . OFFUTT, AS HAS BEEN SEEN, was a man of resource and decision. He
came ashore from his flat-boat and resolutely rented the very mill of which
the dam had caused his disaster, together with an old store-room, which
he filled with a stock of goods, and gave in the clerkly charge of Abraham
Lincoln, with the munificent salary of fifteen dollars a month.

Lincoln had already made his first speech. General W. L. D. Ewing, and
a politician named Posey, who afterward achieved notoriety in the Black
Hawk war, had addressed the freemen of Macon the year previous, "on
the issues of the day." Mr. Posey had, however, in violation of venerable

precedent and sacred etiquette, failed to invite the sovereigns to drink something. They were justly indignant, and persuaded Lincoln to reply, in the expectation that he would possibly make himself offensive to Posey. Lincoln, however, took the stump with characteristic modesty, and begging his friends not to laugh if he broke down, treated very courteously the two speakers who had preceded him, discussed questions of politics, and in his peroration eloquently pictured the future of Illinois. There was sense and reason in his arguments, and his imaginative flight tickled the State pride of the Illinoisans. It was declared that Lincoln had made the best speech of the day; and he, to his great astonishment, found himself a prophet among those of his own household, while his titled fellow-orator cordially complimented his performance.

At New Salem, he now found the leisure and the opportunity to initiate a system of self-education. At last, he had struggled to a point, where he could not only take breath, but could stoop and drink from those springs of knowledge, which a hopeless poverty, incessant toil, and his roving, uncertain life, had, till then, forbidden to his lips.

There seems never to have been any doubt of his ability among Lincoln's acquaintances, any more than there was a doubt of his honesty, his generosity, and gentle-heartedness. When, therefore, he began to make rapid progress in his intellectual pursuits, it surprised none of them — least of all, Lincoln's shrewd patron, Offutt, who had been known to declare, with pardonable enthusiasm, that Lincoln was the smartest man in the United States.

The first branch of learning which he took up, was English grammar, acquiring that science from the dry and meager treatise of Kirkham. The book was not to be had in the immediate vicinity, and Lincoln walked seven or eight miles to borrow a copy. He then devoted himself to the study with the whole strength of his resolute nature; and in three weeks he had gained a fair practical knowledge of the grammar. No doubt the thing was hard to the uncultivated mind, though that mind *was* of great depth and fertility. One of his friends relates that Lincoln used to take him aside, and require explanations of the sententious Kirkham, whenever he visited New Salem.

This young backwoodsman had the stubborn notion that because the Lincolns had always been people of excellent sense, he, a Lincoln, might become a person of distinction. He had talked, he said, with men who were regarded as great, and he did not see where they differed so much from others. He reasoned, probably, that the secret of their success lay in the fact of original capacity, and untiring industry. He was conscious of his own powers; he was a logician, and could not resist logical conclusions. If he studied, why might not he achieve?

And Kirkham fell before him. One incident of his study, was a dispute with the learned man of the place, — a very *savant* among the unlettered pioneers — in regard to a grammatical nicety, and the question being referred to competent authority, it was decided in Lincoln's favor, to his pride and exultation.

Concluding his grammatical studies with Kirkham, he next turned his attention to mathematics, and took up a work on surveying, with which he made himself thoroughly acquainted.

So great was his ardor in study, at this time, that shrewd suspicions with regard to Offutt's clerk got abroad; the honest neighbors began to question whether one who would voluntarily spend all his leisure in "poring over miserable books," could be altogether right in his mind.

The peculiar manner in which he afterward pursued his law studies, was not calculated to allay popular feelings. He bought an old copy of Blackstone, one day, at auction, in Springfield, and on his return to New Salem, attacked the work with characteristic energy.

His favorite place of study was a wooded knoll near New Salem, where he threw himself under a wide-spreading oak, and expansively made a reading desk of the hillside. Here he would pore over Blackstone day after day, shifting his position as the sun rose and sank, so as to keep in the shade, and utterly unconscious of everything but the principles of common law. People went by, and he took no account of them; the salutations of acquaintances ere returned with silence, or a vacant stare; and altogether the manner of the absorbed student was not unlike that of one distraught.

Since that day, his habits of study have changed somewhat, but his ardor remains unabated, and he is now regarded as one of the best informed, as he is certainly the ablest, man in Illinois.

When practicing law, before hie election to Congress, a copy of Burns was his inseparable companion on the circuit; and this he perused so constantly, that it is said he has now by heart every line of his favorite poet. He is also a diligent student of Shakespeare, "to know whom is a liberal education."

The bent of his mind, however, is mathematical and metaphysical, and he is therefore pleased with the absolute and logical method of Poe's tales and sketches, in which the problem of mystery is given, and wrought out into every-day facts by processes of cunning analysis. It is said that he suffers no year to pass without the perusal of this author.

Books, of all sorts, the eager student devoured with an insatiable appetite; and newspapers were no less precious to him. The first publication for which he ever subscribed, was the *Louisville Journal*, which he paid for when he could secure the intellectual luxury only at the expense of physical comfort.

It was a day of great rejoicing with Lincoln, when President Jackson appointed him postmaster at New Salem. He was a Whig, but the office was of so little pecuniary significance, that it was bestowed irrespective of politics. Lincoln, indeed, was the only person in the community whose accomplishments were equal to the task of making out the mail returns for the Department.

An acquaintance says that the Presidency can never make our candidate happier than the post-office did then. He foresaw unlimited opportunities for reading newspapers, and of satisfying his appetite for knowledge.

But it was not through reading alone that Lincoln cultivated his intellect. The grave and practical American mind has always found entertainment and profit in disputation, and the debating clubs are what every American youth is subject to. They are useful in many ways. They safely vent the mental exuberance of youth; these whom destiny intended for the bar and the Senate, they assist; those who have a mistaken vocation to oratory, they mercifully extinguish.

Even in that day, and that rude country, where learning was a marvelous and fearful exception, the debating school flourished, in part as a literary institution, and in part as a rustic frolic.

Lincoln delighted in practicing polemics, as it was called, and used to walk six and seven miles through the woods to attend the disputation in his neighborhood. Of course, many of the debates were infinitely funny, for the disputants were, frequently, men without education. Here, no doubt, Lincoln stored his mind with anecdote and comic illustration, while he delighted his auditors with his own wit and reason, and added to his growing popularity.

This popularity had been early founded by a stroke of firmness and bravery on Lincoln's part, when he first came into Sangamon county. . . .

A pleasant story connected with this part of his political career is related by Hon. John D. Stuart. Lincoln and Stuart were both candidates for the legislature in 1834. Stuart's election was conceded, while that of Lincoln was thought to be comparatively uncertain. The two candidates happened to be present together at a backwoods frolic, when some disaffected of Stuart's party took Lincoln aside, and offered to withdraw votes enough from Stuart to elect him. He rejected the proposal, and at once disclosed the scheme to Stuart, declaring that he would not make such a bargain for any office.

It is by such manly and generous acts that Lincoln has endeared himself to all his old neighbors. It may be said of him without extravagance that he is beloved of all — even by those against whose interests he has conscientiously acted. When in the practice of the law he was never known to undertake a cause which he believed founded in wrong and injustice. "You are not strictly in the right," he said to a person who once wished him to bring a certain suit, and who now tells the story with profound admiration. "I might give the other parties considerable trouble, and perhaps beat them at law, but there would be no justice in it. I am sorry — I cannot undertake your case." "I never knew Lincoln to do a mean act in his life," said Stuart, the veteran lawyer, who first encouraged Lincoln to adopt his profession. "God never made a finer man," exclaimed the old backwoods-man, Close, when applied to for reminiscences of Lincoln. So by the testimony of all, and in the memory of every one who has known him, Lincoln is a pure, candid, and upright man, unblemished by those vices which so often disfigure greatness, utterly incapable of falsehood, and without one base or sordid trait.

During the legislative canvass of 1834, John D. Stuart advised Lincoln to study law, and after the election he borrowed some of Stuart's books, and began to read. Other warm and influential friends, (Wm. Butler, the present Treasurer of State in Illinois, was one of these,) came to Lincoln's material aid and encouragement, and assisted him to retrieve his early errors of generosity. With the support of these friends — for Lincoln is a man who could receive benefits as nobly as he conferred them — and the slender revenues of his surveyorship, he struggled through the term of his law studies, and was admitted to the bar in 1836. Business flowed in upon him, and quitting New Salem, he took up his residence at Springfield, where he united his professional fortunes with those of Major Stuart. The two old friends remained in partnership until Stuart's election to Congress, by

which time Lincoln had elevated himself to a position among the first lawyers of the place. In the midst of affairs, however, he never relaxed his habits of study; taking up, one by one, the natural sciences, and thoroughly ac-
quainting himself with the most abstruse metaphysics. He remains to this
day a severe and indefatigable student never suffering any subject to which
he directs his attention, to pass without profound investigation.

William Dean Howells, *The Life of Abraham Lincoln*. 1860 (Bloomington: Indiana UP, 1960), 28–33, 46–47.

From "Eulogy for Henry Clay" (1852)

ABRAHAM LINCOLN

> Lincoln venerated the great statesman from Kentucky, Henry Clay (1777–1852), considering the U.S. Senator to be the greatest orator in the nation. Like Clay, Lincoln aimed to ensure that all public moments "were made for practical effect," and one of his intentions was to garner support for his brand of ideology and build the consensus necessary to save the Union.[1] To integrate the diverse aspects of the American heritage, Lincoln invented in the First Inaugural his well-known metaphor of the "mystic chords of memory" as a central image uniting all the rest. Quite literally, these chords appear to stretch from place to place, forming a massive weblike network by which all true-blooded Americans are joined. This "mystic chords" image can be noted here in Lincoln's description of Henry Clay: "[Clay] truly touches the chords of human sympathy. . . . All his efforts were made for practical effect. He never spoke merely to be heard." In this crucial point, Lincoln wished to follow in Clay's footsteps. Both agreed that a successful writer and rhetor must somehow weave "chords" to connect with the listener or reader.
>
> Lincoln delivered this eulogy at the Illinois State House in Springfield on July 6, 1852.

ON THE FOURTH DAY of July, 1776, the people of a few feeble and oppressed colonies of Great Britain, inhabiting a portion of the Atlantic coast of North America, publicly declared their national independence, and made their appeal to the justice of their cause, and to the God of battles, for the maintainance of that declaration. That people were few in numbers, and without resources, save only their own wise heads and stout hearts. Within the first year of that declared independence, and while its maintenance was yet problematical—while the bloody struggle between those resolute rebels, and their haughty would-be-masters, was still waging, of undistinguished parents, and in an obscure district of one of those colonies, Henry Clay was born. The infant nation, and the infant child began the race of life together. For three quarters of a century they have travelled hand in hand.

They have been companions ever. The nation has passed its perils, and is free, prosperous, and powerful. The child has reached his manhood, his middle age, his old age, and is dead. In all that has concerned the nation the man ever sympathised; and now the nation mourns for the man. . . .

Henry Clay was born on the 12th of April 1777, in Hanover County, Virginia. Of his father, who died in the fourth or fifth year of Henry's age, little seems to be known, except that he was a respectable man, and a preacher of the Baptist persuasion. Mr. Clay's education, to the end of his life, was comparatively limited. I say *"to the end of his life"* because I have understood that, from time to time, he added something to his education during the greater part of his whole life. Mr. Clay's lack of a more perfect early education, however it may be regretted generally, teaches at least one profitable lesson; it teaches that in this country, one can scarcely be so poor, but that, if he *will*, he *can* acquire sufficient education to get through the world respectably. In his twenty-third year Mr. Clay was licensed to practice law, and emigrated to Lexington, Kentucky. Here he commenced and continued the practice till the year 1803, when he was first elected to the Kentucky Legislature. By successive elections he was continued in the Legislature till the latter part of 1806, when he was elected to fill a vacancy, of a single session, in the United States Senate. In 1807 he was again elected to the Kentucky House of Representatives, and by that body, chosen its speaker. In 1808 he was re-elected to the same body. In 1809 he was again chosen to fill a vacancy of two years in the United States Senate. In 1811 he was elected to the United States House of Representatives, and on the first day of taking his seat in that body, he was chosen its speaker. In 1813 he was again elected Speaker. Early in 1814, being the period of our last British war, Mr. Clay was sent as commissioner, with others, to negotiate a treaty of peace, which treaty was concluded in the latter part of the same year. On his return from Europe he was again elected to the lower branch of Congress, and on taking his seat in December 1815 was called to his old post—the speaker's chair, a position in which he was retained, by successive elections, with one brief intermission, till the inauguration of John Q. Adams in March 1825. He was then appointed Secretary of State, and occupied that important station till the inauguration of Gen. Jackson in March 1829. After this he returned to Kentucky, resumed the practice of the law, and continued it till the Autumn of 1831, when he was by the Legislature of Kentucky, again placed in the United States Senate. By a re-election he was continued in the

Senate till he resigned his seat, and retired, in March 1842. In December 1849 he again took his seat in the Senate, which he again resigned only a few months before his death.

By the foregoing it is perceived that the period from the beginning of Mr. Clay's official life, in 1803, to the end of it in 1852, is but one year short of half a century; and that the sum of all the intervals in it, will not amount to ten years. But mere duration of time in office, constitutes the smallest part of Mr. Clay's history. Throughout that long period, he has constantly been the most loved, and most implicitly followed by friends, and the most dreaded by opponents, of all living American politicians. In all the great questions which have agitated the country, and particularly in those great and fearful crises, the Missouri question — the Nullification question, and the late slavery question, as connected with the newly acquired territory, involving and endangering the stability of the Union, his has been the leading and most conspicuous part. In 1824 he was first a candidate for the Presidency, and was defeated; and, although he was successively defeated for the same office in 1832, and in 1844, there has never been a moment since 1824 till after 1848 when a very large portion of the American people did not cling to him with an enthusiastic hope and purpose of still elevating him to the Presidency. With other men, to be defeated, was to be forgotten; but to him, defeat was but a trifling incident, neither changing him, or the world's estimate of him. Even those of both political parties, who have been preferred to him for the highest office, have run far briefer courses than he, and left him, still shining, high in the heavens of the political world. Jackson, Van Buren, Harrison, Polk, and Taylor, all rose *after*, and set long before him. The spell — the long enduring spell — with which the souls of men were bound to him, is a miracle. Who can compass it? It is probably true he owed his pre-eminence to no one quality, but to a fortunate combination of several. He was surpassingly eloquent; but many eloquent men fail utterly; and they are not, as a class, generally successful. His judgment was excellent; but many men of good judgment, live and die unnoticed. His will was indomitable; but this quality often secures to its owner nothing better than a character for useless obstinacy. These then were Mr. Clay's leading qualities. No one of them is very uncommon; but all taken together are rarely combined in a single individual; and this is probably the reason why such men as Henry Clay are so rare in the world.

Mr. Clay's eloquence did not consist, as many fine specimens of eloquence does [do], of types and figures — of antithesis, and elegant arrangement of words and sentences; but rather of that deeply earnest and impassioned tone, and manner, which can proceed only from great sincerity and a thorough conviction, in the speaker of the justice and importance of his cause. This it is, that truly touches the chords of human sympathy; and those who heard Mr. Clay, never failed to be moved by it, or ever afterwards, forgot the impression. All his efforts were made for practical effect. He never spoke merely to be heard. He never delivered a Fourth of July Oration, or an eulogy on an occasion like this. As a politician or statesman, no one was so habitually careful to avoid all sectional ground. Whatever he did, he did for the whole country. In the construction of his measures he ever carefully surveyed every part of the field, and duly weighed every conflicting interest. Feeling, as he did, and as the truth surely is, that the world's best hope depended on the continued Union of these States, he was ever jealous of, and watchful for, whatever might have the slightest tendency to separate them.

Mr. Clay's predominant sentiment, from first to last, was a deep devotion to the cause of human liberty — a strong sympathy with the oppressed every where, and an ardent wish for their elevation. With him, this was a primary and all controlling passion. Subsidiary to this was the conduct of his whole life. He loved his country partly because it was his own country, but mostly because it was a free country; and he burned with a zeal for its advancement, prosperity and glory, because he saw in such, the advancement, prosperity and glory, of human liberty, human right and human nature. He desired the prosperity of his countrymen partly because they were his countrymen, but chiefly to show to the world that freemen could be prosperous. . . .

But he is gone. Let us strive to deserve, as far as mortals may, the continued care of Divine Providence, trusting that, in future national emergencies, He will not fail to provide us the instruments of safety and security.

Note

1. Waldo Braden, *Abraham Lincoln: Public Speaker* (Baton Rouge: Louisiana State UP, 1988), 44.

Basler, ed., *Collected Works*, 2:121–32.

From *Herndon's Lincoln* (1889)

WILLIAM HENRY HERNDON AND JESSE W. WEIK

William Herndon (1818–1891) was Lincoln's law partner, beginning in 1844, and later became one of the key biographers and collectors of Lincoln materials for the remainder of his life. He clerked in Joshua Speed's store, where he became intimate with Speed and Lincoln. He is best known today for the immense number of materials he gathered from friends, family members, and co-workers of Lincoln, after the president's death. His collaboration with Jesse Weik, known as *Herndon's Lincoln* and containing extensive primary materials, was published in 1889. Herndon was highly controversial during his lifetime and remains so today, largely for his idiosyncratic readings of Lincoln materials, including his popularizing of the Ann Rutledge incident and his disputing of the dead president's commitments to Christian orthodoxy. Herndon's views of Lincoln were often questionable and sometimes simply wrong, yet much of his insight and information about Lincoln is invaluable and unavailable from any other source.

HISTORY FURNISHES few characters whose lives and careers were so nearly parallel as those of Lincoln and [Stephen] Douglas. They met for the first time at the Legislature in Vandalia in 1834, where Lincoln was a member of the House of Representatives and Douglas was in the lobby. The next year Douglas was also a member. In 1839 both were admitted to practice in the Supreme Court of Illinois on the same day. In 1841 both courted the same young lady. In 1846 both represented Illinois in Congress at Washington, the one in the upper and the other in the lower House. In 1858 they were opposing candidates for United States Senator; and finally, to complete the remarkable counterpart, both were candidates for the Presidency in 1860. While it is true that their ambitions ran in parallel lines, yet they were exceedingly unlike in all other particulars. Douglas was short, — something over five feet high, — heavy set, with a large head, broad shoulders, deep chest, and striking features. He was polite and affable, but fearless. He had that unique trait, magnetism, fully developed in his nature, and that attracted a host of friends and readily made him a popular idol. He had had extensive experience in debate, and had been trained by contact for years with the great minds and orators in Congress. He was full of political history, well informed on general topics, eloquent almost to the point of brilliancy, self-confident to the point of arrogance, and a dangerous competitor in every respect. What he lacked in ingenuity he made up in strategy, and if in debate he could not tear down the structure of his opponent's argument by a direct and violent attack, he was by no means reluctant to resort to a strained restatement of the latter's position or to the extravagance of ridicule. Lincoln knew his man thoroughly and well. He had often met Douglas on the stump; was familiar with his tactics, and though fully aware of his "want of fixed political morals," was not averse to measuring swords with the elastic and flexible "Little Giant."

Lincoln himself was constructed on an entirely different foundation. His base was plain common-sense, direct statement, and the inflexibility of logic. In physical make-up he was cold — at least not magnetic — and made no effort to dazzle people by his bearing. He cared nothing for a following, and though he had often before struggled for a political prize, yet in his efforts he never had strained his well-known spirit of fairness or open love of the truth. He analyzed everything, laid every statement bare, and by dint of his broad reasoning powers and manliness of admission inspired his hearers with deep conviction of his earnestness and honesty. Douglas may have electrified the crowds with his eloquence or charmed them with his majestic bearing and dexterity in debate, but as each man, after the meetings were over and the applause had died away, went to his home, his head rang with Lincoln's logic and appeal to manhood.

A brief description of Mr. Lincoln's appearance on the stump and of his manner when speaking may not be without interest. When standing erect he was six feet four inches high. He was lean in flesh and ungainly in figure. Aside from the sad, pained look due to habitual melancholy, his face had no characteristic or fixed expression. He was thin through the chest, and hence slightly stoop-shouldered. When he arose to address courts, juries, or crowds of people, his body inclined forward to a slight degree. At first he was very awkward, and it seemed a real labor to adjust himself to his surroundings. He struggled for a time under a feeling of apparent diffidence and sensitiveness, and these only added to his awkwardness. I have often seen and sympathized with Mr. Lincoln during these moments. When he began speaking, his voice was shrill, piping, and unpleasant. His manner, his attitude, his dark, yellow face, wrinkled and dry, his oddity of pose, his diffident movements — everything seemed to be against him, but only for a short time. After having arisen, he generally placed his hands behind him, the back of his left hand in the palm of his right, the thumb and fingers of his right hand clasped around the left arm at the wrist. For a few moments he played the combination of awkwardness, sensitiveness, and diffidence. As he proceeded he became somewhat animated, and to keep in harmony with his growing warmth his hands relaxed their grasp and fell to his side. Presently he clasped them in front of him, interlocking his fingers, one thumb meanwhile chasing another. His speech now requiring more emphatic utterance, his fingers unlocked and his hands fell apart. His left arm was thrown behind, the back of his hand resting against his body, his right hand seeking his side. By this time he had gained sufficient composure, and his real speech began. He did not gesticulate as much with his hands as with his head. He used the latter frequently, throwing it with vim this way and that. This movement was a significant one when he sought to enforce his statement. It sometimes came with a quick jerk, as if throwing off electric sparks into combustible material. He never sawed the air nor rent space into tatters and rags as some orators do. He never acted for stage effect. He was cool, considerate, reflective — in time self-possessed and self-reliant. His style was clear, terse, and compact. In argument he was logical, demonstrative, and fair. He was careless of his dress, and his clothes, instead of fitting neatly as did the garments of Douglas on the latter's well-rounded form, hung loosely on his giant frame. As he moved along in his speech he became freer and less uneasy in his movements; to that extent he was graceful. He had a perfect naturalness, a strong individuality; and to that extent he was dignified. He despised glitter, show, set forms, and shams. He spoke with effectiveness and to move the judgment as well as the emotions of men. There was a world of meaning and emphasis in the long, bony finger of his right hand as he dotted the ideas on the minds of his hearers. Sometimes, to express joy or pleasure, he would raise both hands at an angle of about fifty degrees, the palms upward, as if desirous of embracing the spirit of that which he loved. If the sentiment was one of detestation — denunciation of slavery, for example — both arms, thrown upward and fists clenched, swept through the air, and he expressed an execration that was truly sublime. This was one of his most effective gestures, and signified most vividly

[41]

a fixed determination to drag down the object of his hatred and trample it in the dust. He always stood squarely on his feet, toe even with toe; that is, he never put one foot before the other. He neither touched nor leaned on anything for support. He made but few changes in his positions and attitudes. He never ranted, never walked backward and forward on the platform. To ease his arms he frequently caught hold, with his left hand, of the lapel of his coat, keeping his thumb upright and leaving his right hand free to gesticulate. The designer of the monument recently erected in Chicago has happily caught him in just this attitude. As he proceeded with his speech the exercise of his vocal organs altered somewhat the tone of his voice. It lost in a measure its former acute and shrilling pitch, and mellowed into a more harmonious and pleasant sound. His form expanded, and, notwithstanding the sunken breast, he rose up a splendid and imposing figure. In his defence of the Declaration of Independence—his greatest inspiration—he was "tremendous in the directness of his utterances; he rose to impassioned eloquence, unsurpassed by Patrick Henry, Mirabeau, or Vergniaud, as his soul was inspired with the thought of human right and Divine justice" [from Horace White, reporter for the *Chicago Tribune*]. His little gray eyes flashed in a face aglow with the fire of his profound thoughts; and his uneasy movements and diffident manner sunk themselves beneath the wave of righteous indignation that came sweeping over him. Such was Lincoln the orator.

We can somewhat appreciate the feeling with which Douglas, aggressive and fearless though he was, welcomed a contest with such a man as Lincoln. Four years before, in a joint debate with him, he had asked for a cessation of forensic hostilities, conceding that his opponent of rail-splitting fame had given him "more trouble than all the United States Senate together." Now he was brought face to face with him again.

It is unnecessary and not in keeping with the purpose of this work to reproduce here the speeches made by either Lincoln or Douglas in their justly renowned debate. Briefly stated, Lincoln's position was announced in his opening speech at Springfield: "'A house divided against itself cannot stand.' I believe this Government cannot endure permanently half slave and half free. I do not expect the Union to be dissolved, I do not expect the house to fall—but I do expect it will cease to be divided. It will become all the one thing or the other. Either the opponents of slavery will arrest the further spread of it and place it where the public mind shall rest in the belief that it is in the course of ultimate extinction; or its advocates will push it forward till it becomes alike lawful in all the states, old as well as new, North as well as South." The position of Douglas on the question of slavery was one of indifference. He advocated with all his power the doctrine of "Popular Sovereignty," a proposition, as quaintly put by Lincoln, which meant that, "if one man chooses to enslave another, no third man has a right to object." At the last joint discussion in Alton, Lincoln, after reflecting on the patriotism of any man who was so indifferent to the wrong of slavery that he cared not whether it was voted up or down, closed his speech with this stirring summary: "That [slavery] is the real issue. That is the issue that will continue in this country when these poor tongues of Judge Douglas and myself shall be silent. It is the eternal struggle between these two principles—right and wrong—throughout the world. They are the two principles that have stood face to face from the beginning of time, and will ever continue to struggle. The one is the common right of humanity, and the other the divine right of kings. It is the same principle, in whatever shape it develops itself. It is the same spirit that says: 'You work and toil and earn bread, and I eat it.' No matter in what shape it comes, whether from the mouth of a king who seeks to bestride the people of his own nation and live by the fruit of their labor, or from one race of men as an apology for enslaving another race, it is the same tyrannical principle."

William Henry Herndon and Jesse W. Weik, *Herndon's Lincoln: The True Story of a Great Life* (Chicago: Belford, Clarke, 1889), 2:403–10.

From *The Real Lincoln* (1922)

Jesse W. Weik

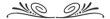

Best known as William H. Herndon's collaborator on his famous biography
of Lincoln, Jesse William Weik (1857–1930) was born in Greencastle, Indiana,
and lived there most of his life. When he was eighteen years old, Weik wrote
Herndon requesting a Lincoln autograph and received a reply containing one
of Lincoln's earliest written pieces—six years later.[1]

Forced by poor health to quit his job, Weik began a writing career with
an article on Lincoln for which he solicited Herndon's aid. Ultimately, Herndon became convinced that he and Weik should collaborate on a book, and
Weik leaped at the opportunity. Herndon wrote rough and rambling drafts of
chapters on particular subjects which Weik turned into readable and often
elegant literature. Herndon and Weik's book went through several editions,
and the manuscripts they collected became the principal source of information on Lincoln's early life.

THE MOMENT THE train steamed out of Springfield the newspaper men, one
of them being the late, Henry Villard, gathered about Lincoln and asked
him to furnish them with a copy of his speech; reminding him that they
were given no chance to take it down as delivered. He answered that his
remarks were extempore and therefore not in manuscript form, but he assured them that he would write the speech in full. He therefore beckoned
to Nicolay, who provided paper and pencil, and he proceeded to comply
with the request. He penciled a few lines, then halted and turned the paper
over to Nicolay, who began writing where he left off, Lincoln meanwhile
dictating to him. Presently at his request Nicolay returned the paper to him
and he resumed the writing himself, but erelong, due to nervousness or the
motion of the train, he desisted a second time and again invoked the aid
of Nicolay, who continued the task, all of which verifies the statement that
the farewell address at Springfield published in the "Century Magazine"
in connection with the Nicolay and Hay "Life of Lincoln," was correctly
printed from the original manuscript, having been written immediately

after the train started, partly by Lincoln's own hand and partly by that of his private secretary from his dictation. When I visited Mr. Nicolay he showed me not only this manuscript, but a number of others also in Lincoln's handwriting, explaining that before he left Springfield Lincoln was so solicitous and careful regarding his utterances *en route* to Washington that he prepared and wrote out in advance such speeches as he expected to make. The manuscripts were enclosed in separate envelopes and properly labeled. Knowing that I was a native of Indiana he withdrew from a package one envelope and turned it over to me to peruse. On it Lincoln had endorsed "For Indianapolis." It proved to be the manuscript of the speech intended for delivery to the Legislature of Indiana containing his definition of coercion and invasion, and a brief but ingenious dissertation on the sacredness of a State. I read it with the deepest interest.

As a rule Lincoln was well poised. He could not be called cold, but in the delivery of a speech or on public occasions he was dignified if not invariably serious; the result was that he never bubbled over — rarely ever wept or otherwise betrayed his emotion. That condition, however, did not prevail the morning he separated from his friends and neighbors in February, 1861, headed for Washington. On that occasion he was deeply moved. My authority for that statement comes from an intimate friend of Lincoln, James C. Conkling, a man in whom Lincoln reposed the fullest confidence and who stood within a few feet and immediately in front of him when he bade his neighbors farewell from the platform of his car. The testimony is in the handwriting of Mr. Conkling himself. Describing the incident, he says:

> It was quite affecting. Many eyes were filled to overflowing as Mr. Lincoln uttered those few and simple words of farewell. His own breast heaved with emotion and he could scarcely command his feelings sufficiently to commence. There was scarcely a dry eye in all that vast crowd.

The following, which is the farewell incident as described in the "Springfield Journal," was the work of the editor Edward L. Baker:

> It was a most impressive scene. We have known Mr. Lincoln for many years; we have heard him speak upon a hundred different occasions; but we never saw him so profoundly affected, nor did he ever utter an address which seemed to us so full of simple and touching eloquence, so exactly adapted to the occasion, so worthy of the man and the hour. Although it was raining fast when he began to speak, every hat was lifted and every head bent forward to catch the

last words of the departing chief. When he said, with the earnestness of a sudden inspiration of feeling, that with God's help he should not fail, there was an uncontrollable burst of applause. At precisely eight o'clock city time the train moved off bearing our honored townsman, our noble chief, Abraham Lincoln, to the scenes of his future labors and, as we firmly believe, of his glorious triumph. God bless honest Abraham Lincoln!

Note

1. Mark Neely, *The Abraham Lincoln Encyclopedia*, 289.

Jesse W. Weik, *The Real Lincoln: A Portrait* (Boston: Houghton Mifflin, 1922), 313–14.

[Autobiographical Statement, 1859]

ABRAHAM LINCOLN

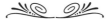

Lincoln wrote this second autobiography for Jesse W. Fell, a longtime Illinois Republican friend who was a native of Pennsylvania. Fell used his influence to get the piece incorporated into an article appearing in a Pennsylvania newspaper on February 11, 1860. Lincoln enclosed the autobiography in a letter to Fell dated December 20, 1859, which began, "Herewith is a little sketch, as you requested. There is not much of it, for the reason, I suppose, that there is not much of me.

"If any thing be made out of it, I wish it to be modest, and not to go beyond the materials. If it were thought necessary to incorporate any thing from any of my speeches, I suppose there would be no objection. Of course it must not appear to have been written by myself. Yours very truly A. Lincoln"

I WAS BORN Feb. 12, 1809, in Hardin County, Kentucky. My parents were both born in Virginia, of undistinguished families — second families, perhaps I should say. My mother, who died in my tenth year, was of a family of the name of Hanks, some of whom now reside in Adams, and others in Macon counties, Illinois. My paternal grandfather, Abraham Lincoln, emigrated from Rockingham County, Virginia, to Kentucky, about 1781 or 2, where, a year or two later, he was killed by indians, not in battle, but by stealth, when [where?] he was laboring to open a farm in the forest. His ancestors, who were quakers, went to Virginia from Berks County, Pennsylvania. An effort to identify them with the New-England family of the same name ended in nothing more definite, than a similarity of Christian names in both families, such as Enoch, Levi, Mordecai, Solomon, Abraham, and the like.

My father, at the death of his father, was but six years of age; and he grew up, literally without education. He removed from Kentucky to what is now Spencer County, Indiana, in my eighth year. We reached our new home about the time the State came into the Union. It was a wild region, with many bears and other wild animals still in the woods. There I grew up.

[47]

There were some schools, so called; but no qualification was ever required of a teacher, beyond *"readin, writin, and cipherin,"* to the Rule of Three. If a straggler supposed to understand Latin, happened to sojourn in the neighborhood, he was looked upon as a wizard. There was absolutely nothing to excite ambition for education. Of course when I came of age I did not know much. Still somehow, I could read, write, and cipher to the Rule of Three; but that was all. I have not been to school since. The little advance I now have upon this store of education, I have picked up from time to time under the pressure of necessity.

I was raised to farm work, which I continued till I was twenty two. At twenty one I came to Illinois, and passed the first year in Macon county. Then I got to New-Salem (at that time in Sangamon, now in Menard county), where I remained a year as a sort of Clerk in a store. Then came the Black-Hawk war; and I was elected a Captain of Volunteers — a success which gave me more pleasure than any I have had since. I went the campaign, was elated, ran for the Legislature the same year (1832) and was beaten — the only time I ever have been beaten by the people. The next, and three succeeding biennial elections, I was elected to the Legislature. I was not a candidate afterwards. During this Legislative period I had studied law, and removed to Springfield to practice it. In 1846 I was once elected to the lower House of Congress. Was not a candidate for re-election. From 1849 to 1854, both inclusive, practiced law more assiduously than ever before. Always a whig in politics, and generally on the whig electoral tickets, making active canvasses. I was losing interest in politics, when the repeal of the Missouri Compromise aroused me again. What I have done since then is pretty well known.

If any personal description of me is thought desirable, it may be said, I am, in height, six feet, four inches, nearly; lean in flesh, weighing, on an average, one hundred and eighty pounds; dark complexion, with coarse black hair, and grey eyes — no other marks or brands recollected. Yours very truly A. Lincoln

Basler, ed., *Collected Works*, 3:511–12.

[Autobiographical Statement, 1860]

ABRAHAM LINCOLN

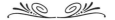

When Lincoln first ran for president, John L. Scripps of the *Chicago Press and Tribune* asked him for an account of his life so he could write a campaign biography. This third-person account, dated June 1860, is the result. The many misspellings and errors of usage testify to the speed with which the author penned it. Nevertheless it is the longest and most detailed of the Lincoln autobiographies and offers fascinating information about his early years.

ABRAHAM LINCOLN was born Feb. 12, 1809, then in Hardin, now in the more recently formed county of Larue, Kentucky. His father, Thomas, & grandfather, Abraham, were born in Rockingham county Virginia, whither their ancestors had come from Berks county Pennsylvania. His lineage has been traced no farther back than this. The family were originally quakers, though in later times they have fallen away from the peculiar habits of that people. The grand-father Abraham, had four brothers — Isaac, Jacob, John & Thomas. So far as known, the descendants of Jacob and John are still in Virginia. Isaac went to a place near where Virginia, North Carolina, and Tennessee, join; and his decendants are in that region. Thomas came to Kentucky, and after many years, died there, whence his decendants went to Missouri. Abraham, grandfather of the subject of this sketch, came to Kentucky, and was killed by indians about the year 1784. He left a widow, three sons and two daughters. The eldest son, Mordecai, remained in Kentucky till late in life, when he removed to Hancock county, Illinois, where soon after he died, and where several of his descendants still reside. The second son, Josiah, removed at an early day to a place on Blue River, now within Harrison [Hancock] county, Indiana; but no recent information of him, or his family, has been obtained. The eldest sister, Mary, married Ralph Crume and some of her descendants are now known to be in Breckenridge county Kentucky. The second sister, Nancy, married William Brumfield, and her family are not known to have left Kentucky, but there is no recent information from them. Thomas, the youngest son, and father of the present subject, by the early death of his father, and very narrow circumstances of his mother, even in childhood was a wandering laboring boy, and grew up litterally without education. He never did more in the way of writing than to bunglingly sign his own name. Before he was grown, he passed one year as a hired hand with his uncle Isaac on Wata[u]ga, a branch of the Holsteen [Holston] River. Getting back into Kentucky, and having reached his 28th. year, he married Nancy Hanks—mother of the present subject—in the year 1806. She also was born in Virginia; and relatives of hers of the name of Hanks, and of other names, now reside in Coles, in Macon, and in Adams counties, Illinois, and also in Iowa. The present subject has no brother or sister of the whole or half blood. He had a sister, older than himself, who was grown and married, but died many years ago, leaving no child. Also a brother, younger than himself, who died in infancy. Before leaving Kentucky he and his sister were sent for short periods, to A.B.C. schools, the first kept by Zachariah Riney, and the second by Caleb Hazel.

At this time his father resided on Knob-creek, on the road from Bardstown Ky. to Nashville Tenn. at a point three, or three and a half miles South or South-West of Atherton's ferry on the Rolling Fork. From this place he removed to what is now Spencer county Indiana, in the autumn of 1816, A. then being in his eighth year. This removal was partly on account of slavery; but chiefly on account of the difficulty in land titles in Ky. He settled in an unbroken forest; and the clearing away of surplus wood was the great task a head. A. though very young, was large of his age, and had an axe put into his hands at once; and from that till within his twenty-third year, he was almost constantly handling that most useful instrument—less, of course, in plowing and harvesting seasons. At this place A. took an early start as a hunter, which was never much improved afterwards. (A few days before the completion of his eigth year, in the absence of his father, a flock of wild turkeys approached the new log-cabin, and A. with a rifle gun, standing inside, shot through a crack, and killed one of them. He has never since pulled a trigger on any larger game.) In the autumn of 1818 his mother died; and a year afterwards his father married Mrs. Sally Johnston, at Elizabeth-Town, Ky—a widow, with three children of her first marriage. She proved a good and kind mother to A. and is still living in Coles Co. Illinois. There were no children of this second marriage. His father's residence continued at the same place in Indiana, till 1830.

While here A. went to A.B.C. schools by littles, kept successively by Andrew Crawford, — Sweeney, and Azel W. Dorsey. He does not remember any other. The family of Mr. Dorsey now reside in Schuyler Co. Illinois. A. now thinks that the agregate of all his schooling did not amount to one year. He was never in a college or Academy as a student; and never inside of a college or accademy building till since he had a law-license. What he has in the way of education, he has picked up. After he was twentythree, and had separated from his father, he studied English grammar, imperfectly of course, but so as to speak and write as well as he now does. He studied and nearly mastered the Six-books of Euclid, since he was a member of Congress. He regrets his want of education, and does what he can to supply the want. In his tenth year he was kicked by a horse, and apparently killed for a time. When he was nineteen, still residing in Indiana, he made his first trip upon a flat-boat to New-Orleans. He was a hired hand merely; and he and a son of the owner, without other assistance, made the trip. The nature of part of the cargo-load, as it was called — made it necessary for them to linger and trade along the Sugar coast — and one night they were attacked by seven negroes with intent to kill and rob them. They were hurt some in the melee, but succeeded in driving the negroes from the boat, and then "cut cable" "weighed anchor" and left.

March 1st. 1830 — A. having just completed his 21st. year, his father and family, with the families of the two daughters and sons-in-law, of his step-mother, left the old homestead in Indiana, and came to Illinois. Their mode of conveyance was waggons drawn by ox-teams, or A. drove one of the teams. They reached the county of Macon, and stopped there some time within the same month of March. His father and family settled a new place on the North side of the Sangamon river, at the junction of the timber-land and prairie, about ten miles Westerly from Decatur. Here they built a log-cabin, into which they removed, and made sufficient of rails to fence ten acres of ground, fenced and broke the ground, and raised a crop of sow[n] corn upon it the same year. These are, or are supposed to be, the rails about which so much is being said just now, though they are far from being the first, or only rails ever made by A.

The sons-in-law, were temporarily settled at other places in the county. In the autumn all hands were greatly afflicted with augue and fever, to which they had not been used, and by which they were greatly discouraged — so much so that they determined on leaving the county. They remained how-

ever, through the succeeding winter, which was the winter of the very celebrated "deep snow" of Illinois. During that winter, A. together with his
step-mother's son, John D. Johnston, and John Hanks, yet residing in Macon county, hired themselves to one Denton Offutt, to take a flat boat from
Beardstown Illinois to New-Orleans; and for that purpose, were to join
him — Offut — at Springfield, Ills so soon as the snow should go off. When
it did go off which was about the 1st. of March 1831 — the county was so
flooded, as to make traveling by land impracticable; to obviate which difficulty the[y] purchased a large canoe and came down the Sangamon river
in it. This is the time and the manner of A's first entrance into Sangamon
County. They found Offutt at Springfield, but learned from him that he had
failed in getting a boat at Beardstown. This lead to their hiring themselves
to him at $12 per month, each; and getting the timber out of the trees and
building a boat at old Sangamon Town on the Sangamon river, seven miles
N.W. of Springfield, which boat they took to New-Orleans, substantially
upon the old contract. It was in connection with this boat that occurred
the ludicrous incident of sewing up the hogs eyes. Offutt bought thirty
odd large fat live hogs, but found difficulty in driving them from where
[he] purchased them to the boat, and thereupon conceived the whim that
he could sew up their eyes and drive them where he pleased. No sooner
thought of than decided, he put his hands, including A. at the job, which
they completed — all but the driving. In their blind condition they could
not be driven out of the lot or field they were in. This expedient failing,
they were tied and hauled on carts to the boat. It was near the Sangamon
River, within what is now Menard county.

During this boat enterprize acquaintance with Offutt, who was previously an entire stranger, he conceved a liking for A. and believing he could
turn him to account, he contracted with him to act as clerk for him, on his
return from New-Orleans, in charge of a store and Mill at New-Salem, then
in Sangamon, now in Menard county. Hanks had not gone to New-Orleans,
but having a family, and being likely to be detained from home longer than
at first expected, had turned back from St. Louis. He is the same John
Hanks who now engineers the "rail enterprize" at Decatur; and is a first
cousin to A's mother. A's father, with his own family & others mentioned,
had, in pursuance of their intention, removed from Macon to Coles county.
John D. Johnston, the step-mother's son, went to them; and A. stopped indefinitely, and, for the first time, as it were, by himself at New-Salem, be-

fore mentioned. This was in July 1831. Here he rapidly made acquaintances and friends. In less than a year Offutt's business was failing—had almost failed,—when the Black-Hawk war of 1832—broke out. A joined a volunteer company, and to his own surprize, was elected captain of it. He says he has not since had any success in life which gave him so much satisfaction. He went the campaign, served near three months, met the ordinary hardships of such an expedition, but was in no battle. He now owns in Iowa, the land upon which his own warrants for this service, were located. Returning from the campaign, and encouraged by his great popularity among his immediate neighbors, he, the same year, ran for the Legislature and was beaten—his own precinct, however, casting it's votes 277 for and 7, against him. And this too while he was an avowed Clay man, and the precinct the autumn afterwards, giving a majority of 115 to Genl. Jackson over Mr. Clay. This was the only time A was ever beaten on a direct vote of the people. He was now without means and out of business, but was anxious to remain with his friends who had treated him with so much generosity, especially as he had nothing elsewhere to go to. He studied what he should do—thought of learning the black-smith trade—thought of trying to study law—rather thought he could not succeed at that without a better education. Before long, strangely enough, a man offered to sell and did sell, to A. and another as poor as himself, an old stock of goods, upon credit. They opened as merchants; and he says that was *the* store. Of course they did nothing but get deeper and deeper in debt. He was appointed Post-master at New-Salem—the office being too insignificant, to make his politics an objection. The store winked out. The Surveyor of Sangamon, offered to depute to A that portion of his work which was within his part of the county. He accepted, procured a compass and chain, studied Flint, and Gibson a little, and went at it. This procured bread, and kept soul and body together. The election of 1834 came, and he was then elected to the Legislature by the highest vote cast for any candidate. Major John T. Stuart, then in full practice of the law, was also elected. During the canvass, in a private conversation he encouraged A. [to] study law. After the election he borrowed books of Stuart, took them home with him, and went at it in good earnest. He studied with nobody. He still mixed in the surveying to pay board and clothing bills. When the Legislature met, the law books were dropped, but were taken up again at the end of the session. He was re-elected in 1836, 1838, and 1840. In the autumn of 1836 he obtained a law licence, and on

April 15, 1837 removed to Springfield, and commenced the practice, his old friend, Stuart taking him into partnership. March 3rd. 1837, by a protest entered upon the Ills. House Journal of that date, at pages 817, 818, A. with Dan Stone, another representative of Sangamon, briefly defined his position on the slavery question; and so far as it goes, it was then the same that it is now. The protest is as follows — . . . In 1838, & 1840 Mr. L's party in the Legislature voted for him as Speaker; but being in the minority, he was not elected. After 1840 he declined a re-election to the Legislature. He was on the Harrison electoral ticket in 1840, and on that of Clay in 1844, and spent much time and labor in both those canvasses. In Nov. 1842 he was married to Mary, daughter of Robert S. Todd, of Lexington, Kentucky. They have three living children, all sons — one born in 1843, one in 1850, and one in 1853. They lost one, who was born in 1846. In 1846, he was elected to the lower House of Congress, and served one term only, commencing in Dec. 1847 and ending with the inaugeration of Gen. Taylor, in March 1849. All the battles of the Mexican war had been fought before Mr. L. took his seat in congress, but the American army was still in Mexico, and the treaty of peace was not fully and formally ratified till the June afterwards. Much has been said of his course in Congress in regard to this war. A careful examination of the Journals and Congressional Globe shows, that he voted for all the supply measures which came up, and for all the measures in any way favorable to the officers, soldiers, and their families, who conducted the war through; with this exception that some of these measures passed without yeas and nays, leaving no record as to how particular men voted. The Journals and Globe also show him voting that the war was unnecessarily and unconstitutionally begun by the President of the United States. This is the language of Mr. Ashmun's amendment, for which Mr. L. and nearly or quite all, other whigs of the H. R. voted.

Mr. L's reasons for the opinion expressed by this vote were briefly that the President had sent Genl. Taylor into an inhabited part of the country belonging to Mexico, and not to the U.S. and thereby had provoked the first act of hostility — in fact the commencement of the war; that the place, being the country bordering on the East bank of the Rio Grande, was inhabited by native Mexicans, born there under the Mexican government; and had never submitted to, nor been conquered by Texas, or the U.S. nor transferred to either by treaty — that although Texas claimed the Rio Grande as her boundary, Mexico had never recognized it, the people on the ground had never recognized it, and neither Texas nor the U.S. had ever enforced it — that there was a broad desert between that, and the country over which Texas had actual control — that the country where hostilities commenced, having once belonged to Mexico, must remain so, until it was somehow legally transferred, which had never been done.

Mr. L. thought the act of sending an armed force among the Mexicans, was *unnecessary*, inasmuch as Mexico was in no way molesting, or menacing the U.S. or the people thereof; and that it was *unconstitutional*, because the power of levying war is vested in Congress, and not in the President. He thought the principal motive for the act, was to divert public attention from the surrender of "Fifty-four, forty, or fight" to Great Brittain, on the Oregon boundary question.

Mr. L. was not a candidate for re-election. This was determined upon, and declared before he went to Washington, in accordance with an understanding among whig friends, by which Col. Hardin, and Col. Baker had each previously served a single term in the same District.

In 1848, during his term in congress, he advocated Gen. Taylor's nomination for the Presidency, in opposition to all others, and also took an active part for his election, after his nomination — speaking a few times in Maryland, near Washington, several times in Massachusetts, and canvassing quite fully his own district in Illinois, which was followed by a majority in the district of over 1500 for Gen. Taylor.

Upon his return from Congress he went to the practice of the law with greater earnestness than ever before. In 1852 he was upon the Scott electoral ticket, and did something in the way of canvassing, but owing to the hopelessness of the cause in Illinois, he did less than in previous presidential canvasses.

In 1854, his profession had almost superseded the thought of politics in his mind, when the repeal of the Missouri compromise aroused him as he had never been before.

In the autumn of that year he took the stump with no broader practical aim or object that [than?] to secure, if possible, the re-election of Hon Richard Yates to congress. His speeches at once attracted a more marked attention than they had ever before done. As the canvass proceeded, he was drawn to different parts of the state, outside of Mr. Yates' district. He did not abandon the law, but gave his attention, by turns, to that and politics. The State agricultural fair was at Springfield that year, and Douglas was announced to speak there.

In the canvass of 1856, Mr. L. made over fifty speeches, no one of which, so far as he remembers, was put in print. One of them was made at Galena, but Mr. L. has no recollection of any part of it being printed; nor does he remember whether in that speech he said anything about a Supreme court decision. He may have spoken upon that subject; and some of the newspapers may have reported him as saying what is now ascribed to him; but he thinks he could not have expressed himself as represented.

Basler, ed., *Collected Works*, 4:61–67.

"Chiefly about War Matters" (1862)

Nathaniel Hawthorne

One of the great American authors of the century, Nathaniel Hawthorne grew up in Salem, Massachusetts, and went to college at Bowdoin in Maine, where he was a college roommate of future president Franklin Pierce. Hawthorne learned his craft as a writer of short fiction while working at the Boston Custom House. Later he published such important works as *The Scarlet Letter* (1850) and *The House of the Seven Gables* (1851). His mixed response to the anti-slavery movements is reflected in the fact that at the height of his national fame, Hawthorne supported for the presidency in 1852 his good friend Pierce, a pro-Southern politician who later became a sharp critic of the Lincoln administration. Hawthorne even agreed to write Pierce's campaign biography, a gesture Pierce never forgot. (He was with Hawthorne when the novelist died.)

Hawthorne visited the sitting president in March of 1862. Although his disapproval of the Lincoln administration was much milder than that of his friend Pierce, the lengthy report that came out of that meeting, excerpted here, was seen as potentially harmful to the reputation of one of New England's elite writers. Evidently there seemed to be something about Lincoln's physical presence and speaking style that bothered Hawthorne. As his friend Edward Dicey put it, "The impression . . . made upon him by the personal manner and behaviour of President Lincoln was so inconsistent with his own ideas of dignity."[1] Hawthorne's editor at the *Atlantic Monthly*, James T. Fields, immediately discerned that the essay, while "excellently well done throughout," "contained a personal description of President Lincoln . . . [that] would not be wise or tasteful to print."[2] Fields made a number of suggested cuts, to which Hawthorne agreed. Here Hawthorne's original words are restored.

OF COURSE, there was one other personage, in the class of statesmen, whom I should have been truly mortified to leave Washington without seeing; since (temporarily, at least, and by force of circumstances) he was the man of men. But a private grief had built up a barrier about him, impeding the customary free intercourse of Americans with their chief-magistrate;

so that I might have come away without a glimpse of his very remarkable physiognomy, save for a semi-official opportunity of which I was glad to take advantage. The fact is, we were invited to annex ourselves, as super-numeraries, to a deputation that was about to wait upon the President, from a Massachusetts whip-factory, with a present of a splendid whip.

Our immediate party consisted only of four or five, (including Major Ben Perley Poore, with his note-book and pencil,) but we were joined by several other persons, who seemed to have been lounging about the pre-cincts of the White House, under the spacious porch, or within the hall, and who swarmed in with us to take the chances of a presentation. Nine o'clock had been appointed as the time for receiving the deputation, and we were punctual to the moment, but not so the President, who sent us word that he was eating his breakfast, and would come as soon as he could. His appetite, we were glad to think, must have been a pretty fair one; for we waited about half-an-hour, in one of the ante-chambers, and then were ushered into a reception-room, in one corner of which sat the Secretaries of War and of the Treasury, expecting, like ourselves, the termination of the presidential breakfast. During this interval, there were several new ad-ditions to our groupe, one or two of whom were in a working-garb; so that we formed a very miscellaneous collection of people, mostly unknown to each other, and without any common sponsor, but all with an equal right to look our head-servant in the face. By-and-by, there was a little stir on the staircase and in the passage-way; and in lounged a tall, loose-jointed figure, of an exaggerated Yankee port and demeanor, whom, (as being about the homeliest man I ever saw, yet by no means repulsive or disagreeable,) it was impossible not to recognize as Uncle Abe.

Unquestionably, Western man though he be, and Kentuckian by birth, President Lincoln is the essential representative of all Yankees, and the ver-itable specimen, physically, of what the world seems determined to regard as our characteristic qualities. It is the strangest, and yet the fittest thing in the jumble of human vicissitudes, that he, out of so many millions, un-looked-for, unselected by any intelligible process that could be based upon his genuine qualities, unknown to those who chose him, and unsuspected of what endowments may adapt him for his tremendous responsibility, should have found the way open for him to fling his lank personality into the chair of state — where, I presume, it was his first impulse to throw his legs on the council-table, and tell the cabinet-ministers a story. There is

no describing his lengthy awkwardness, nor the uncouthness of his movement; and yet it seemed as if I had been in the habit of seeing him daily, and
had shaken hands with him a thousand times in some village-street; so true
was he to the aspect of the pattern American, though with a certain extravagance which, possibly, I exaggerated still further by the delighted eagerness
with which I took it in. If put to guess his calling and livelihood, I should
have taken him for a country-schoolmaster, as soon as anything else. He
was dressed in a rusty black frock-coat and pantaloons, unbrushed, and
worn so faithfully that the suit had adapted itself to the curves and angu-
larities of his figure, and had grown to be an outer skin of the man. He had
shabby slippers on his feet. His hair was black, still unmixed with gray,
stiff, somewhat bushy, and had apparently been acquainted with neither
brush nor comb, that morning, after the disarrangement of the pillow; and
as to a night-cap, Uncle Abe probably knows nothing of such effeminacies.
His complexion is dark and sallow, betokening, I fear, an insalubrious atmosphere around the White House; he has thick black eyebrows and an
impending brow; his nose is large, and the lines about his mouth are very
strongly defined.

The whole physiognomy is as coarse a one as you would meet anywhere
in the length and breadth of the States; but, withal, it is redeemed, illumi-
nated, softened, and brightened, by a kindly though serious look out of his
eyes, and an expression of homely sagacity, that seems weighted with rich
results of village-experience. A great deal of native sense; no bookish culti-
vation, no refinement; honest at heart, and thoroughly so, and yet, in some
sort, sly — at least, endowed with a sort of tact and wisdom that are akin to
craft, and would impel him, I think, to take an antagonist in flank, rather
than to make a bull-run at him right in front. But, on the whole, I liked this
sallow, queer, sagacious visage, with the homely human sympathies that
warmed it; and, for my small share in the matter, would as lief have Uncle
Abe for a ruler as any man whom it would have been practicable to put in
his place.

Immediately on his entrance, the President accosted our Member of
Congress, who had us in charge, and, with a comical twist of his face, made
some jocular remark about the length of his breakfast. He then greeted us
all round, not waiting for an introduction, but shaking and squeezing everybody's hand with the utmost cordiality, whether the individual's name
was announced to him or not. His manner towards us was wholly without

pretence, but yet had a kind of natural dignity, quite sufficient to keep the forwardest of us from clapping him on the shoulder and asking for a story. A mutual acquaintance being established, our leader took the whip out of its case, and began to read the address of presentation. The whip was an exceedingly long one, its handle wrought in ivory, (by some artist in the Massachusetts state-prison, I believe,) and ornamented with a medallion of the President, and other equally beautiful devices; and along its whole length, there was a succession of golden bands and ferules. The address was shorter than the whip, but equally well made, consisting chiefly of an explanatory description of these artistic designs, and closing with a hint that the gift was a suggestive and emblematic one, and that the President would recognize the use to which such an instrument should be put.

This suggestion gave Uncle Abe rather a delicate task in his reply, because, slight as the matter seemed, it apparently called for some declaration, or intimation, or faint foreshadowing of policy in reference to the conduct of the war, and the final treatment of the rebels. But the President's Yankee aptness and not-to-be-caughtness stood him in good stead, and he jerked or wriggled himself out of the dilemma with an uncouth dexterity that was entirely in character; although, without his gesticulation of eye and mouth—and especially the flourish of the whip, with which he imagined himself touching up a pair of fat horses—I doubt whether his words would be worth recording, even if I could remember them. The gist of the reply was, that he accepted the whip as an emblem of peace, not punishment; and this great affair over, we retired out of the presence in high good humor, only regretting that we could not have seen the President sit down and fold up his legs, (which is said to be a most extraordinary spectacle,) or have heard him tell one of those delectable stories for which he is so celebrated. A good many of them are afloat upon the common talk of Washington, and are certainly the aptest, pithiest, and funniest little things imaginable; though, to be sure, they smack of the frontier freedom, and would not always bear repetition in a drawing-room, or on the immaculate page of the Atlantic.

Good Heavens, what liberties have I been taking with one of the potentates of the earth, and the man on whose conduct more important consequencies depend, than on that of any other historical personage of the century! But with whom is an American citizen entitled to take a liberty, if not with his own chief-magistrate? However, lest the above allusions to President Lincoln's little peculiarities (already well-known to the country and to the world) should be misinterpreted, I deem it proper to say a word or two, in regard to him, of unfeigned respect and measurable confidence. He is evidently a man of keen faculties, and, what is still more to the purpose, of powerful character. As to his integrity, the people have that intuition of it which is never deceived. Before he actually entered upon his great office, and for a considerable time afterwards, there is no reason to suppose that he adequately estimated the gigantic task about to be imposed on him, or, at least, had any distinct idea how it was to be managed; and, I presume, there may have been more than one veteran politician who proposed to himself to take the power out of President Lincoln's hands into his own, leaving our honest friend only the public responsibility for the good or ill-success of the career. The extremely imperfect development of his statesmanly qualities, at that period, may have justified such designs. But the President is teachable by events, and has now spent a year in a very arduous course of education; he has a flexible mind, capable of much expansion, and convertible towards far loftier studies and activities than those of his early life; and, if he came to Washington as a backwoods humorist, he has already transformed himself into as good a statesman (to speak moderately) as his prime-minister.

We hesitated to admit the above sketch, and shall probably regret our decision in its favor. It appears to have been written in a benign spirit, and perhaps conveys a not inaccurate impression of its august subject; but it lacks reverence, and it pains us to see a gentleman of ripe age, and who has spent years under the corrective influence of foreign institutions, falling into the characteristic and most ominous fault of Young America.

Notes

1. Edward Dicey, "Nathaniel Hawthorne," in *Hawthorne in His Own Time*, ed. Ronald A. Bosco and Jillmarie Murphy (Iowa City: U of Iowa P, 2007), 120.

2. James T. Fields, "Our Whispering Gallery," in *Hawthorne in His Own Time*, 146.

Nathaniel Hawthorne, "Chiefly about War Matters," in *Tales, Sketches, and Other Papers* (Boston: Houghton Mifflin, 1883), 299–345.

"Extracts from an Unpublished Manuscript" [1860s?]

Rev. P. D. Gurley

Phineas Densmore Gurley (1816–1868) was born in Hamilton, New York, and graduated in 1837 from Union College in New York, after which he attended Princeton Theological Seminary. Following lengthy pastorates in Indianapolis and Dayton, Gurley ministered for the remainder of his life at the New York Avenue Presbyterian Church in Washington, D.C., where he also became chaplain of the U.S. Senate in 1859. Gurley numbered among his worshiping congregation President Abraham Lincoln and Mary Todd Lincoln, and became a frequent guest at the White House. He was at Lincoln's deathbed, and preached his funeral sermon on April 19, 1865, at the White House. On that somber occasion, Gurley said, "Never shall I forget the emphasis and the deep emotion with which he said in this very room, to a company of clergymen and others, who called to pay him their respects in the darkest days of our civil conflict: 'Gentlemen, my hope of success in this great and terrible struggle rests on that immutable foundation, the justice and goodness of God. And when events are very threatening, and prospects very dark, I still hope that in some way which man can not see all will be well in the end, because our cause is just, and God is on our side.' Such was his sublime and holy faith, and it was an anchor to his soul, both sure and steadfast."[1]

Gurley spent much time in the presence of Lincoln and made extensive notes about their interactions that he hoped one day could be published, but they never were during his lifetime. His observations regarding Lincoln's spirituality during the White House years are prized for their insight and their intimacy, as here, where he writes of the president's great interest in a tender sermon delivered at the death of Willie in 1862.

MR. LINCOLN WAS very much impressed with an address made over the coffin of his little son Willie. The day after the funeral he wrote me a note and asked me to write it out for him so he could give copies to his friends.

He often spoke to me of how he liked to read it over. This address was as follows: "Sad and solemn is the occasion that brings us here today. A dark shadow of affliction has fallen upon this habitation and upon the hearts of its inmates. The news thereof has already gone forth to the extremities of the country. The nation has heard it with deep and tender emotion. The eye of the nation is moistened with tears as it turns today to the Presidential mansion. The heart of the nation sympathizes with its chief magistrate while to the unprecedented weight of civil care which presses upon him is added the burden of this great domestic sorrow, and the prayers of the nation ascend to heaven on his behalf and on behalf of his weeping family that God's grace may be sufficient for them, and that in this hour of sore bereavement and trial they may have the presence and succor of Him who said: 'Come unto Me all ye that labor and are heavy laden and I will give you rest.' Oh, that they may be enabled to lay their heads upon His infinite bosom and find, as many other smitten ones have found, that He is their truest refuge and strength and a very present help in trouble.

"The beloved youth whose death we now and here lament was a child of bright intelligence and of peculiar promise. He possessed many excellent qualities of mind and heart which greatly endeared him not only to the family circle but to all his youthful acquaintances and friends. His mind was active, he was inquisitive and conscientious; his disposition was amiable and affectionate. His impulses kind and generous; his words and manners were gentle and attractive. It is easy to see how a child thus endowed could, in the course of eleven years entwine himself around the hearts of those who knew him best; nor can we wonder that the grief of his affectionate mother today is like that of Rachel weeping for her children and refusing to be comforted, because they were not.

"His sickness was a attack of fever threatening from the first and painfully productive of mental wandering and delirium. All that the most tender parental care and watching and the most assiduous and skillful medical treatment could do was done, and though at times even in the last stages of the disease his symptoms were regarded as favorable and inspired a faint and wavering hope of his recovery, still the insidious malady pursued its course unchecked, and on Thursday last, at the hour of five in the afternoon, the golden bowl was broken and the emancipated spirit returned to the God who gave it. That departure was a sore bereavement to parents and brothers, and while they weep they also rejoice in the confidence that their loss is his gain, for they believe as well they may, that he has gone to Him who said: 'Suffer little children to come to Me and forbid them not, for of such is the kingdom of heaven'; and that now with kindred spirits, and with a little brother he never saw on earth, he beholds the glory and sings the praises of the Redeemer. Blessed by God!

> There is a world above
> Where sorrow is unknown,
> A long eternity of love
> Formed for the good alone.
> And faith beholds the dying here,
> Translated to that glorious sphere.[2]

"It is well for us and very comforting on such an occasion as this to get a clear and scriptural view of the Providence of God. His kingdom ruleth over all. All those events which in any wise affect our condition and happiness are in His hands and at His disposal. Disease and death are His messengers; they go forth at His bidding and their fearful work is limited or extended according to the good pleasure of His will. Not a sparrow falls to the ground without His care much less one of the human family, for we are of more value than many sparrows. These bereaved parents may be sure that their affliction has not come forth of the dust nor has their trouble sprung out of the ground. It is the well-ordered procedure of their Father and their God. A mysterious dealing they may consider it; but still it is His dealing and while they mourn He is saying to them, as the Lord Jesus once said to His disciples when they were perplexed: 'What I do ye know not now, but ye shall know hereafter.' What we need in the hour of trial, and what we should seek by earnest prayer is confidence in Him who sees the end from the beginning and doeth all things well. Let us bow in His presence with a humble and teachable spirit; let us be still and know that He is God; let us acknowledge His hand and hear His voice; inquire after His will and seek His Holy Spirit, as our counselor and guide, and all will be well in the end. In His light shall we see light; by His grace our sorrows will be sanctified and made a blessing to our souls, and by and by we shall have occasion to say with blended gratitude and rejoicing, 'It is good for us that we have been afflicted.'"

Soon after this the President and Mrs. Lincoln presented me with a beautiful ebony cane; the head and six inches in length, of small gold roses, and the following was engraved upon it: "Rev. P.D. Gurley, D.D., from Mr. and Mrs. Abraham Lincoln, 1862." It was in February, 1862, that this address was delivered in the room in which Willie died and from which he was buried. On account of the nature of the disease (varioloid) his funeral was private as possible. I was with the President and Mrs. Lincoln often during these dark hours.

Willie's death was a great blow to Mr. Lincoln, coming as it did in the midst of the war, when his burdens seemed already greater than he could bear. The little boy was always interested in the war and used to go down to the White House stables and read the battle news to the employees and talk over the outcome. These men all loved him and thought, for one of his years, he was most unusual. When he was dying he said to me, "Doctor Gurley, I have six one dollar gold pieces in my bank over there on the mantel. Please send them to the missionaries for me." After his death those six one dollar pieces were shown to my Sunday school and the scholars were informed of Willie's request. He died in what was always called the "Prince of Wales Room," as the prince occupied it when visiting President Buchanan.

After his son's death, Mr. Lincoln was greatly annoyed by the report that he was interested in spiritualism. He told me he thought the report originated from the fact that a medium had chanced to call on Mrs. Lincoln. "A simple faith in God is good enough for me, and beyond that I don't concern myself very much," he added.

Willie was laid away in Oak Hill cemetery, Georgetown, D.C. Later, when his father's body was taken to Springfield, the child's remains were also taken.

Notes

1. From Gurley's sermon as reprinted in the *New York Times* on April 20, 1865.

2. From British poet James Montgomery (1771–1854), whose lament, "Friends," became one of the most widely-known consolation poems of the nineteenth century.

Ervin Chapman, ed., *Latest Light on Abraham Lincoln and War-Time Memories* (New York: Fleming H. Revell, 1917), 501–07.

From *Behind the Scenes* (1868)

Elizabeth Keckley

> Born a slave in Virginia, a mulatto whose father may have been her white master, Elizabeth Keckley (1818?–1907) rose to prominence in Washington society as a seamstress and modiste, becoming an intimate of Mary Todd Lincoln and a regular part of the White House scene for the years of the Lincoln presidency. She learned her trade as a slave in St. Louis, bought her own freedom and that of her child in 1855, and later designed dresses for the likes of Jefferson Davis's wife. Another influential client introduced her to Mrs. Lincoln, and in the war years Keckley became the First Lady's confidante, particularly after the death of Willie in 1862. (Keckley had already suffered the death of her own son, in a battle in Missouri.) With great insight into the temperaments and foibles of both Lincolns, her sensitive portrayals of some of their most human moments as husband and wife are among the best ever recorded. One example is Keckley's depiction of the illness and death of Willie, and the bereavement of the president over his lost son.

THE CHILDREN, Tad and Willie, were constantly receiving presents. Willie was so delighted with a little pony, that he insisted on riding it every day. The weather was changeable, and exposure resulted in a severe cold, which deepened into fever. He was very sick, and I was summoned to his bedside. It was sad to see the poor boy suffer. Always of a delicate constitution, he could not resist the strong inroads of disease. The days dragged wearily by, and he grew weaker and more shadow-like. He was his mother's favorite child, and she doted on him. It grieved her heart sorely to see him suffer. When able to be about, he was almost constantly by her side. When I would go in her room, almost always I found blue-eyed Willie there, reading from an open book, or curled up in a chair with pencil and paper in hand. He had decidedly a literary taste, and was a studious boy. . . .

On the evening of the reception Willie was suddenly taken worse. His mother sat by his bedside a long while, holding his feverish hand in her own, and watching his labored breathing. The doctor claimed there was no cause for alarm. I arranged Mrs. Lincoln's hair, then assisted her to dress. Her dress was white satin, trimmed with black lace. The trail was very long, and as she swept through the room, Mr. Lincoln was standing with his back to the fire, his hands behind him, and his eyes on the carpet. His face wore a thoughtful, solemn look. The rustling of the satin dress attracted his attention. He looked at it a few moments; then, in his quaint, quiet way remarked—

"Whew! our cat has a long tail to-night."

Mrs. Lincoln did not reply. The President added:

"Mother, it is my opinion, if some of that tail was nearer the head, it would be in better style"; and he glanced at her bare arms and neck. She had a beautiful neck and arm, and low dresses were becoming to her. She turned away with a look of offended dignity, and presently took the President's arm, and both went down-stairs to their guests, leaving me alone with the sick boy.

The reception was a large and brilliant one, and the rich notes of the Marine Band in the apartments below came to the sick-room in soft, subdued murmurs, like the wild, faint sobbing of far-off spirits. Some of the young people had suggested dancing, but Mr. Lincoln met the suggestion with an emphatic veto. The brilliance of the scene could not dispel the sadness that rested upon the face of Mrs. Lincoln. During the evening she came upstairs several times, and stood by the bedside of the suffering boy. She loved him with a mother's heart, and her anxiety was great. The night passed slowly; morning came, and Willie was worse. He lingered a few days, and died. God called the beautiful spirit home, and the house of joy was turned into the house of mourning. I was worn out with watching, and was not in the room when Willie died, but was immediately sent for. I assisted in washing him and dressing him, and then laid him on the bed, when Mr. Lincoln came in. I never saw a man so bowed down with grief. He came to the bed, lifted the cover from the face of his child, gazed at it long and earnestly, murmuring, "My poor boy, he was too good for this earth. God has called him home. I know that he is much better off in heaven, but then we loved him so. It is hard, hard to have him die!"

Great sobs choked his utterance. He buried his head in his hands, and his tall frame was convulsed with emotion. I stood at the foot of the bed, my eyes full of tears, looking at the man in silent, awe-stricken wonder. His grief unnerved him, and made him a weak, passive child. I did not dream that his rugged nature could be so moved. I shall never forget those solemn moments — genius and greatness weeping over love's idol lost. There is a grandeur as well as a simplicity about the picture that will never fade. With me it is immortal — I really believe that I shall carry it with me across the dark, mysterious river of death.

Mrs. Lincoln's grief was inconsolable. The pale face of her dead boy threw her into convulsions. Around him love's tendrils had been twined, and now that he was dressed for the tomb, it was like tearing the tendrils out of the heart by their roots. Willie, she often said, if spared by Providence, would be the hope and stay of her old age. But Providence had not spared him. The light faded from his eyes, and the death-dew had gathered on his brow.

In one of her paroxysms of grief the President kindly bent over his wife, took her by the arm, and gently led her to the window. With a stately, solemn gesture, he pointed to the lunatic asylum.

"Mother, do you see that large white building on the hill yonder? Try and control your grief, or it will drive you mad, and we may have to send you there."

Mrs. Lincoln was so completely overwhelmed with sorrow that she did not attend the funeral. Willie was laid to rest in the cemetery, and the White House was draped in mourning. Black crape everywhere met the eye, contrasting strangely with the gay and brilliant colors of a few days before. Party dresses were laid aside, and every one who crossed the threshold of the Presidential mansion spoke in subdued tones when they thought of the sweet boy at rest —

"Under the sod and the dew."

Previous to this I had lost my son. Leaving Wilberforce, he went to the battle-field with the three months troops, and was killed in Missouri — found his grave on the battle-field where the gallant General Lyon fell. It was a sad blow to me, and the kind womanly letter that Mrs. Lincoln wrote to me when she heard of my bereavement was full of golden words of comfort. For two years after Willie's death the White House was the scene of no fashionable display. The memory of the dead boy was duly respected. In some things Mrs. Lincoln was an altered woman. Sometimes, when in her room, with no one present but myself, the mere mention of Willie's name would excite her emotion, and any trifling memento that recalled him would move her to tears. She could not bear to look upon his picture;

and after his death she never crossed the threshold of the Guest's Room in which he died, or the Green Room in which he was embalmed. There was something supernatural in her dread of these things, and something that she could not explain. Tad's nature was the opposite of Willie's, and he was always regarded as his father's favorite child. His black eyes fairly sparkled with mischief.

The war progressed, fair fields had been stained with blood, thousands of brave men had fallen, and thousands of eyes were weeping for the fallen at home. There were desolate hearthstones in the South as well as in the North, and as the people of my race watched the sanguinary struggle, the ebb and flow of the tide of battle, they lifted their faces Zionward, as if they hoped to catch a glimpse of the Promised Land beyond the sulphurous clouds of smoke which shifted now and then but to reveal ghastly rows of new-made graves. Sometimes the very life of the nation seemed to tremble with the fierce shock of arms. In 1863 the Confederates were flushed with victory, and sometimes it looked as if the proud flag of the Union, the glorious old Stars and Stripes, must yield half its nationality to the tri-barred flag that floated grandly over long columns of gray. These were sad, anxious days to Mr. Lincoln, and those who saw the man in privacy only could tell how much he suffered. One day he came into the room where I was fitting a dress on Mrs. Lincoln. His step was slow and heavy, and his face sad. Like a tired child he threw himself upon a sofa, and shaded his eyes with his hands. He was a complete picture of dejection. Mrs. Lincoln, observing his troubled look, asked:

"Where have you been, father?"

"To the War Department," was the brief, almost sullen answer.

"Any news?"

"Yes, plenty of news, but no good news. It is dark, dark everywhere."

He reached forth one of his long arms, and took a small Bible from a stand near the head of the sofa, opened the pages of the holy book, and soon was absorbed in reading them. A quarter of an hour passed, and on glancing at the sofa the face of the President seemed more cheerful. The dejected look was gone, and the countenance was lighted up with new resolution and hope. The change was so marked that I could not but wonder at it, and wonder led to the desire to know what book of the Bible afforded so much comfort to the reader. Making the search for a missing article an excuse, I walked gently around the sofa, and looking into the open book, I discovered that Mr. Lincoln was reading that divine comforter, Job. He read with Christian eagerness, and the courage and hope that he derived from the inspired pages made him a new man. I almost imagined that I could hear the Lord speaking to him from out the whirlwind of battle: "Gird up thy loins now like a man: I will demand of thee, and declare thou unto me." What a sublime picture was this! A ruler of a mighty nation going to the pages of the Bible with simple Christian earnestness for comfort and courage, and finding both in the darkest hours of a nation's calamity. Ponder it, O ye scoffers at God's Holy Word, and then hang your heads for very shame!

Elizabeth Keckley, *Behind the Scenes; Or, Thirty Years a Slave, and Four Years in the White House* (New York: G. W. Carleton, 1868), 55–99.

[Sketch on the Funeral for Willie Lincoln, 1862]

Nathaniel Parker Willis

Nathaniel Parker Willis (1806–1867) was born in Portland, Maine, and moved with his family in 1812 to Boston, where he would embark on a long career as a magazine editor. Working at first for others, Willis quickly went on to establish his own magazine, the *American Monthly Magazine*, which folded in 1831. Willis moved to New York City, where he took up the position of co-editor of the *New York Mirror*, and later spent five years in Europe as a correspondent for the *Mirror*. As an editor, he employed both Walt Whitman and Edgar Allan Poe. Meanwhile his sister Sara, whom he famously spurned as a potential writer, developed the pen name Fanny Fern and during the 1850s became one of America's most financially successful writers, male or female. In her novel *Ruth Hall* (1854), Fern paints a very unflattering picture of her condescending brother. During the Civil War he lived in Washington, D.C., as the *Home Journal*'s correspondent. Willis's popularity and prominence in antebellum literary circles came under reconsideration due to his interest in the social world of the wealthy, causing many to see him as simply a literary man about town. While American literary history has come to remember Willis as a snob and a writer of trifles, his role in the development of a distinctly national literary culture was important.

Willis's talent for the telling detail and his powerful use of sentiment is obvious. As Willie Lincoln's death after a two-week illness had plunged his mother into inconsolable grief, the words Willis wrote about Willie in the *Home Journal* were of great comfort to the grieving mother. This brief essay was printed throughout the nation and was "very much admired by Mrs. Lincoln," who kept a copy and pasted it into her scrapbook, according to Elizabeth Keckley, who reprinted the sketch in her memoir *Behind the Scenes* (1868).[1]

THIS LITTLE FELLOW had his acquaintances among his father's friends, and I chanced to be one of them. He never failed to seek me out in the crowd, shake hands, and make some pleasant remark; and this, in a boy of ten years of age, was, to say the least, endearing to a stranger. But he had more than mere affectionateness. His self-possession—*aplomb*, as the French call it—was extraordinary. I was one day passing the White House, when he was outside with a play-fellow on the side-walk. Mr. Seward drove in, with Prince Napoleon and two of his suite in the carriage; and, in a mock-heroic way—terms of intimacy evidently existing between the boy and the Secretary—the official gentleman took off his hat, and the Napoleon did the same, all making the young prince President a ceremonious salute. Not a bit staggered with the homage, Willie drew himself up to his full height, took off his little cap with graceful self-possession, and bowed down formally to the ground, like a little ambassador. They drove past, and he went on unconcernedly with his play: the impromptu readiness and good judgment being clearly a part of his nature. His genial and open expression of countenance was none the less ingenuous and fearless for a certain tincture of fun; and it was in this mingling of qualities that he so faithfully resembled his father.

With all the splendor that was around this little fellow in his new home he was so bravely and beautifully *himself*—and that only. A wild flower transplanted from the prairie to the hothouse, he retained his prairie habits, unalterably pure and simple, till he died. His leading trait seemed to be a fearless and kindly frankness, willing that everything should be as different as it pleased, but resting unmoved in his own conscious single-heartedness. I found I was studying him irresistibly, as one of the sweet problems of childhood that the world is blessed with in rare places; and the news of his death (I was absent from Washington, on a visit to my own children, at the time) came to me like a knell heard unexpectedly at a merry-making.

On the day of the funeral I went before the hour, to take a near farewell look at the dear boy; for they had embalmed him to send home to the West—to sleep under the sod of his own valley—and the coffin-lid was to be closed before the service. The family had just taken their leave of him, and the servants and nurses were seeing him for the last time—and with tears and sobs wholly unrestrained, for he was loved like an idol by every one of them. He lay with eyes closed—his brown hair parted as we had known it—pale in the slumber of death; but otherwise unchanged, for he was dressed as if for the evening, and held in one of his hands, crossed upon his breast, a bunch of exquisite flowers—a message coming from his mother, while we were looking upon him, that those flowers might be preserved for her. She was lying sick in her bed, worn out with grief and overwatching.

The funeral was very touching. Of the entertainments in the East Room the boy had been — for those who now assembled more especially — a most life-giving variation. With his bright face, and his apt greetings and replies, he was remembered in every part of that crimson-curtained hall, built only for pleasure — of all the crowds, each night, certainly the one least likely to be death's first mark. He was his father's favorite. They were intimates — often seen hand in hand. And there sat the man, with a burden on his brain at which the world marvels — bent now with the load at both heart and brain — staggering under a blow like the taking from him of his child! His men of power sat around him — McClellan, with a moist eye when he bowed to the prayer, as I could see from where I stood; and Chase and Seward, with their austere features at work; and senators, and ambassadors, and soldiers, all struggling with their tears — great hearts sorrowing with the President as a stricken man and a brother. That God may give him strength for all his burdens is, I am sure, at present the prayer of a nation.

Note

1. Keckley, *Behind the Scenes*, 110.

Keckley, *Behind the Scenes*, 106–10.

"Reminiscences of Abraham Lincoln" (1895)

GRACE GREENWOOD

Grace Greenwood was the pen name of Sara Jane Clarke (1823–1904), one of America's most prominent writers. She was born in Pompey, New York, the daughter of Thaddeus Clarke, a physician, and Deborah Baker. Not long after her birth, the family moved to nearby Fabius and later to Rochester, where she was educated. While in her teens, she started contributing verse to the local papers.

In 1844 Clarke began contributing letters to the New York *Mirror and Home Journal*, signing them "Grace Greenwood," a name she started using socially as well. These contributions secured her literary reputation, and she was soon writing for some of the most important periodicals of the day, ranging in topic from sentimental fiction and verse to commentary on the current state of literature and politics. In 1849 she became an editorial assistant for *Godey's Lady's Book*, but Louis Godey dismissed her the following year for an antislavery essay she contributed to the abolitionist *National Era*. Gamaliel Bailey, the editor of the *National Era*, subsequently offered her a position and asked her to move to Washington, D.C. She accepted the offer and simultaneously became the Washington correspondent for the *Saturday Evening Post*. Starting in 1850, she began gathering and publishing her periodical contributions as separate works. *Greenwood Leaves*, a collection of sentimental sketches, literary burlesques, and journalistic letters, was the earliest of her many popular books. In 1853 she married Leander K. Lippincott, with whom she had one daughter. The following is her record of a meeting with Abraham Lincoln.

MY ACTUAL ACQUAINTANCE with President Lincoln was slight, but the place it fills in my memory seems great, and is a very sacred one. During a visit to Washington, in late war time, I received an informal invitation to a reception *extraordinaire* at the White House. It was to meet Mr. And Mr. Charles S. Stratton — "General Tom Thumb" — and his wife, Lavinia, then on their bridal tour. I suppose that Mr. Barnum, a good loyal Republican, had solicited an audience for his then most famous, comely and *comme il faut* human curiosities, and that the President and Mrs. Lincoln, with an amiable desire to share a novel little entertainment with their friends, had sent out a limited number of invitations. I think Mr. Lincoln's quick sense of fitness led him to pass over all members of their circle, so stiffened by social starch or official solemnity as to be likely to find the occasion *infra dig*, and so, unenjoyable.

I was presented to the President and Mrs. Lincoln by Mr. Lovejoy, and was made very happy and a little proud by being received by them as already "a friend," having become known to them in their home in Springfield through my work in magazines and newspapers — especially the *National Era*, the *Independent*, and my own publication, the *Little Pilgrim*; so I felt at home speedily.

Yet Mr. Lincoln, before I heard his sweet-toned voice, and saw his singularly sympathetic smile, was certainly an awesome personage to me. So tall, gaunt and angular was his figure — so beyond all question, plain, was his face, furrowed and harrowed by unexampled cares and infinite perplexities, while over all was a simple dignity which was more than sacerdotal — a peculiar, set-apart look, which I have never seen in any other man, never shall see.

Mr. Lincoln's dress was somber black, unrelieved except by gloves of white or very light kid, which had a rather ghastly effect on his large, bony hands. But Mrs. Lincoln was gay enough in attire — a low-necked gown of rich pink silk, with flounces climbing high up, over a hoop-skirt trellis, and pink roses in her hair. She was not handsome, but her manner was pleasant and kindly. She must have had a good heart, after all said, for her husband loved her. She must have had a more than ordinary intelligence, for Charles Sumner respected her opinions, and he knew her well. She certainly lacked worldly wisdom, tact and judgment — fatal lackings in her case. The dizzy elevation of her storm-rocked position, and its perils, unsettled her brain in effect, and the tragedy which shook the world, cast her "quite, quite down." Most desolate and misunderstood of women was she at the last.

Of the President's household present that evening, I remember two young men, who I thought ought to make careers for themselves, not alone because they looked clever, thoughtful and scholarly, but because their daily association with Abraham Lincoln must be a liberal education in noble ideas and aims, in manliness and mansuetude. These young gentlemen were the President's son, Robert, and his secretary, John Hay.

Rather to my surprise the high-toned and austere Secretary of the Treasurey, Mr. Chase, was one of the guests, coming in early, as though in boyish haste to see the show. He was then but little past his prime, and a superb looking man. With him was his darling daughter, Kate — "the prettiest Kate in Christendom" — tall, graceful, her small Greek head borne royally, her lovely, piquant face untouched by care or sorrow, her exquisite dark eyes with their heavily fringed lids, full of a certain entangling charm.

Secretary Stanton was not there, to my disappointment, as in our younger days we had been familiar friends. Doubtless he thought this occasion a bit of fooling, unsuited to this most critical and sorrowful time of the imperiled Republic, when "men must work, and women must weep," their hardest and bitterest. He always was awfully in earnest. A pun once nearly cost me his friendship, and it was a good pun, too.

That night I first saw General Butler. It appears to me that he never changed much in all the years that followed till he died, in the house next to this — only yesterday, it seems. A little heavier grew that powerful face, a little less arrogant and audacious in expression, a little balder became that masterful, low, broad head without any "bump" of veneration, till in his coffin it looked like an antique bust of an old Roman emperor of the Augustan line — hard, but grand.

As was natural, perhaps, the autocrat of New Orleans had little sympathy with the quaint Commander-in-Chief, whose big, soft heart so often played the mischief with military discipline through a flagrant exercise of the pardoning power; but he had to respect the moral steadfastness and purity of the man.

The reception took place in the East room; and when, following the loud announcement, "Mr. And Mrs. Charles Stratton," the guests of honor entered from the corridor, and walked slowly up the long *salon*, to where Mr. and Mrs. Lincoln stood, to welcome them, the scene became interesting, though a little bizarre. The pigmy "General," at that time still rather goodlooking, though slightly *blasé*, wore his elegant wedding suit, and his wife, a plump but symmetrical little woman, with a bright, intelligent face, her wedding dress — the regular white satin, with point lace orange blossoms and pearls — while a train some two yards long swept out behind her. I well remember the "pigeon-like stateliness" with which they advanced, almost to the feet of the President, and the profound respect with which they looked up, up, to his kindly face.

It was pleasant to see their tall host bend, and the bend, to take their little hands in his great palm, holding Madame's with especial chariness, as though it were a robin's egg, and he were fearful of breaking it. Yet he did not *talk* down to them, but made them feel from the first as though he regarded them as real "folks," sensible, and knowing a good deal of the world. He presented them, very courteously and soberly, to Mrs. Lincoln, and in his compliments and congratulations there was not the slightest touch of the exaggeration which a lesser man might have been tempted to make use of, for the quiet amusement of on-lookers; in fact, nothing to reveal to that shrewd little pair of his keen sense of the incongruity of the scene. He was, I think, most amused by the interest and curiosity of his "little Tad," who seemed disposed to patronize the diminutive gentleman and lady, grown up and married, yet lacking his lordly inches. When refreshments were being served, he graciously superintended his mother's kindly arrangements, by which the distinguished little folk were able to take their cake, wine and ices comfortably, off a chair.

Later, while the bride and groom were taking a quiet promenade by themselves up and down the big drawing-room, I noticed the President gazing after them with a smile of quaint humor; but, in his beautiful, sorrow shadowed eyes, there was something more than amusement—a gentle, human sympathy in the apparent happiness and good-fellowship of this curious wedded pair—come to him out of fairyland.

After they were gone I had my little talk with, or rather from, Mr. Lincoln; for, naturally, I said but little during those golden moments. He was in one of his most genial moods; and judging, perhaps, from my newspaper connections that I was not a fool, he even favored me with a few of his "little stories," which he told very simply and tersely, yet with inimitable drollery. As was characteristic of him, he evidently was most amused by one wherein the joke was against himself. As I recall it, the story ran that a certain honest old farmer, visiting the capital for the first time, was taken by the member from his "deestrick" to some large gathering or entertainment, at which he was told he could see the President. Unfortunately, Mr. Lincoln did not appear; and the Congressman, being a bit of a wag and not liking to have his constituent disappointed, pointed out Mr. R., of Minnesota, a gentleman of a particularly round and rubicund countenance; the worthy farmer, greatly astonished, exclaimed: "Is that Old Abe? Well I du declare? He's a better-lookin' man than I expected to see; but it does seem as if his troubles had driven him to drink."

After this evening I only saw Mr. Lincoln at two of his public receptions, when the people — or torrent of humanity — surged into the White House, and swept past him, every soul-wave mirroring clear his pale, patient face, and taking a glint from his kindly eyes. Each time I was made happy by an instant and smiling recognition and a few words of special welcome.

To pass into the presence, as one of a great crowd, even, was to receive from Mr. Lincoln a real, honest, hearty handshake, which you felt to the tips of your toes. Nowadays the official fashion is less neighborly and more perfunctory. The great man touches your fingers an instant, while looking over your shoulder for the next comer, or clutches your hand any way, pulls you forward and passes you on. You *think* he has said a word or two, but you are not quite sure.

Every moment that I found it possible on those occasions to linger near Mr. Lincoln, I spent in studying the face of the man on whose single life hung the destinies of a country and the redemption of a race. It was always the same impression. Under the pleasantest light of his eyes, I divined a depth of melancholy unfathomable.

Yet I recognized then, almost as clearly as I do now, the "saving grace" of those gifts of imagination and humor, which gave him temporary "surcease from sorrow," and the soul-weariness of helpless pity, through poetry, the drama, and those droll "little stories," so often wisdom in homely disguise — parables of subtle significance. It takes nothing from my respect for him as a hero and a Christian, to know that he kept on the stand by the side of his bed, volumes of his favorite humorists. When, in the dreary watches of the night the bitter waters of his "sea of troubles" were rising to his lips, I doubt not he found the buoyant wit of "Pickwick" more potent to bear him up than the bat-wings of Young's "Night Thoughts." Doubtless there was for him more heart-lightenings in Artemus Ward than in Isaac Watts; and he may have found in the homely diet of Hosea Biglow more stimulating mental aliments than in all the philosophy of Athens or Concord. I believe that one good, hearty laugh did him more good than any number of those recitations of "O Why should the Spirit of Mortals be Proud?" he was addicted to in his low and sentimental moods.

[78]

Not till that woeful time when a tidal wave of national mourning swept across the continent, did I look again on the face of Abraham Lincoln. It was at Philadelphia — one of the stations in the great funeral progress. He lay in state, in Independence Hall, where one could almost believe that he had a double guard of honor, one invisible to us — the august shades of men whose patriotic act made that chamber glorious forever.

According to a private view, I was able to remain as long as I could bear to stay beside the casket, gazing down on what seemed to me a dread *simulacrum* of the face of our great friend — so unlike was it, though so like. The color was not the pallor I remembered, but a sort of ashen gray; the mouth looked stern, and then, the total eclipse of those benignant eyes! People said the face was "peaceful"; but it was an awful peace, there remained such touching shadows of mortal sorrow, struggle and strain. It was as though the soul, sunk deep beyond deep in God's rest, had left in its garment of flesh the perfect mould of its mortal cares, its piteous yearnings, its unspeakable weariness.

I have always pitied those who have only such recollections of Abraham Lincoln, and have been fervently thankful that while he yet lived I looked on that now historic figure and found it heroic in its grand ungainliness; on that worn and rugged face, and found it both lovable and impressive; that my hand has been grasped, in greeting and farewell, by the hand that performed the grandest work of the century; that my eyes have gazed full into those sad, prophetic eyes, whose tired lids were pressed down at last by the long-prayed-for Angel of Peace.

And I am thankful that it was my privilege to know some of his greatest generals, and those splendid aids of his, the "war governors" of the North and West, and also the faithful statesmen and patriots, who here at the Capital "upheld his hands" — Stanton, Chase and Seward, Henry Wilson, Hannibal Hamlin, Thaddeus Stevens, Joseph Holt, all gone — the type gone!

William Hayes Ward, *Abraham Lincoln: Tributes from His Associates* (New York: Thomas Crowell, 1895), 108–15.

"Lincoln's Colonial Scheme" (1862)

[ABRAHAM LINCOLN]

> This unsigned entry is described as an interview with the president from August 1862, but in fact it is mostly Lincoln himself talking—about his view of race, African American freedom, and the possibility of colonizing the slaves, once they were freed, to locations such as Liberia in western Africa or somewhere in Central America. As far back as 1854, Lincoln had shown some favor toward colonization schemes, and in December of 1861 he had recommended such an action in his message to the U.S. Congress. Despite his reputation as the Great Emancipator and as a liberal and progressive champion of African Americans, this piece is sobering in its presentation of the vast racial issues facing Americans in the midst of the greatest domestic crisis in their history.

THEY WERE INTRODUCED by the Rev. J. Mitchell, Commissioner of Emigration. E. M. Thomas, the Chairman, remarked that they were there . . . to hear what the Executive had to say to them. Having all been seated, the President, after a few preliminary observations, informed them that a sum of money had been appropriated by Congress, and placed at his disposition for the purpose of aiding the colonization in some country of the people, or a portion of them, of African descent, thereby making it his duty, as it had for a long time been his inclination, to favor that cause; and why, he asked, should the people of your race be colonized, and where? Why should they leave this country? That is, perhaps, the first question for proper consideration. You and we are different races. We have between us a broader difference than exists between almost any other two races. Whether it is right or wrong I need not discuss, but this physical difference is a great disadvantage to us both, as I think your race suffer very greatly, many of them by living among us, while ours suffer from your presence. In a word we suffer on each side. If this is admitted, it affords a reason at least why we should be separated. You here are freemen I suppose.

A VOICE: Yes, sir.

The President—Perhaps you have long been free, or all your lives. Your race are suffering, in my judgment, the greatest wrong inflicted on any people. But even when you cease to be slaves, you are yet far removed from being placed on an equality with the white race. You are cut off from many of the advantages which the other race enjoy. The aspiration of men is to enjoy equality with the best when free, but on this broad continent, not a single man of your race is made the equal of a single man of ours. Go where you are treated the best, and the ban is still upon you.

I do not propose to discuss this, but to present it as a fact with which we have to deal. I cannot alter it if I would. It is a fact, about which we all think and feel alike, I and you. We look to our condition, owing to the existence of the two races on this continent. I need not recount to you the effects upon white men, growing out of the institution of Slavery. I believe in its general evil effects on the white race. See our present condition—the country engaged in war!—our white men cutting one another's throats, none knowing how far it will extend; and then consider what we know to be the truth. But for your race among us there could not be war, although many men engaged on either side do not care for you one way or the other. Nevertheless, I repeat, without the institution of Slavery and the colored race as a basis, the war could not have an existence.

It is better for us both, therefore, to be separated. I know that there are free men among you, who even if they could better their condition are not as much inclined to go out of the country as those, who being slaves could obtain their freedom on this condition. I suppose one of the principal difficulties in the way of colonization is that the free colored man cannot see that his comfort would be advanced by it. You may believe you can live in Washington or elsewhere in the United States the remainder of your life, perhaps more so than you can in any foreign country, and hence you may come to the conclusion that you have nothing to do with the idea of going to a foreign country. This is (I speak in no unkind sense) an extremely selfish view of the case.

But you ought to do something to help those who are not so fortunate as yourselves. There is an unwillingness on the part of our people, harsh as it may be, for you colored people to remain with us. Now, if you could give a start to white people, you would open a wide door for many to be made free. If we deal with those who are not free at the beginning, and whose intellects are clouded by Slavery, we have very poor materials to start with. If intelligent colored men, such as are before me, would move in this matter, much might be accomplished. It is exceedingly important that we have men at the beginning capable of thinking as white men, and not those who have been systematically oppressed.

There is much to encourage you. For the sake of your race you should sacrifice something of your present comfort for the purpose of being as grand in that respect as the white people. It is a cheering thought throughout life that something can be done to ameliorate the condition of those who have been subject to the hard usage of the world. It is difficult to make a man miserable while he feels he is worthy of himself and claims kindred to the great God who made him. In the American Revolutionary war sacrifices were made by men engaged in it; but they were cheered by the future. Gen. Washington himself endured greater physical hardship than if he had remained a British subject. Yet he was a happy man, because he was engaged in benefiting his race—something for the children of his neighbors, having none of his own.

The colony of Liberia has been in existence a long time. In a certain sense it is a success. The old President of Liberia, [Joseph Jenkins] Roberts, has just been with me—the first time I ever saw him. He says they have within the bounds of that colony between 300,000 and 400,000 people, or more than in some of our old states, such as Rhode Island or Delaware, or in some of our newer States, and less than in some of our larger ones. They are not all American colonists, or their descendants. Something less than 12,000 have been sent thither from this country. Many of the original settlers have died, yet, like people elsewhere, their offspring outnumber those deceased.

The question is if the colored people are persuaded to go anywhere, why not there? One reason for an unwillingness to do so is that some of you would rather remain within reach of the country of your nativity. I do not know how much attachment you may have toward our race. It does not strike me that you have the greatest reason to love them. But still you are attached to them at all events.

The place I am thinking about having for a colony is in Central America. It is nearer to us than Liberia—not much more than one-fourth as far as Liberia, and within seven days' run by steamers. Unlike Liberia it is on a great line of travel—it is a highway. The country is a very excellent one for any people, and with great natural resources and advantages, and

[82]

especially because of the similarity of climate with your native land — thus being suited to your physical condition.

The particular place I have in view is to be a great highway from the Atlantic or Caribbean Sea to the Pacific Ocean, and this particular place has all the advantages for a colony. On both sides there are harbors among the finest in the world. Again, there is evidence of very rich coal mines. A certain amount of coal is valuable in any country, and there may be more than enough for the wants of the country. Why I attach so much importance to coal is, it will afford an opportunity to the inhabitants for immediate employment till they get ready to settle permanently in their homes.

If you take colonists where there is no good landing, there is a bad show; and so where there is nothing to cultivate, and of which to make a farm. But if something is started so that you can get your daily bread as soon as you reach there, it is a great advantage. Coal land is the best thing I know of with which to commence an enterprise.

To return, you have been talked to upon this subject, and told that a speculation is intended by gentlemen, who have an interest in the country, including the coal mines. We have been mistaken all our lives if we do not know whites as well as blacks look to their self-interest. Unless among those deficient of intellect everybody you trade with makes something. You meet with these things here as elsewhere.

If such persons have what will be an advantage to them, the question is whether it cannot be made of advantage to you. You are intelligent, and know that success does not as much depend on external help as on self-reliance. Much, therefore, depends upon yourselves. As to the coal mines, I think I see the means available for your self-reliance.

I shall, if I get a sufficient number of you engaged, have provisions made that you shall not go wronged. If you will engage in the enterprise I will spend some of the money entrusted to me. I am not sure you will succeed. The Government may lose the money, but we cannot succeed unless we try; but we think, with care, we can succeed.

The political affairs in Central America are not in quite as satisfactory condition as I wish. There are contending factions in that quarter; but it is true all the factions agree alike on the subject of colonization, and want it, and are more generous than we are here. To your colored race they have no objection. Besides, I would endeavor to have you made equals, and have the best assurance that you should be the equals of the best.

The practical thing I want to ascertain is whether I can get a number of able-bodied men, with their wives and children, who are willing to go, when I present evidence of encouragement and protection. Could I get a hundred tolerably intelligent men, with their wives and children, to "cut their own fodder," so to speak? Can I have fifty? If I could find twenty-five able-bodied men, with a mixture of women and children, good things in the family relation, I think I could make a successful commencement.

I want you to let me know whether this can be done or not. This is the practical part of my wish to see you. These are subjects of very great importance, worthy of a month's study, [not] of a speech delivered in an hour. I ask you then to consider seriously not pertaining to yourselves merely, nor for your race, and ours, for the present time, but as one of the things, if successfully managed, for the good of mankind — not confined to the present generation, but as

> From age to age descends the lay,
> To millions yet to be,
> Till far its echoes roll away,
> Into eternity.

The above is merely given as the substance of the President's remarks.

From an unsigned article in the *New York Tribune*, August 15, 1862. Reprinted in *Conversations with Lincoln*, Charles M. Segal, ed. (New York: G. P. Putnam's Sons, 1961), 188–92.

From *They Knew Lincoln* (1942)

JOHN E. WASHINGTON

Dr. John E. Washington (1880–1964) was an African American artist, educa-tor, and dentist who collected the testimonies and anecdotes of hundreds of African Americans to produce his unusual volume, *They Knew Lincoln*, published in 1942. In the book's preface, Washington states that his goal is to produce "a true picture of Lincoln as he appeared to the ignorant slave and his offspring. To do this, hundreds of visits and interviews were held in backwoods sections of various parts of the land." He proudly presents there a letter from the preeminent Lincoln scholar of his day, J. G. Randall, whose encouragement spurred Washington onward to completion: "Except for your efforts, the story of the colored people who knew Lincoln is lost. There is a remarkable story there but it is difficult to recover it."[1] Washington was one of the first to see the value in collecting these tales from that generation of African Americans who lived when Lincoln lived; this important work gave voice to those who perceived themselves as most powerfully impacted by the dead president. Yet the tone of Randall's comments hints at the fact that these accounts were published at a time when black army troops weren't al-lowed to serve alongside white—more than a full decade before Brown vs. Board of Education, Rosa Parks, and the death of Emmett Till jump-started the civil rights movement.

Uncle Ben's Story of Divine Preparation

Uncle Ben told the old E Street people a story about Lincoln which I shall never forget. He said:

"When the Children of Israel were in bondage God raised up Moses to lead them out of it; but Moses was not to lead an ignorant horde that was uncultured and despised — a group without tradition, but was called to lead the Israelites out of bondage. He was one of them and knew his people.

"In America where there was a group of God's children of a different color struggling in bondage and under the oppressor's lash, begging him not for salvation for themselves but for their children and their children's children, God needed more than a Moses of the Israelite kind, and needed one of a type unknown before. So God in answering the prayers of the oppressed deliberately created an individual to His own liking and planned his education in a manner that his language could be understood by all whom he was to lead. In short, this person had to be made to suit the purpose of Almighty God. He had to be a child of the soil, speaking the same language and experiencing the same hardships as those people who looked up to him. He had to be unlettered and uncultured in the beginning, as they were. He had come through the fiery furnace of hardships as did the Hebrew children and had to be as fearless in so doing as Daniel was in the lion's den. He had to have a heart for the most despised and rejected of people. Therefore God created Lincoln as the rough person needed for this great task. Then in His school of training He placed this child where he could know the abilities and ideas of men of a different race and color and brought him up in it."

Uncle Ben told us that he believed that Almighty God created someone to teach his chosen prophet, Lincoln, by example all that a Negro could attain with freedom and equal opportunity, and although he had never heard about anyone who had done this, he believed that some day the person would be found.

Old Aunt Phoebe Bias: Her Story of the
"Big Watch-Meeting" before the Emancipation Proclamation

In recalling these old New Year's gatherings, I shall never forget the last one attended by old Aunt Phoebe Bias, before the pale horse rider carried her away to Glory.

Although she was nearly as old as old Aunt Eliza, she was nevertheless very active in spite of the fact that she was lame and bent over. The white folks for whom she worked were relatively newcomers and called themselves "F.F.V.'s." They certainly must have been the First Families of Virginia for they had nothing, and I heard lost all they had in the war.

She said that her family were slaves in Old Virginia. Once, because her husband had carelessly passed by some tobacco worms on a plant, the new master attempted to beat him. She and her son jumped into the fray and stopped him. For so doing all were severely flogged. The men were sold away down in Georgia, but she who had been severely crippled in the fight was allowed to remain on the farm since she was scarred for life and unable to do heavy work.

When General Benjamin T. Butler brought his troops into Virginia near the farm on which she lived, she just took herself up and joined his army. Soon a big boat came to his camp and carried a load of colored women to Washington. She was one of them. It wasn't long before she found work with a good old Northern family and joined the Union Bethel church on M Street.

Here is her last story told at a Watch-Meeting in our house.

During the Christmas Holidays of '62, she heard people everywhere talking about the Big Watch-Meeting to be held in her church where important white and colored men would speak about President Lincoln and the Emancipation Proclamation. She made up her mind to go.

When the last day of the old year rolled around, people from all over the city arrived early in order to get seats. She went early to get her seat on the front row, which had been reserved for the lame, aged, sick, and blind who wished to attend.

Before sundown the church was filled. To pass away the time until the services should begin at 10 o'clock, the brothers and sisters sang, prayed and spoke of their earthly experiences, just as they had done in class meetings.

Exactly at the appointed hour the pastor opened the Bible and began this memorable service with prayers, after which he preached about God, old Satan, Lincoln and the coming day of eternal freedom. After the service, a white man spoke about freedom, and the war, and then read every word in the Emancipation Proclamation from a copy which he had brought in his pocket and told them just how Lincoln had fought for it.

Now the meeting was turned over to the congregation and oh! how it sang and prayed. The very roof of the church seemed to be tumbling down.

Five minutes before 12 o'clock the minister told everybody present that he wanted no one to pray standing up with bowed head; nobody sitting down, with bended necks praying; and no brother kneeling on one knee, because his pants were too tight for him, but to get down on *both knees* to thank Almighty God for his freedom and President Lincoln too.

At first all was still as death, then as the hands on the old church clock moved toward 12, you could hear some brother or sister cry, moan or pray out loud for God to keep on guiding them when the hour of freedom came, just as He had led them out of bondage; and also they cried in loud voices for God to guide, support and strengthen the hand of the man who had brought to them their freedom.

When the city bells rang in the New Year — the year of their freedom, men and women jumped to their feet, yelled for joy, hugged and kissed each other and cried for joy. Many could not stand the excitement and fell into trances all over the house while the crowd yelled "Praise God," and kept yelling "Freed at last," "I'm so glad," "I'm freed at last," and "Before I'd be a slave I'll be carried to my grave," and many other old songs of freedom and hope. They had prayed for freedom. That night it came. One older brother who was blind as a bat yelled out loud that he was thankful to God that he had lived to *see* the day of freedom come.

After a prolonged period of religious excitement, shouting, and singing, the pastor reminded these old people that it was really a Happy New Year. Then, suddenly, like a clap of thunder the sounds of "What a Happy New Year" rang out as it never was heard before and after singing the Doxology, the parting blessing from the pulpit was said.

Although the meeting was now over, it was such a Happy New Year for everybody, that only a few persons left this house of God until daybreak the next morning. Men and women just wept, sang and gave thanks to God Who had set them free and to old Abe Lincoln who had been the Moses who their Maker had ordered to tell the old slave owners to let his people go.

Note

1. Washington, ed., *They Knew Lincoln*, 15, 19.

John E. Washington, ed., *They Knew Lincoln* (New York: E. P. Dutton, 1942), 61–62, 89–91.

"Army Memories of Lincoln: A Chaplain's Reminiscences" (1913)

Joseph H. Twichell

Joseph Hopkins Twichell (1838–1918) was one of the best-known ministers in New England during his years leading the Asylum Hill Congregational Church near the trendy Nook Farm neighborhood of Hartford, Connecticut. Among his flock were next-door neighbors Harriet Beecher Stowe and Mark Twain; he also ministered to Charles Dudley Warner and Isabella Beecher, among others. His association with Twain, which included travels with the famous writer to Europe and elsewhere, was especially noteworthy in terms of his growing reputation and esteem. A graduate of Yale and Andover, Twichell was mentored by Horace Bushnell, one of the century's most influential churchmen. He served in the Union Army as chaplain of a brigade from New York under General Dan Sickles, and witnessed many of the most dramatic battles firsthand, including Fredericksburg, Chancellorsville, and Gettysburg. A popular public speaker, Twichell often appeared at civil-religious ceremonies marking historical anniversaries and dedications, as he did on July 2, 1888, at the laying of a cornerstone on the Gettysburg battlefield.[1] On that day he said, "Abraham Lincoln, you will recall, in that transcendent utterance of his which has passed into the liturgy of freedom forever, spoken above the ashes of these same dead, summoned the living to take from them increased devotion to the cause, their devotion to which, given here in its last full measure, had itself hallowed this ground far above the power of any to add or to detract. . . . No graves were ever so eloquent as these."[2]

WITH *THE CONGREGATIONALIST*'s request that, in view of the approaching semi-centennial anniversary of the Emancipation Proclamation, I contribute to its columns my personal memories of Mr. Lincoln, I am very willing to comply, though I have not much to relate. I saw him on three different occasions that I recall. The first was on July 8, 1862, when he, in company with Secretary Stanton, paid a visit to the Army of the Potomac, in which I served, while after the fierce wrestle of the Seven Days' Battles it was resting at Harrison's Landing on the James River.

In telling how he then and there appeared to my young eyes I can probably do no better than to transcribe, with unimportant changes, mostly in the way of abridgment, the account thereof I gave to my father at home the day following, in a letter now in my possession.

The circumstance that it was expected to be read in the privacy of the family circle only, will explain and excuse certain freedoms of description by which it was characterized and which derive their sole interest from the contemporary date of the record.

In this letter I said: "As they (Mr. Lincoln and Mr. Stanton) rode along the lines the boys cheered stoutly like good and loyal soldiers, but with the feeling (so I fancied), 'We are the chaps to be admired. It is you—Abraham and Edwin—that ought to do the cheering!' The President's visit was a surprise. At about the middle of the afternoon a salute fired by the gunboats (in the James River) announced his coming. We were called out into line and before nightfall he went the rounds.

"The first real information I had of his arrival was from colored 'Ben' (the cook of our mess), whom we 'stole' out of Maryland (where we had been quartered the winter before). He was out foraging and came in, his black face all shining and cloven with a mighty grin; and with keen delight exclaimed, 'I'se seed ole Uncle Linkum!' It is wonderful how these Negro slaves contract their political views.

"'Ben' says that he never heard a white man speak of Mr. Lincoln in any terms except those of denunciation. He was described to the Negroes as a monster. Yet in those simple hearts the President had attained the reverence due to a benefactor—and that without abolition tracts or teachings. They hardly accounted him a real man, but rather as some half-mythical, far-off omen of good, which some day would break the clouds above them. Simple minds apprehend *persons* rather than *principles*; and Ben says that when our division came (last fall) to the Lower Potomac, the slaves did not regard it as the Union Army, but as a visible sign of the coming of the long-expected, benign reign of 'Old Uncle Linkum.' The story moistened my eyes."

A Ludicrous Sight

"I have seldom witnessed a more ludicrous sight than our worthy Chief Magistrate presented on horseback yesterday. While I lifted my cap with respect for the man raised up by Providence to rule our troubled times, I quickly lowered it to cover a smile that overmastered me. McClellan was beside him, short, stout, stiffly erect, sitting his horse like a dragoon, and the contrast between the two was complete.

"It did seem as though every moment the President's legs would become entangled with those of the horse he rode, and both come down together; while his arms were apparently liable to similar mishap. That with which he held the rein, in its angles and position, resembled the hind leg of a grasshopper — the hand before, the elbow away back over the horse's tail. The removal of his hat in front of each regiment was also a source of laughter in the style of its execution; the quick trot of the horse making it a feat of some difficulty, while, from the same cause, his hold on it seemed precarious. I shall remember the picture a long time. But *the boys* liked him. In fact, his popularity in the army is and has been universal. Many of our rulers and leaders fall into odium, but all have faith in Lincoln. 'When he finds it out (they say of this or that matter of complaint) it will be stopped.' I heard an officer of rank yesterday make the earnest remark (to whom or to what referring I cannot now say), 'With all their palaver and princes and dukes, I don't believe they'll be able to pull the wool over old Lincoln's eyes!'

"His benignant smile as he passed on was a real reflection of his honest, kindly heart; but deeper, under the surface of that marked and not all uncomely face, were the unmistakable signs of care and anxiety. God bless him and give answer to the prayers for guidance I am sure he offers."

So much for my first sight of him. To me it is memorable. The next was nearly a year later, at Falmouth, Va., in April, 1863, shortly before the Battle of Chancellorsville, when he again came down to see us.

At Falmouth, Va., in '63

Of this visit, particularly of one thing connected with it that was of special interest to me, I wrote home thus:

"Tuesday the officers of the Third Corps were invited to meet at General Sickles' headquarters at the Fitzhugh House, for the purpose of welcoming Mr. Lincoln. Three o'clock was the hour appointed, but it was five o'clock before the distinguished visitor appeared. The day was raw and gusty, and it was cold business waiting, but plenty of food and drink kept the crowd patient and good-natured; so that a hearty reception was accorded to our good President when at length he did come.

"We all shook hands with him, and I took occasion to thank him for the Day of Fasting and Prayer he had recently appointed. He looked pale and careworn, yet not dispirited. It is said that he was highly pleased with the appearance of the army."

An incident of the reception that impressed me greatly and was pleasant to witness was this: A good way down the long line of officers, several hundred in number, coming up in single file to be presented to him, he spied an old acquaintance — an Illinoian presumably — and the two began, at a distance, to exchange signals of recognition. When, finally, that officer's turn for introduction was reached, Mr. Lincoln seized him by the hand and spun him round and round, boy fashion, manifesting every token of delight at their meeting.

In the Last Weary Days

The third time I saw him was later still, in Washington, whither I had come up from the army to look after the sick and wounded men of my regiment, in hospital there. I then met him picking his way through the mud of one of the narrow streets adjacent to the War Department. He was carrying under his arm what appeared to be a large rolled-up map of some sort, and he was entirely alone.

I had only a momentary glimpse of his face as he passed me, yet could not fail to note in it, as I had done before, the unmistakable pathetic marks of the awful burden he was bearing.

That face I saw but once more. It was in April, 1865, as he lay in his coffin in the city of New York on the way to the grave. And in place of the look of weariness it had worn on the foregoing occasions I have described, was the peace of the eternal sleep.

Notes

1. Harold K. Bush, *Mark Twain and the Spiritual Crisis of His Age* (Tuscaloosa: U of Alabama P, 2007), 161–75.

2. *Hartford Evening Post*, July 17, 1888.

From *Congregationalist and Christian World*, January 30, 1913.

[Three Civil War Letters of Consolation, 1861–1864]

ABRAHAM LINCOLN

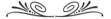

In these examples of the many letters of grief that Lincoln authored during the great conflict, we get a sense of the profound sympathies with which he observed the loss of numerous friends and acquaintances in battle. If, as Allen Guelzo has argued, Lincoln continued until the end his lifelong "dalliance with old school Calvinism,"[1] here we note his fervent hope that the fates of these lost loved ones might serve some larger purpose, in accordance with Romans 8:28, which teaches that "all things work together for good." Most importantly, Lincoln wishes that all be comforted by the divine presence.

The first letter is to the parents of a close friend, Elmer Ellsworth, who died a sudden and rather bizarre death in May of 1861. After taking down a Confederate flag that hung before a hotel, Ellsworth was confronted by the hotel's owner and shot dead. Upon hearing the news, Lincoln was convulsed with weeping. The second letter is to Fanny Washington, whose father, Lieutenant Colonel William McCullough of the Fourth Illinois Cavalry, was killed in a night battle near Coffeeville, Mississippi, on December 5, 1862. As clerk of the McLean County Circuit Court at Bloomington, McCullough had been well known to Lincoln. Third is the well-known letter consoling Lydia Bixby for the death of five sons, made even more famous when it was utilized as a plot device in Steven Spielberg's D-Day film *Saving Private Ryan*; the letter was possibly written all or in part by John Hay. Bixby, who was likely a Confederate sympathizer, lost only two sons; two others deserted.[2]

To the Father and Mother of Col. Elmer E. Ellsworth, May 25. 1861

My dear Sir and Madam, In the untimely loss of your noble son, our affliction here, is scarcely less than your own. So much of promised usefulness to one's country, and of bright hopes for one's self and friends, have rarely been so suddenly dashed, as in his fall. In size, in years, and

in youthful appearance, a boy only, his power to command men, was surpassingly great. This power, combined with a fine intellect, an indomitable
energy, and a taste altogether military, constituted in him, as seemed to
me, the best natural talent, in that department, I ever knew. And yet he
was singularly modest and deferential in social intercourse. My acquaintance with him began less than two years ago; yet through the latter half of
the intervening period, it was as intimate as the disparity of our ages, and
my engrossing engagements, would permit. To me, he appeared to have
no indulgences or pastimes; and I never heard him utter a profane, or an
intemperate word. What was conclusive of his good heart, he never forgot
his parents. The honors he labored for so laudably, and, in the sad end, so
gallantly gave his life, he meant for them, no less than for himself.

In the hope that it may be no intrusion upon the sacredness of your sorrow, I have ventured to address you this tribute to the memory of my young
friend, and your brave and early fallen child.

May God give you that consolation which is beyond all earthly power.
Sincerely your friend in a common affliction —

A. Lincoln

Executive Mansion, December 23, 1862.

Dear Fanny Washington,

It is with deep grief that I learn of the death of your kind and brave Father; and, especially, that it is affecting your young heart beyond what is
common in such cases. In this sad world of ours, sorrow comes to all; and,
to the young, it comes with bitterest agony, because it takes them unawares.
The older have learned to ever expect it. I am anxious to afford some al-
leviation of your present distress. Perfect relief is not possible, except with
time. You can not now realize that you will ever feel better. Is not this so?
And yet it is a mistake. You are sure to be happy again. To know this, which
is certainly true, will make you some less miserable now. I have had experience enough to know what I say; and you need only to believe it, to feel
better at once. The memory of your dear Father, instead of an agony, will
yet be a sad sweet feeling in your heart, of a purer, and holier sort than you
have known before.

Please present my kind regards to your afflicted mother.

Your sincere friend A. Lincoln.

Executive Mansion, Washington, Nov. 21, 1864.

Dear Madam, —I have been shown in the files of the War Department a statement of the Adjutant General of Massachusetts, that you are the mother of five sons who have died gloriously on the field of battle.

I feel how weak and fruitless must be any words of mine which should attempt to beguile you from the grief of a loss so overwhelming. But I cannot refrain from tendering to you the consolation that may be found in the thanks of the Republic they died to save.

I pray that our Heavenly Father may assuage the anguish of your bereavement, and leave you only the cherished memory of the loved and lost, and the solemn pride that must be yours, to have laid so costly a sacrifice upon the altar of Freedom. Yours, very sincerely and respectfully, A. Lincoln.

Notes

1. Allen C. Guelzo, *Abraham Lincoln*: *Redeemer President* (Grand Rapids: Eerdmans, 2003), 9.

2. Michael Burlingame, "The Trouble with the Bixby Letter," *American Heritage* 50.4 (1999): 64–67.

Basler, ed., *Collected Works*, 4:385–86; 6:16–17; and 8:116–17.

"Lincoln's Vigil" (1895)

William O. Stoddard

William Osborne Stoddard (1835–1925), born in Homer, New York, became editor in 1858 of the *Central Illinois Gazette*, a pro-Republican newspaper in Champaign. It was in that newspaper's office that he first met Abraham Lincoln on April 17, 1859. The following January, Stoddard wrote an editorial endorsing Lincoln for the presidency. It is widely believed that this was the first such endorsement from any paper in the nation.

After Lincoln's election in November 1860, Stoddard sought a position within the new administration, but it was not until July 1861 that he finally secured the post of clerk in the U.S. Department of the Interior, where he was assigned to the White House to sign Lincoln's name on land patents. He soon expanded his tedious duties by taking on full responsibility for the president's growing correspondence, which eventually totaled some five hundred letters and parcels a day.[1] As the "third secretary"—behind John G. Nicolay and John Hay—Stoddard also performed numerous other duties for Lincoln, especially when his superiors were away on assignment.

Stoddard became a prolific writer on the subject of Lincoln. He produced twelve behind-the-scenes recollections entitled "White House Sketches," which appeared as a series in the *New York Citizen* between September and November 1866. His major biography, *Abraham Lincoln: The True Story of a Great Life*, appeared in 1884, and Stoddard said he wrote the book so that Americans might honor "a man who seems to have been in himself our embodiment and personification of all that is best in American national life."[2] In this tale of Lincoln's anxiety as he awaited news from the battlegrounds, Stoddard presents a memorable account of the commander-in-chief's travails and perseverance at one of the most troubling moments of the war years.

THEY SEEM FAR AWAY and almost unreal, as if they had never been, those long, overheated years with Lincoln in the White House. Very few remain of the men whose names and faces are associated in memory with the events of that time. Yet it often seems strange, unnatural, to find that the people met and talked with in every-day life, all of them who are of less than middle age, are but vaguely informed concerning those events and the actors in them. Probably most of these must, indeed, be forgotten, they were so many and there is so much else that this generation must needs study and always assume to know.

One tall figure, however, still stands forth, distinctly visible always, as if it belonged to the present as much as to the past and would march along forever, keeping step, shoulder to shoulder, with the continuous history of the Republic.

Lincoln cannot be forgotten. He is even better and better understood by thinking men. But there seems to be floating around, in the minds of many, something of the idea so curiously presented by one of the dead President's old Illinois neighbors:

"Linkin?" said the prairie man; "oh yes, I knowed him. Knowed his folks, too. They was torn-down poor. He wasn't much up to the War; that was what made him. Tell ye what, they wouldn't let on so much 'bout him now, 'f he hadn't been killed. That helped him, powerful. People kind o' sympathize with him, ye know. It made him pop'lar. He saved suthin' w'ile he was President, but I don't reckon he left much propity. Oh yes, I knowed Linkin."

In strong contrast with this crude skepticism is the marvelous keenness of the general popular instinct which then recognized, accepted, trusted, and sustained its God-appointed leader. That he was of God's appointment must be apparent to any man whose creed contains a confession of a living God, mindful of human affairs.

It may be noted, without any surprise whatever, that many intelligent persons who had associated with Lincoln in his earlier years were never, to the end, able to see anything but what may be called their first mental photographs of him, badly taken, on defective negatives. These were at best but surface pictures and contained only something of the man as he was seen before, say, the year 1858. One of his oldest, most intimate professional associates and late biographers, for instance, was hardly acquainted with him at all; for he did not even see him after 1860.

During long years prior to the War, the actual growth of so deep and strong a nature was necessarily hidden, even from himself; and when its disclosure came, through trial after trial, there was something of a surprise attaching to each successive manifestation of capacity. His slow and somewhat ponderous inability to hesitate; his apparently overconfident readiness to accept responsibilities; his forward stride to grapple unflinchingly with unknown, untellable difficulties, were only the unexpected expressions of his silent consciousness of power. This subtle, unformulated assertion of the strength that was in him was itself a serious offence, often, to men who thought they knew him, but did not, and to others who could not believe it possible for any man to do the things which he undertook and accomplished.

One remarkable feature of his development, or of its expression, was the suddenness with which, in 1861, he ceased to be a party man, or merely the head of a party, and became the man of the nation. It was true that his party itself underwent a change, welding in with the great mass of American patriotism, but its after relations with him contained little or no mere partisanship. It was once said of a President elect: "Well, he was big enough for so small a State as ours [his own]; but I'm thinking he'll show kind o' thin when you come to spread him out over the whole country." The thin spot in Lincoln's spreading has not yet been discovered.

When he went to Washington, in 1861, and the first great army from the North and West poured in around him, with their haversacks crammed with recommendations for appointment to office, there was yet another large tribe who were sorely astonished and disappointed. They had known him years and years, had heard him tell stories and try law cases, or they had even higher claims upon him, and they wondered at the heartless ingratitude with which he ignored them in making his appointments. They never forgave him; for they could not and would not understand that to him the public service was first, and personal relations not so much second as simply somewhere else. He did not even make his own father a brigadier nor invite Dennis Hanks to a seat in his Cabinet.

Lincoln's work as President and, to a certain extent, as General-in-Chief in charge of the military operations which were already not only inevitable but actually progressing, began even before his election. It is no exaggeration to say that thenceforward his toil did not cease until the end. When not asleep he was at his task.

The White House, the Executive Mansion as it is otherwise described, was much simpler and narrower in its official staff and management than it is now. Part of it was a family residence, but all the rest, including the reception rooms, was merely a workshop. There were a few days, truly, in the spring of 1861, while Washington City was a frontier post, almost cut off from the North, that the great East Room was a camp, perhaps a fort, garrisoned at night by a regiment of office seekers who had provided themselves with rifles and were prepared to defend the citadel of their prospects for appointment.

It was a remarkably silent workshop, considering how much was going on there. The very air seemed heavy with the pressure of the times, centering toward that place. There was only now and then a day bright enough to send any great amount of sunshine into the house, especially upstairs. It was not so much that coming events cast their shadow before, although they may have done so, as that the shadows, the ghosts, if you will, of all sorts of events, past, present and to come, trooped in and flitted around the halls and lurked in the corners of the rooms. The greater part of them came over from the War Office, westward, in company with messengers carrying telegraphic dispatches. Troops of them used to follow Stanton or Halleck right into Lincoln's rooms. Seward, too, was sometimes a gloomy messenger; but he was always diplomatically cheerful about it, and nobody could tell by his face but what he was bringing good news. The President could receive any kind of tidings with less variation of face or manner than any other man, and there was a reason for it. He never seemed to hear anything with reference to itself, but solely with a quick forward grasping for the consequences, for what must be done next. The announcement of a defeat or disaster did not bring to him the blow only, but rather the consideration of the counterstroke. When the cannon ball struck Charles the Twelfth in the head, it did not kill him so quickly that his sword was not half drawn before he fell.

Lincoln's characteristic as a worker was his persistency, his tirelessness; and for this he was endowed with rare toughness of bodily and mental fiber. There was not a weak spot in his whole animal organism, and his brain was thoroughly healthy; his White House life, therefore, was a continual stepping from one duty to another. There was also what to a host of men was a provoking way of stepping over or across unessential things, with an instinctive perception of their lack of value. Some things that he stepped over seemed vastly important to those who had them in hand, but at the same time he discovered real importance where others failed to see them.

He had vast capacity for work, and also the exceedingly valuable faculty of putting work upon others. He could load, up to their limit or beyond it, his Cabinet officers, generals, legislative supporters, and so forth. He could hold them responsible, sharply; but he never really interfered with them, "bothered them," at their work, or found undue fault with its execution. A false idea obtained circulation at one time concerning his hardness, his exacting dealings with his immediate co-workers and subordinates. Perhaps this arose from the numerous changes made in his civil and military appointments. He was the very reverse of exacting. For illustration, I do not know or believe that he ever found fault with one of his private secretaries in all the onerous and delicate duties with which they were charged. I know that during all the years of my own service he never uttered a criticism or expressed disapproval, and yet such a mass of work could not possibly have all been perfect. He was the most kindly and lenient of men, even when, through days and days of gloom and over-work, he would pass us, invariably, without speaking, as if we were not there, until business gave us the right to speak.

Did he never at any time reel or stagger under his burden? Oh yes, once. He could feel a hit or a stab at any time; but the things which hurt him, that made him suffer, that were slowly killing him, as he himself declared, did not interfere with the perpetual efficiency of his work. If there were hours when despondency came and when he doubted the result, the final triumph of the national arms, he did not tell anybody; but there was one night when his wrestle with despair was long and terrible.

In the opinion of Edwin M. Stanton, concurred in by other good judges, the darkest hour of the Civil War came in the first week of May, 1863. The Army of the Potomac, under General Hooker, had fought the bloody battle of Chancellorsville. The record of their dead and wounded told how bravely they had fought; but they were defeated, losing the field of battle, and seventeen thousand men. The Confederate commanders acknowledged a loss of only thirteen thousand, but their Army of Northern Virginia was dreadfully cut up. How severe a disaster this costly victory had been to them could not be understood by the people of the North.

The country was weary of the long war, with its draining taxes of gold and blood. Discontent was everywhere raising its head, and the opponents of the Lincoln administration were savage in their denunciations. Many of his severest critics were men of unquestionable patriotism. The mail desk in the Secretary's office at the White House was heaped with letters, as if the President could read them. He knew their purport well enough without reading. He knew of the forever vacant places in a hundred thousand households before Chancellorsville. If more than a third of each day's mail already consisted of measureless denunciation; if another large part was made up of piteous pleas for peace, for a termination of the long murder of the Civil War, what would it be when tidings of this last slaughter should go out and send back echoes from the heart-stricken multitude? Had not enough been endured, and was there not imminent peril that the country would refuse to endure any more? This question was, perhaps, the darkest element in the problem presented to Mr. Lincoln; for the armies, east or west, were ample in force and ready to fight again.

There were callers at the White House the day on which the news of the defeat was brought; but they were not the customary throng. Members of the Senate and House came, with gloomy faces; the members of the Cabinet came, to consult or to condole with the President. There were army and navy officers, but only such as were sent for. The house was as if a funeral were going forward, and those who entered or left it trod softly, as people always do around a coffin, for fear they may wake the dead.

That night, the last visitors in Lincoln's room were Stanton and Halleck. They went away together in silence, at somewhere near nine o'clock, and the President was left alone. Not another soul was on that floor except the one secretary, who was busy with the mail in his room across the hall from the President's; and the doors of both rooms were ajar, for the night was warm. The silence was so deep that the ticking of a clock would have been noticeable; but another sound came that was almost as regular and ceaseless. It was the tread of the President's feet as he strode slowly back and forth across the chamber in which so many Presidents of the United States had done their work. Was he to be the last of the line? The last President of the entire United States? At that hour that very question had been asked of him by the battle of Chancellorsville. If he had wavered, if he had failed in faith or courage or prompt decisions, then the nation, and not the Army of the Potomac, would have lost its great battle.

Ten o'clock came, without a break in the steady march, excepting now and then a pause in turning at either wall.

There was an unusual accumulation of letters, for that was a desk hard worked with other duties also, and it was necessary to clear it before leaving it. It seemed as if they contained a double allowance of denunciation, threats, ribaldry. Some of them were hideous, some were tear-blistered. Some would have done Lincoln good if he could have read them; but, over there in his room, he was reading the lesson of Chancellorsville and the future of the Republic. Eleven o'clock came, and then another hour of that ceaseless march so accustomed the ear to it that when, a little after twelve, there was a break of several minutes, the sudden silence made one put down letters and listen.

The President may have been at his table writing, or he may — no man knows or can guess; but at the end of the minutes, long or short, the tramp began again. Two o'clock, and he was walking yet, and when, a little after three, the secretary's task was done and he slipped noiselessly out, he turned at the head of the stairs for a moment. It was so — the last sound he heard as he went down was the footfall in Lincoln's room.

That was not all, however. The young man had need to return early, and he was there again before eight o'clock. The President's room door was open and he went in. There sat Mr. Lincoln eating breakfast alone. He had not been out of his room; but there was a kind of cheery, hopeful, morning light on his face, instead of the funeral battle-cloud from Chancellorsville. He had watched all night, but a dawn had come, for beside his cup of coffee lay the written draft of his instructions to General Hooker to push forward, to fight again. There was a decisive battle won that night in that long vigil with disaster and despair. Only a few weeks later the Army of the Potomac fought it over again as desperately — and they won it — at Gettysburg.

Notes

1. William O. Stoddard, *Lincoln's Third Secretary: The Memoirs of William O. Stoddard* (New York: Exposition Press, 1955), 6.

2. Harold Holzer, "William Osborn Stoddard," in *American National Biography* online (October 2008).

Ward, *Abraham Lincoln*, 41–49.

From *Lincoln at Gettysburg* (1906)

Clark E. Carr

Clark Ezra Carr (1836–1919) was a local politician in Galesburg, Illinois, who went on to become postmaster of the city and, later, ambassador to Denmark from 1889 to 1893. He also was a newspaper editor and prolific author; besides his book on Lincoln, he wrote one on Stephen Douglas, another on the state of Illinois, and another on the railway business, of which he and his family were prominent leaders. Carr became friends with Lincoln after serving as the youngest member of the commission in charge of the Gettysburg National Cemetery. He suggested that President Lincoln be invited to speak, and persevered when many on the commission dismissed what they considered impetuous youthful ideas. And yet now history notes that perhaps Lincoln's presence at Gettysburg should be attributed largely to Carr's persistence. He was an eyewitness to the Gettysburg Address in November of 1863 and here provides one of the best accounts of Lincoln's performance and the speech's immediate reception.

WHEN THE PRESIDENT thus appeared it was the first opportunity the people really had to see him. There was the usual craning of necks, the usual exclamations of "Down in front!" the usual crowding to get places to see, and much confusion. He waited patiently for the audience to become quiet, and there was absolute silence while he spoke. He began in those high, clarion tones, which the people of Illinois had so often heard, to which he held to the close. His was a voice that, when he made an effort, could reach a great multitude, and he always tried to make every one hear. He held in his left hand two or three pages of manuscript, toward which he glanced but once. He spoke with deliberation, but cannot have continued more than three or four, some said two, minutes.

A moment's reflection will convince any one that before the great multitude of people, nearly all of whom were standing, could have prepared themselves to listen intelligently—before they had, I may say, become poised, before their thoughts had become sufficiently centered upon the speaker to take up his line of thought and follow him — he had finished and returned to his seat.

People Disappointed in Lincoln's Address

So short a time was Mr. Lincoln before them that the people could scarcely believe their eyes when he disappeared from their view. They were almost dazed. They could not possibly in so short a time, mentally grasp the ideas that were conveyed, nor even their substance. Time and again expressions of disappointment were made to me. Many persons said to me that they would have supposed that on such a great occasion the President would have made a speech. Every one thought, as expressed by Mr. Wills four days later (to which reference has been made), that instead of Mr. Lincoln's delivering an address, he only made a very few "dedicatory remarks."

We on the platform heard every word. And what did we hear? A dozen commonplace sentences, scarcely one of which contained anything new, anything that when stated was not self-evident.

I am aware, because I noted it at the time, that in the Associated Press report, which appeared in the morning papers, there were the punctuation of "applause," "long continued applause," etc., according to the invariable custom in those days. Except when he concluded, I did not observe it, and at the close the applause was not especially marked. The occasion was too solemn for any kind of boisterous demonstrations.

Why the Audience Was Not Impressed

In concluding his comments upon Mr. Lincoln's address, Mr. Nicolay, in his "Century" article to which reference has been made, says, "They [the hearers] were therefore totally unprepared for what they heard, and could not immediately realize that his words, and not those of the carefully selected orator, were to carry the concentrated thought of the occasion like a trumpet peal to the farthest posterity."

My own recollection, which is more clear as to occurrences in those troublous times, especially those upon that occasion, the responsibilities of which devolved in a great degree upon a board of which I was a member, coincides with that of Mr. Lamon and Mr. Nicolay. It is true, as Mr. Nicolay says, the hearers were totally unprepared for what they heard, and could not immediately realize how able and far-reaching was Mr. Lincoln's address. My recollection also confirms that of Mr. Lamon, that no one there present saw the marvelous beauties of that wonderful speech. I did not hear the expressions of Mr. Seward and Mr. Everett in regard to it, as my seat was with the members of our Commission, but from the expressions of opinion I did hear, I have no doubt that they were made.

I heard every word and every articulation of Mr. Lincoln, and had no realization that he did anything more than make "a few dedicatory remarks." His expressions were so plain and homely, without any attempt at rhetorical periods, and his statements were so axiomatic, and I may say, matter of fact, and so simple, that I had no ideas that as an address it was anything more than ordinary.

Mr. Lincoln's Manner and Bearing

I was very much struck, many times as I had heard him, by the appearance of Mr. Lincoln when he arose and stood before the audience. It seemed to me that I had never seen any other human being who was so stately, and, I may say, majestic, and yet benignant. His features had a sad, mournful, almost haggard, and still hopeful expression. Every one was impressed with his sincerity and earnestness.

Clark E. Carr, *Lincoln at Gettysburg: An Address* (Chicago: A. C. McClure, 1906), 56–68.

"Abraham Lincoln" (1864)

Harriet Beecher Stowe

> The novelist Harriet Beecher Stowe (1811–1896) became one of the century's literary superstars with the publication of her most famous work, *Uncle Tom's Cabin*, first as a magazine serial and then as a two-volume work published in 1852. Besides its status as one of the great antislavery polemics of its time, the extremely popular novel features a very long cast of interesting characters, a wide geographical sweep, and extensive examples of the rhetorical debates that were common in the decade leading up to the Civil War. As such, the emotional responses to the story were considered to be among the most important precursors of the war, so much so that the legend developed that Lincoln said to her, upon their first meeting in 1862, "Is this the little woman who made this great war?" Whether or not these specific words, or even this sort of observation in general, came from President Lincoln, it did become a standard myth of the American experience.[1] Stowe continued writing throughout her life, and although she produced significant works after *Uncle Tom's Cabin* (most importantly *Dred* [1856], *The Minister's Wooing* [1859], and *Oldtown Folks* [1869]), she never surpassed it in either sales or prestige. But she became a famous cultural spokesperson for the American civil religion of the time, and for a vision of "Christian Union" founded on a strong embrace of Scripture, elements of which are seen in this piece she published in 1864.

THE REVOLUTION through which the American nation is passing is not a mere local convulsion. It is a war for a principle which concerns all mankind. It is THE WAR for the rights of the working classes of mankind, as against the usurpation of privileged aristocracies. You can make nothing else of it. That is the reason why, like a shaft of light in the judgment day, it has gone through all nations, dividing to the right and the left the multitudes. *For* us and our cause, all the common working classes of Europe — all that toil and sweat and are oppressed. *Against* us, all privileged classes, nobles, princes, bankers, and great manufacturers, and all who live at ease. A silent instinct, piercing to the dividing of soul and spirit, joints and marrow, has gone through the earth, and sent every soul with instinctive certainty where it belongs. The poor laborers of Birmingham and Manchester, the poor silk weavers of Lyons, to whom our conflict has been present starvation and lingering death, have stood bravely *for* us. No sophistries could blind or deceive *them*; they knew that *our* cause was *their* cause, and they have suffered their part heroically, as if fighting by our side, because they knew that our victory was to be their victory. On the other side, all aristocrats and holders of exclusive privileges have felt the instinct of opposition, and the sympathy with a struggling aristocracy, for they, too, feel that our victory will be their doom.

This great contest has visibly been held in the hands of Almighty God, and is a fulfilment of the solemn prophecies with which the Bible is sown thick as stars, that he would spare the soul of the needy, and judge the cause of the poor. It was he who chose the instrument for this work, and he chose him with a visible reference to the rights and interests of the great majority of mankind, for which he stands.

Abraham Lincoln is in the strictest sense a man of the working classes. All his advantages and abilities are those of *a man of the working classes*; all his disadvantages and disabilities are those of a man of the working classes; and his position now at the head of one of the most powerful nations of the earth, is a sign to all who live by labor that their day is coming. Lincoln was born to the inheritance of hard work as truly as the poorest laborer's son that digs in our fields. At seven years of age he was set to work, axe in hand, to clear up a farm in a Western forest. Until he was seventeen his life was that of a simple farm laborer, with only such intervals of schooling as farm laborers get. Probably the school instruction of his whole life would not amount to more than one year. At nineteen he made a trip to New Orleans as a hired hand on a flat boat, and on his return he split the rails for a log cabin and built it, and enclosed ten acres of land with a rail fence of his own handiwork. The next year he hired himself for twelve dollars a month to build a flat boat and take her to New Orleans; and any one who knows what the life of a Mississippi boatman was in those days, must know that it involved every kind of labor. In 1832, in the Black Hawk Indian War, the hardy boatman volunteered to fight for his country, and was unanimously elected a captain, and served with honor for a season in frontier military life. After this, while serving as a postmaster, he began his law studies, borrowing the law books he was too poor to buy, and studying by the light of his evening fire. He acquired a name in the country about as a man of resources and shrewdness; he was one that people looked to for counsel in exigencies, and to whom they were ready to depute almost any enterprise which needed skill and energy. The surveyor of Sangamon County being driven with work, came to him to take the survey of a tract off from his hands. True, he had never studied surveying — but what of that? He accepted the "job," procured a chain, a treatise on surveying, and *did the work*. Do we not see in this a parable of the wider wilderness which in later years he has undertaken to survey and fit for human habitation *without* chart or surveyor's chain?

In 1836 our backwoodsman, flat-boat hand, captain, surveyor, obtained a license to practise law, and, as might be expected, rose rapidly.

His honesty, shrewdness, energy, and keen practical insight into men and things soon made him the most influential man in his State. He became the reputed leader of the Whig party, and canvassed the State as stump speaker in the time of Henry Clay, and in 1846 was elected representative to Congress.

Here he met the grinding of the great question of the day — the upper and nether millstone of slavery and freedom revolving against each other. Lincoln's whole nature inclined him to be a harmonizer of conflicting parties rather than a committed combatant on either side. He was firmly and from principle an enemy to slavery — but the ground he occupied in Congress was in some respects a middle one between the advance guard of the anti-slavery and the spears of the fire-eaters. He voted with John Quincy Adams for the receipt of anti-slavery petitions; he voted with Giddings for a committee of inquiry into the constitutionality of slavery in the District of Columbia, and the expediency of abolishing slavery in that District; he voted for the various resolutions prohibiting slavery in the territories to be acquired from Mexico, and he voted forty-two times for the Wilmot Proviso. In Jan. 16, 1849, he offered a plan for abolishing slavery in the District of Columbia, by compensation from the national treasury, with the consent of a majority of the citizens. He opposed the annexation of Texas, but voted for the bill to pay the expenses of the war.

But at the time of the repeal of the Missouri Compromise he took the field, heart and soul, against the plot to betray our territories to slavery. It was mainly owing to his exertions that at this critical period a Republican Senator was elected from Illinois, when a Republican Senator in the trembling national scales of the conflict was worth a thousand times his weight in gold.

Little did the Convention that nominated Abraham Lincoln for President know what they were doing. Little did the honest, fatherly, patriotic man, who stood in his simplicity on the platform at Springfield, asking the prayers of his townsmen and receiving their pledges to remember him, foresee how awfully he was to need those prayers, the prayers of all this nation, and the prayers of all the working, suffering common people throughout the world. God's hand was upon him with a visible protection, saving first from the danger of assassination at Baltimore and bringing him safely to our national capital. Then the world has seen and wondered at the greatest sign and marvel of our day, to wit; a plain working man of the people, with no more culture, instruction, or education than any such working man may obtain for himself, called on to conduct the passage of a great people through a crisis involving the destinies of the whole world. The eyes of princes, nobles, aristocrats, of dukes, earls, scholars, statesmen, warriors, all turned on the plain backwoodsman, with his simple sense, his imperturbable simplicity, his determined self-reliance, his impracticable and incorruptible honesty, as he sat amid the war of conflicting elements, with unpretending steadiness, striving to guide the national ship through a channel at whose perils the world's oldest statesmen stood aghast. The brilliant courts of Europe levelled their opera-glasses at the phenomenon. Fair ladies saw that he had horny hands and disdained white gloves. Dapper diplomatists were shocked at his system of etiquette; but old statesmen, who knew the terrors of that passage, were wiser than court ladies and dandy diplomatists, and watched him with a fearful curiosity, simply asking, "*Will* that awkward old backwoodsman really get that ship through? If he does, it will be time for us to look about us."

Sooth to say, our own politicians were somewhat shocked with his state-papers at first. Why not let us make them a little more conventional, and file them to a classical pattern? "No," was his reply, "I shall write them myself. *The people will understand them.*" "But this or that form of expression is not elegant, not classical." "*The people will understand it,*" has been his invariable reply. And whatever may be said of his state-papers, as compared with the classic standards, it has been a fact that they have always been wonderfully well understood by the people, and that since the time of Washington, the state-papers of no President have more controlled the popular mind. And one reason for this is, that they have been informal and undiplomatic. They have more resembled a father's talks to his children than a state-paper. And they have had that relish and smack of the soil, that appeal to the simple human heart and head, which is a greater power in writing than the most artful devices of rhetoric. Lincoln might well say with the apostle, "But though I be rude in speech yet not in knowledge, but we have been thoroughly *made manifest among you* in all things." His rejection of what is called fine writing was as deliberate as St. Paul's, and for the same reason — because he felt that he was speaking on a subject which must be made clear to the lowest intellect, though it should fail to captivate the highest. But we say of Lincoln's writing, that for all true, manly purposes of writing, there are passages in his state-papers that could not be better put; they are absolutely perfect. They are brief, condensed, intense, and with a power of insight and expression which make them worthy to be inscribed in letters of gold. Such are some passages of the celebrated Springfield letter, especially that masterly one where he compares the conduct of the patriotic and loyal blacks with that of the treacherous and disloyal whites. No one can read this letter without feeling the influence of a mind both strong and generous.

Lincoln is a strong man, but his strength is of a peculiar kind; it is not aggressive so much as passive, and among passive things, it is like the strength not so much of a stone buttress as of a wire cable. It is strength swaying to every influence, yielding on this side and on that to popular needs, yet tenaciously and inflexibly bound to carry its great end; and probably by no other kind of strength could our national ship have been drawn safely thus far during the tossings and tempests which beset her way.

Surrounded by all sorts of conflicting claims, by traitors, by half-hearted, timid men, by Border States men, and Free States men, by radical Abolitionists and Conservatives, he has listened to all, weighed the words of all, waited, observed, yielded now here and now there, but in the main kept one inflexible, honest purpose, and drawn the national ship through.

In times of our trouble Abraham Lincoln has had his turn of being the best abused man of our nation. Like Moses leading his Israel through the wilderness, he has seen the day when every man seemed ready to stone him, and yet, with simple, wiry, steady perseverance, he has held on, conscious of honest intentions, and looking to God for help. All the nation have felt, in the increasing solemnity of his proclamations and papers, how deep an education was being wrought in his mind by this simple faith in God, the ruler of nations, and this humble willingness to learn the awful lessons of his providence.

We do not mean to give the impression that Lincoln is a religious man in the sense in which that term is popularly applied. We believe he has never made any such profession, but we see evidence that in passing through this dreadful national crisis he has been forced by the very anguish of the struggle to look upward, where any rational creature must look for support. No man in this agony has suffered more and deeper, albeit with a dry, weary, patient pain, that seemed to some like insensibility. "Whichever way it ends," he said to the writer, "I have the impression that *I* sha'n't last long after it's over." After the dreadful repulse of Fredericksburg, his heavy eyes and worn and weary air told how our reverses wore upon him, and yet there was a never-failing fund, of patience at bottom that sometimes rose to the surface in some droll, quaint saying, or story, that forced a laugh even from himself.

There have been times with many, of impetuous impatience, when our national ship seemed to lie water-logged and we have called aloud for a deliverer of another fashion,—a brilliant general, a dashing, fearless statesman, a man who could dare and do, who would stake all on a die, and win or lose by a brilliant *coup de main*. It may comfort our minds that since He who ruleth in the armies of nations set no such man to this work, that perhaps He saw in the man whom He did send some peculiar fitness and aptitudes therefore.

Slow and careful in coming to resolutions, willing to talk with every person who has anything to show on any side of a disputed subject, long in weighing and pondering, attached to constitutional limits and time-honored landmarks, Lincoln certainly was the *safest* leader a nation could have at a time when the *habeas corpus* must be suspended, and all the constitutional and minor rights of citizens be thrown into the hands of their military leader. A reckless, bold, theorizing, dashing man of genius might have wrecked our Constitution and ended us in a splendid military despotism.

Among the many accusations which in hours of ill-luck have been thrown out upon Lincoln, it is remarkable that he has never been called self-seeking, or selfish. When we were troubled and sat in darkness, and looked doubtfully towards the presidential chair, it was never that we doubted the goodwill of our pilot—only the clearness of his eyesight. But Almighty

God has granted to him that clearness of vision which he gives to the true-hearted, and enabled him to set his honest foot in that promised land of freedom which is to be the patrimony of all men, black and white — and from henceforth nations shall rise up to call him blessed.

Note

1. For the "official" Stowe family account of this episode, see the material presented in Susan Belasco, ed., *Stowe in Her Own Time* (Iowa City: U of Iowa P, 2009), 149–51.

The Living Age, February 6, 1864, 282–84.

From "Abraham Lincoln" (1865)

JAMES RUSSELL LOWELL

One of the great literary minds of his age, James Russell Lowell (1819–1891) was a poet, essayist, lecturer, critic, and diplomat. Along with his contemporaries Henry Wadsworth Longfellow, John Greenleaf Whittier, and Oliver Wendell Holmes, Lowell was often grouped as one of the "Fireside Poets" who reigned supreme as New England's spokespersons for the genteel life of the American mind. Replacing Longfellow, Lowell taught languages at Harvard and, preceding William Dean Howells, he spent some years editing the *Atlantic Monthly*. In this selection, Lowell gives one of the most profound reflections on the meaning of Lincoln's achievements that was published during the war years, with particular praise for his attempt to save the Union and his simple-yet-elegant style of speech. Lowell brings a keen and searching sensibility to bear on Lincoln's brilliance with words—one of the best analyses of Lincoln's genius ever produced in the nineteenth century.

AT THE BEGINNING of the war there was, indeed, occasion for the most anxious apprehension. A President known to be infected with the political heresies, and suspected of sympathy with the treason, of the Southern conspirators, had just surrendered the reins, we will not say of power, but of chaos, to a successor known only as the representative of a party whose leaders, with long training in opposition, had none in the conduct of affairs; an empty treasury was called on to supply resources beyond precedent in the history of finance; the trees were yet growing and the iron unmined with which a navy was to be built and armored; officers without discipline were to make a mob into an army; and, above all, the public opinion of Europe, echoed and reinforced with every vague hint and every specious argument of despondency by a powerful faction at home, was either contemptuously sceptical or actively hostile. It would be hard to over-estimate the force of this latter element of disintegration and discouragement among a people where every citizen at home, and every soldier in the field, is a reader of newspapers. The peddlers of rumor in the North were the most effective allies of the rebellion. A nation can be liable to no more insidious treachery than that of the telegraph, sending hourly its electric thrill of panic along the remotest nerves of the community, till the excited imagination makes every real danger loom heightened with its unreal double. . . .

But beside any disheartening influences which might affect the timid or the despondent, there were reasons enough of settled gravity against any over confidence of hope. A war—which, whether we consider the expanse of the territory at stake, the hosts brought into the field, or the reach of the principles involved, may fairly be reckoned the most momentous of modern times—was to be waged by a people divided at home, unnerved by fifty years of peace, under a chief magistrate without experience and without reputation, whose every measure was sure to be cunningly hampered by a jealous and unscrupulous minority, and who, while dealing with unheard-of complications at home, must soothe a hostile neutrality abroad, waiting only a pretext to become war. All this was to be done without warning and without preparation, while at the same time a social revolution was to be accomplished in the political condition of four millions of people, by softening the prejudices, allaying the fears, and gradually obtaining the cooperation, of their unwilling liberators. Surely, if ever there were an occasion when the heightened imagination of the historian might see Destiny visibly intervening in human affairs, here was a knot worthy of her shears. . . .

The Republicans had carried the country upon an issue in which ethics were more directly and visibly mingled with politics than usual. Their leaders were trained to a method of oratory which relied for its effect rather on the moral sense than the understanding. Their arguments were drawn, not so much from experience as from general principles of right and wrong. When the war came, their system continued to be applicable and effective, for here again the reason of the people was to be reached and kindled through their sentiments. It was one of those periods of excitement, gathering, contagious, universal, which, while they last, exalt and clarify the minds of men, giving to the mere words *country, human rights, democracy,* a meaning and a force beyond that of sober and logical argument. They were convictions, maintained and defended by the supreme logic of passion. That penetrating fire ran in and roused those primary instincts that make their lair in the dens and caverns of the mind. What is called the great popular heart was awakened, that indefinable something which may be, according to circumstances, the highest reason or the most brutish unreason.

But enthusiasm, once cold, can never be warmed over into anything better than cant, — and phrases, when once the inspiration that filled them with beneficent power has ebbed away, retain only that semblance of meaning which enables them to supplant reason in hasty minds. Among the lessons taught by the French Revolution there is none sadder or more striking than this, that you may make everything else out of the passions of men except a political system that will work, and that there is nothing so pitilessly and unconsciously cruel as sincerity formulated into dogma. It is always demoralizing to extend the domain of sentiment over questions where it has no legitimate jurisdiction; and perhaps the severest strain upon Mr. Lincoln was in resisting a tendency of his own supporters which chimed with his own private desires, while wholly opposed to his convictions of what would be wise policy.

The change which three years have brought about is too remarkable to be passed over without comment, too weighty in its lesson not to be laid to heart. Never did a President enter upon office with less means at his command, outside his own strength of heart and steadiness of understanding, for inspiring confidence in the people, and so winning it for himself, than Mr. Lincoln. All that was known of him was that he was a good stump speaker, nominated for his *availability*, — that is, because he had no history, — and chosen by a party with whose more extreme opinions he was not in sympathy. It might well be feared that a man past fifty, against whom the ingenuity of hostile partisans could rake up no accusation, must be lacking in manliness of character, in decision of principle, in strength of will; that a man who was at best only the representative of a party, and who yet did not fairly represent even that, would fail of political, much more of popular, support. And certainly no one ever entered upon office with so few resources of power in the past, and so many materials of weakness in the present, as Mr. Lincoln. Even in that half of the Union which acknowledged him as President, there was a large and at that time dangerous minority, that hardly admitted his claim to the office, and even in the party that elected him there was also a large minority that suspected him of being secretly a communicant with the church of Laodicea. All that he did was sure to be virulently attacked as ultra by one side; all that he left undone, to be stigmatized as proof of lukewarmness and backsliding by the other. Meanwhile, he was to carry on a truly colossal war by means of both; he was to disengage the country from diplomatic entanglements of unprecedented peril undisturbed by the help or the hindrance of either, and to win from the crowning dangers of his administration, in the confidence of the people, the means of his safety and their own. He has contrived to do it, and perhaps none of our Presidents since Washington has stood so firm in the confidence of the people as he does after three years of stormy administration.

Mr. Lincoln's policy was a tentative one, and rightly so. . . . Time was his prime-minister, and, we began to think, at one period, his general-in-chief also. At first he was so slow that he tired out all those who see no evidence of progress but in blowing up the engine; then he was so fast, that he took the breath away from those who think there is no getting on safely while there is a spark of fire under the boilers. God is the only being who has time enough; but a prudent man, who knows how to seize occasion, can commonly make a shift to find as much as he needs. Mr. Lincoln, as it seems to us in reviewing his career, though we have sometimes in our impatience thought otherwise, has always waited, as a wise man should, till the right moment brought up all his reserves. *Semper nocuit differre paratis* is a sound axiom, but the really efficacious man will also be sure to know when he is *not* ready, and be firm against all persuasion and reproach till he is.[1]

One would be apt to think, from some of the criticisms made on Mr. Lincoln's course by those who mainly agree with him in principle, that the chief object of a statesman should be rather to proclaim his adhesion to certain doctrines, than to achieve their triumph by quietly accomplishing his ends. In our opinion, there is no more unsafe politician than a conscientiously rigid *doctrinaire*, nothing more sure to end in disaster than a theoretic scheme of policy that admits of no pliability for contingencies. True, there is a popular image of an impossible He, in whose plastic hands the submissive destinies of mankind become as wax, and to whose commanding necessity the toughest facts yield with the graceful pliancy of fiction; but in real life we find that the men who control circumstances, as it is called, are those who have learned to allow for the influence of their eddies, and have the nerve to turn them to account at the happy instant. Mr. Lincoln's perilous task has been a rather shaky raft through the rapids, making fast the unrulier logs as he could snatch opportunity, and the country is to be congratulated that did not think it his duty to run straight at all hazards, but cautiously to assure himself with his setting-pole where the main current was, and keep steadily to that. He is still in wild water, but we have faith that his skill and sureness of eye will bring him out right at last.

People of more sensitive organizations may be shocked, but we are glad that in this our true war of independence, which is to free us forever from the Old World, we have had at the head of our affairs a man whom America made, as God made Adam, out of the very earth, unancestried, unprivileged, unknown, to show us how much truth, how much magnanimity, and how much state-craft await the call of opportunity in simple manhood when it believes in the justice of God and the worth of man. Conventionalities are all very well in their proper place, but they shrivel at the touch of nature like stubble in the fire. The genius that sways a nation by its arbitrary will seems less august to us than that which multiplies and reinforces itself in the instincts and convictions of an entire people. Autocracy may have something in it more melodramatic than this, but falls far short of it in human value and interest.

Experience would have bred in us a rooted distrust of improvised statesmanship, even if we did not believe politics to be a science, which, if it cannot always command men of special aptitude and great powers, at least demands the long and steady application of the best powers of such men as it can command to master even its first principles. It is curious, that, in a country which boasts of its intelligence, the theory should be so generally held that the most complicated of human contrivances, and one which every day becomes more complicated, can be worked at sight by any man able to talk for an hour or two without stopping to think.

Mr. Lincoln is sometimes claimed as an example of a ready-made ruler. But no case could well be less in point; for, besides that he was a man of such fair-mindedness as is always the raw material of wisdom, he had in his profession a training precisely the opposite of that to which a partisan is subjected. His experience as a lawyer compelled him not only to see that there is a principle underlying every phenomenon in human affairs, but that there are always two sides to every question, both of which must be fully understood in order to understand either, and that it is of greater advantage to an advocate to appreciate the strength than the weakness of his antagonist's position. Nothing is more remarkable than the unerring tact with which, in his debate with Mr. Douglas, he went straight to the reason of the question; nor have we ever had a more striking lesson in political tactics than the fact, that, opposed to a man exceptionally adroit in using popular prejudice and bigotry to his purpose, exceptionally unscrupulous in appealing to those baser motives that turn a meeting of citizens into a mob of barbarians, he should yet have won his case before a jury of the people. Mr. Lincoln was as far as possible from an impromptu politician. His wisdom was made up of a knowledge of things as well as of men; his sagacity resulted from a clear perception and honest acknowledgment of difficulties, which enabled him to see that the only durable triumph of political opinion is based, not on any abstract right, but upon so much of justice, the highest attainable at any given moment in human affairs, as may be had in the balance of mutual concession. Doubtless he had an ideal, but it was the ideal of a practical statesman, — to aim at the best, and to take the next best, if he is lucky enough to get even that. His slow, but singularly masculine, intelligence taught him that precedent is only another name for embodied experience, and that it counts for even more in the guidance of communities of men than in that of the individual life. He was not a man who held it good public economy to pull down on the mere chance of rebuilding better. Mr. Lincoln's faith in

God was qualified by a very well-founded distrust of the wisdom of man. Perhaps it was his want of self-confidence that more than anything else won him the unlimited confidence of the people, for felt that there would be no need of retreat from any position he had deliberately taken. The cautious, but steady, advance of his policy during war was like that of a Roman army. He left behind him a firm road on which public confidence could follow; he took America with him where he went; what he gained he occupied, and his advanced posts became colonies. The very homeliness of his genius was its distinction. His kingship was by its workday homespun. Never was ruler so absolute as he, nor so little conscious of it; for he was the incarnate common-sense of the people. With all that tenderness of nature whose sweet sadness touched whoever saw him with something of its own pathos, there was no trace of sentimentalism in his speech or action. He seems to have had but one rule of conduct, always that of practical and successful politics, to let himself be guided by events, when they were sure to bring him out where he wished to go, though by what seemed to unpractical minds, which let go the possible to grasp at the desirable, a longer road. . . .

While every day was bringing the people nearer to the conclusion which all thinking men saw to be inevitable from the beginning, it was wise in

Mr. Lincoln to leave the shaping of his policy to events. In this country, where the rough and ready understanding of the people is sure at last to be the controlling power, a profound common-sense is the best genius for statesmanship. Hitherto the wisdom of the President's measures has been justified by the fact that they have always resulted in more firmly uniting public opinion. One of the things particularly admirable in the public utterances of President Lincoln is a certain tone of familiar dignity, which, while it is perhaps the most difficult attainment of mere style, is also no doubtful indication of personal character. There must be something essentially noble in an elective ruler who can descend to the level of confidential ease without forfeiting respect, something very manly in one who can break through the etiquette of his conventional rank and trust himself to the reason and intelligence of those who have elected him. No higher compliment was ever paid to a nation than the simple confidence, the fireside plainness, with which Mr. Lincoln always addresses himself to the reason of the American people. This was, indeed, a true democrat, who grounded himself on the assumption that a democracy can think. "Come, let us reason together about this matter," has been the tone of all his addresses to the people; and accordingly we have never had a chief magistrate who so won to himself the love and at the same time the judgment of his countrymen. To us, that simple confidence of his in the right-mindedness of his fellowmen is very touching, and its success is as strong an argument as we have ever seen in favor of the theory that men can govern themselves. He never appeals to any vulgar sentiment, he never alludes to the humbleness of his origin; it probably never occurred to him, indeed, that there was anything higher to start from than manhood; and he put himself on a level with those he addressed, not by going down to them, but only by taking it for granted that they had brains and would come up to a common ground of reason. In an article lately printed in "The Nation," Mr. Bayard Taylor mentions the striking fact, that in the foulest dens of the Five Points he found the portrait of Lincoln. The wretched population that makes its hive there threw all its votes and more against him, and yet paid this instinctive tribute to the sweet humanity of his nature. Their ignorance sold its vote and took its money, but all that was left of manhood in them recognized its saint and martyr.

Mr. Lincoln is not in the habit of saying, "This is *my* opinion, or *my* theory," but, "This is the conclusion to which, in my judgment, the time has come, and to which, accordingly, the sooner we come the better for us."

His policy has been the policy of public opinion based on adequate discussion and on a timely recognition of the influence of passing events in shaping the features of events to come.

One secret of Mr. Lincoln's remarkable success in captivating the popular mind is undoubtedly an unconsciousness of self which enables him, though under the necessity of constantly using the capital *I*, to do it without any suggestion of egotism. There is no single vowel which men's mouths can pronounce with such difference of effect. That which one shall hide away as it were, behind the substance of his discourse, or, if he bring it to the front, shall use merely to give an agreeable accent of individuality to what he says, another shall make an offensive challenge to the self-satisfaction of all his hearers, and an unwarranted intrusion upon each man's sense of personal importance, irritating every pore of his vanity, like a dry northeast wind, to a goose-flesh of opposition and hostility. Mr. Lincoln has never studied Quintillian; but he has, in the earnest simplicity and unaffected Americanism of his own character, one art of oratory worth all the rest. He forgets himself so entirely in his object as to give his *I* the sympathetic and persuasive effect of *We* with the great body of his countrymen. Homely, dispassionate, showing all the rough-edged process of his thought as it goes along, yet arriving at his conclusions with an honest kind of everyday logic, he is so eminently our representative man, that, when he speaks, it seems as if the people were listening to their own thinking aloud. The dignity of his thought owes nothing to any ceremonial garb of words, but to the manly movement that comes of settled purpose and an energy of reason that knows not what rhetoric means. There has been nothing of Cleon, still less of Strepsiades striving to underbid him in demagogism, to be found in the public utterances of Mr. Lincoln. He has always addressed the intelligence of men, never their prejudice, their passion, or their ignorance.

On the day of his death, this simple Western attorney, who according to one party was a vulgar joker, and whom the *doctrinaires* among his own supporters accused of wanting every element of statesmanship, was the most absolute ruler in Christendom, and this solely by the hold his good-humored sagacity had laid on the hearts and understandings of his countrymen. Nor was this all, for it appeared that he had drawn the great majority, not only of his fellow-citizens, but of mankind also, to his side. So strong and so persuasive is honest manliness without a single quality of romance or unreal sentiment to help it! A civilian during times of the most captivating military achievement, awkward, with no skill in the lower technicalities of manners, he left behind him a fame beyond that of any conqueror, the memory of a grace higher than that of outward person, and of a gentlemanliness deeper than mere breeding. Never before that startled April morning did such multitudes of men shed tears for the death of one they had never seen, as if with him a friendly presence had been taken away from their lives, leaving them colder and darker. Never was funeral panegyric so eloquent as the silent look of sympathy which strangers exchanged when they met on that day. Their common manhood had lost a kinsman.

Note

1. Delay is always harmful to those who are prepared.

James Russell Lowell, *The Writings of James Russell Lowell*, Vol. 5, *Political Essays* (Cambridge, MA: Riverside Press, 1890), 177–209.

[Excerpts from Letters about Her Husband, 1865–1873]

MARY TODD LINCOLN

Born Mary Anne Todd on December 13, 1818, in Lexington, Kentucky, the daughter of Robert and Eliza Todd, Mary grew up wealthy, well educated, and fascinated by politics. In 1839, she moved to Springfield, Illinois, to live with her sister Elizabeth, and there met Abraham Lincoln. Married in November 1842, their relationship was sometimes vexed as the Lincolns' four sons were born over the next ten years, and Abraham struggled to further his career. One son, Eddie, died in Illinois in 1850 and was buried there.

Mary was unpopular and controversial as First Lady, considered by many fastidious, showy in dress, and bossy toward her husband. Her favored-son Willie's death in 1862, followed three years later by her husband's assassination at her side in a theater box, left her isolated, grief-stricken, and in debt. Another son, Tad, her most frequent companion after Abraham's death, died in 1871, leaving her with only one living son, Robert. Their relationship deteriorated amid her financial and personal instability, and in 1875 Robert had her institutionalized. She successfully sued for her release a year later and moved to France. In 1880, she moved to her sister's house in Springfield, and died there in 1882 after having been bedridden for some time. Though one can disagree with some of her characterizations of her husband, clearly Mary also possessed many telling insights about him as well, as here in letters that speak directly to some of William Herndon's controversial accusations about Lincoln's character and religiosity.

To Josiah G. Holland

Chicago Dec 4th 1865

Private —

My Dear Sir:

. . . It is exceedingly painful to me, *now*, suffering under such an overwhelming bereavement, to recall *that* happy time. My beloved husband, had so entirely devoted himself to me, for two years before my marriage, that I doubtless trespassed, many times & oft, upon his great tenderness & amiability of character. There never existed a more loving & devoted husband & such a Father, has seldom been bestowed on children. Crushed and bowed to the earth, with our *great great* sorrow, for the sake of my poor afflicted boys, I have to strive, to live on, and comfort them, as well, as I can. You are aware, that with all the President's, deep feeling, he was *not*, a demonstrative man, when he felt most deeply, he expressed, the least. There are some very good persons, who are inclined to magnify conversations & incidents, connected with their slight acquaintance, with this great & good man, For instance, the purported conversations, between the President & the Hospital nurse, it was not *his* nature, to commit his griefs and religious feelings so fully to words & that with an entire stranger. Even, between ourselves, when our deep & touching sorrows, were *one* & the same, his expressions were few — Also the lengthy account, of the lady, who *very* wisely, persisted, in claiming a hospital, for her State. My husband, never had the time, to discuss these matters, so lengthily with any person or persons — too many of them came daily, in review before him — And again, I cannot understand, how strangely his temper, could be at so complete a variance, from what it always was, in the home circle. There, he was always, so gentle & kind. Before closing this long letter, which I fear will weary you, ere you get through it — allow me again to assure you, of the great satisfaction the perusal of your Memoirs, have given me. I remain very truly & gratefully,

Mary Lincoln

To James Smith

Marienbad, June 8, 1870

. . . My husband also possessed among his other noble attributes, great truthfulness and sincerity of character — and very naturally, had mentioned all persons, with whom he had been particularly acquainted or intimate in

his life. You may well suppose — that understanding Mr Herndon's style of talking & remembering Mr Lincoln's assurances always to me — that for no other lady, had he ever cared, but myself — When Herndon came out with that pathetic & sensational love story — which he had racked his brains to invent — to bring himself into notice — we who knew Mr Lincoln so well — smiled at his falseness, knowing that time would make it right. It has just been made to appear as it really was — in the recent published note from Mr McNair [McNamar] the Scotch gentleman, to whom the young lady was engaged when she died — and who says, that for *his* life, notwithstanding his own exact story, to Herndon, he cannot tell, why Herndon persists in thus falsyfing. As my husband was known to be the most loving and devoted husband & father we will allow these falsehoods a place where they deserve. We all — the whole world have been greatly shocked — at the fearful ideas — Herndon — has advanced regarding Mr Lincoln's religious views. You, who knew him so well & held so many conversations, with him, as far back as twenty years since, know what they were. A man, who never took the name of his Maker in vain, who always read his Bible diligently, who never failed to rely on God's promises & looked up to him for protection, surely such a man as this, could not have been a disbeliever, or any other but what he was, a true Christian gentleman. No one, but such a man as Herndon could venture — to suggest such an idea. From the time of the death of our little Edward, I believe my husband's heart, was directed towards religion & as time passed on — when Mr Lincoln became elevated to Office — with the care of a great Nation, upon his shoulders — when devastating war was upon us — then indeed to my own knowledge — did his great heart go up daily, hourly, in prayer to God — for his sustaining power. When too — the overwhelming sorrow came upon us, our beautiful, bright, angelic boy, Willie was called away from us, to his Heavenly Home, with God's chastising hand upon us — he turned his heart to Christ —
Pardon this scrawl, for I am too tired to copy.

M. L.

To John Todd Stuart

Chicago, Dec 15th 1874 [1873]

My dear Cousin:

Owing to much indisposition during the past year & whilst in Canada for months, seldom seeing an American paper, the controversy which appears to have been going on regarding my great & good husband's religious views, have entirely escaped me. With very great sorrow & natural indignation have I read of Mr Herndon, placing words in my mouth—*never once* uttered. I remember the call *he* made on me for a few minutes at the [St. Nicholas] hotel as he mentions, *your* welcome entrance a quarter of an hour afterward, naturally prevented a further interview with him. Mr Herndon, had always been an utter stranger to me, he was not considered an habitué, at our house. The office was more, in his line. Very soon after his entrance, I remember well, he branched off to Mr Lincoln's religious beliefs—I told him in positive words, that my husband's heart, was naturally religious—he had often described to me, his noble Mother, reading to him at a very early age, from her Bible, the prayers she offered up for him, that he should become a pious boy & man—and then I told Mr Herndon, what an acceptable book, *that* Great Book, was always to him. In our family bereavements, it was *there*, he first turned for comfort—Sabbath mornings he accompanied me to hear dear good old Dr Smith, preach & moreover, I reminded Mr Herndon, that his last words, to his dear friends on leaving for Washington, with an impending Rebellion before the country were words uttered in great a[n]xiety & sadness "Pray for me"—

These words revealed his *heart*. What more can I say in answer to this man, who when my heart was broken with anguish, issued falsehoods, against me & mine, which were enough to make the Heaven's blush—

Very truly yours
Mary Lincoln

Please show Rev Mr Read [sic] this note.

Justin G. and Linda Levitt Turner, *Mary Todd Lincoln: Her Life and Letters* (New York: Knopf, 1972), 293–94, 567–68, 603–4.

"Dreams and Presentiments" (1895)

Ward Hill Lamon

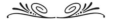

Ward Hill Lamon (1828–1893), a burly and imposing man who enjoyed strong drink, loud arguments, and jovial humor, was an Illinois lawyer that President Lincoln once described as "my particular friend." In 1850 he rode the Eighth Judicial Circuit with Lincoln and David Davis, and from 1852 to 1857 he was Lincoln's associate in numerous legal cases. Although Lamon worked for Lincoln's election to the Senate in 1854 and 1858, he disliked more radically antislavery Republicans like Owen Lovejoy.

Lincoln appointed Lamon marshal of the District of Columbia in 1861, where he performed various official duties, kept the local prison, and served as the president's bodyguard. He was marshal-in-chief of the procession at Gettysburg before Lincoln's famous address and introduced the president on the platform. Lamon constantly worried over Lincoln's personal safety and recommended employing secret spies to ferret out disloyalty in the White House. On April 11, 1865, the president sent Lamon to Richmond; thus he was out of town the night Lincoln was assassinated. In this account, Lamon provides some of the more eerie details regarding Lincoln's interest in and penchant for mystical dreams and other experiences, which sometimes occurred as he slept in his White House bedroom.

THAT "EVERY MAN HAS within him his own Patmos," Victor Hugo was not far wrong in declaring. "Revery," says the great French thinker, "fixes its gaze upon the shadow until there issues from it light. Some power that is very high has ordained it thus." Mr. Lincoln had his Patmos, his "kinship with the shades"; and this is, perhaps, the strangest feature of his character. That his intellect was mighty and of exquisite mould, that it was of a severely logical cast, and that his reasoning powers were employed in the main on matters eminently practical, all men who know anything about the real Lincoln. The father of modern philosophy tells us that "the master of superstition is the people; and in all superstitions wise men follow fools." Lord Bacon, however, was not unwilling to believe that storms might be dispersed by the ringing of bells, — a superstition that is not yet wholly dead, even in countries most distinguished by modern enlightenment. Those whom the great Englishman designated "masters of superstition, — fools," were the common people whose collective wisdom Mr. Lincoln esteemed above the highest gifts of cultured men. That the Patmos of the *plain people* as Mr. Lincoln called them, was his in a large measure he freely acknowledged; and this peculiarity of his nature is shown in his strange dreams and presentiments, which sometimes elated and sometimes disturbed him in a very astonishing degree.

From early youth he seemed conscious of a high mission. Long before his admission to the bar, or his entrance into politics, he believed that he was destined to rise to a great height; that from a lofty station to which he should be called he would be able to confer lasting benefits on his fellow men. He believed also that from a lofty station he should fall. It was a vision of grandeur and of gloom which was confirmed in his mind by the dreams of his childhood, of his youthful days, and of his mature years. The plain people with whom his life was spent, and with whom he was in cordial sympathy, believed also in the marvelous as revealed in presentiments and dreams; and so Mr. Lincoln drifted on through years of toil and exceptional hardship, struggling with a noble spirit for honest promotion, — meditative, aspiring, certain of his star, but appalled at times by its malignant aspect. Many times prior to his election to the Presidency he was both elated and alarmed by what seemed to him a rent in the veil which hides from mortal view what the future holds. He saw, or thought he saw, a vision of glory and of blood, himself the central figure in a scene which his fancy transformed from giddy enchantment to the most appalling tragedy.

On the day of his renomination at Baltimore, Mr. Lincoln was engaged at the War Department in constant telegraphic communication with General Grant, who was then in front of Richmond. Throughout the day he seemed wholly unconscious that anything was going on at Baltimore in which his interests were in any way concerned. At luncheon time he went to the White House, swallowed a hasty lunch, and without entering his private office hurried back to the War Office. On his arrival at the War Department the first dispatch that was shown him announced the nomination of Andrew Johnson for Vice-President.

"This is strange," said he, reflectively; "I thought it was usual to nominate the candidate for President first."

His informant was astonished. "Mr. President," said he, "have you not heard of your own renomination? It was telegraphed to you at the White House two hours ago."

Mr. Lincoln had not seen the dispatch, had made no inquiry about it, had not even thought about it. On reflection, he attached great importance to this singular occurrence. It reminded him, he said, of an ominous incident of mysterious character which occurred just after his election in 1860. It was the double image of himself in a looking-glass, which he saw while lying on a lounge in his own chamber at Springfield. There was Abraham Lincoln's face reflecting the full glow of health and hopeful life; and in the same mirror, at the same moment of time, was the face of Abraham Lincoln showing a ghostly paleness. On trying the experiment at other times, as confirmatory tests, the illusion reappeared, and then vanished as before.

Mr. Lincoln more than once told me that he could not explain this phenomenon; that he had tried to reproduce the double reflection at the Executive Mansion, but without success; that it had worried him not a little; and that the mystery had its meaning, which was clear enough to him. To his mind the illusion was a sign, — the life-like image betokening a safe passage through his first term as President; the ghostly one, that death would overtake him before the close of the second. Wholly unmindful of the events happening at Baltimore, which would have engrossed the thoughts of any other statesman in his place that day, — forgetful, in fact, of all earthly things except the tremendous events of the war, — this circumstance, on reflection, he wove into a volume of prophecy, a sure presage of his re-election. His mind then instantly traveled back to the autumn of 1860; and the vanished wraith — the ghostly face in the mirror, mocking its healthy and hopeful fellow — told him plainly that although certain of re-election to the exalted office he then held, he would surely hear the fatal summons from the silent shore during his second term. With that firm conviction, which no philosophy could shake, Mr. Lincoln moved on through a maze of mighty events, calmly awaiting the inevitable hour of his fall by a murderous hand.

How, it may be asked, could he make life tolerable, burdened as he was with the portentous horror which though visionary, and of trifling import in *our* eyes, was by his interpretation a premonition of impending doom? I answer in a word: His sense of duty to his country; his belief that "the inevitable" is right; and his innate and irrepressible humor.

But the most startling incident in the life of Mr. Lincoln was a dream he had only a few days before his assassination. To him it was a thing of deadly import, and certainly no vision was ever fashioned more exactly like a dread reality. Coupled with other dreams, with the mirror-scene and with other incidents, there was something about it so amazingly real, so true to the actual tragedy which occurred soon after, that more than mortal strength and wisdom would have been required to let it pass without a shudder or a pang. After worrying over it for some days, Mr. Lincoln seemed no longer able to keep the secret. I give it as nearly in his own words as I can, from notes which I made immediately after its recital. There were only two or three persons present. The President was in a melancholy, meditative mood, and had been silent for some time. Mrs. Lincoln, who was present, rallied him on his solemn visage and want of spirit. This seemed to arouse him, and without seeming to notice her sally he said, in slow and measured tones: —

"It seems strange how much there is in the Bible about dreams. There are, I think, some sixteen chapters in the Old Testament and four or five in the New in which dreams are mentioned; and there are many other passages scattered throughout the book which refer to visions. If we believe the Bible, we must accept the fact that in the old days God and His angels came to men in their sleep and made themselves known in dreams. Nowadays dreams are regarded as very foolish, and are seldom told, except by old women and by young men and maidens in love."

Mrs. Lincoln here remarked: "Why, you look dreadfully solemn; do *you* believe in dreams?"

"I can't say that I do," returned Mr. Lincoln; "but I had one the other night which has haunted me ever since. After it occurred, the first time I opened the Bible, strange as it may appear, it was at the twenty-eighth chapter of Genesis, which relates the wonderful dream Jacob had. I turned other passages, and seemed to encounter a dream or a vision wherever I looked. I kept on turning the leaves of the old book, and everywhere my eye fell upon passages recording matters strangely in keeping with my own thoughts, supernatural visitations, dreams, visions, etc."

He now looked so serious and disturbed that Mrs. Lincoln exclaimed: "You frighten me! What is the matter?"

"I am afraid," said Mr. Lincoln, observing the effect his words had upon his wife, "that I have done wrong to mention the subject at all; but somehow the thing has got possession of me, and, like Banquo's ghost, it will not down."

This only inflamed Mrs. Lincoln's curiosity the more, and while bravely disclaiming any belief in dreams, she strongly urged him to tell the dream which seemed to have such a hold upon him, being seconded in this by another listener. Mr. Lincoln hesitated, but at length commenced very deliberately, his brow overcast with a shad of melancholy.

"About ten days ago," said he, "I retired very late. I had been up waiting for important dispatches from the front. I could not have been long in bed when I fell into a slumber, for I was weary. I soon began to dream. There seemed to be a death-like stillness about me. Then I heard subdued sobs, as if a number of people were weeping. I thought I left my bed and wandered downstairs. There the silence was broken by the same pitiful sobbing, but the mourners were invisible. I went from room to room; no living person was in sight, but the same mournful sounds of distress met me as I passed along. It was light in all the rooms; every object was familiar to me; but where were all the people who were grieving as if their hearts would break? I was puzzled and alarmed. What could be the meaning of all this? Determined to find the cause of a state of things so mysterious and so shocking, I kept on until I arrived at the East Room, which I entered. There I met with a sickening surprise. Before me was a catafalque, on which rested a corpse wrapped in funeral vestments. Around it were stationed soldiers who were acting as guards; and there was a throng of people, some gazing mournfully upon the corpse, whose face was covered, others weeping pitifully. 'Who is dead in the White House?' I demanded of one of the soldiers. 'The President,' was his answer; 'he was killed by an assassin!' Then came a loud burst of grief from the crowd, which awoke me from my dream. I slept no more that night; and although it was only a dream, I have been strangely annoyed by it ever since."

"That is horrid!" said Mrs. Lincoln. "I wish you had not told it. I am glad I don't believe in dreams, or I should be in terror from this time forth."

"Well," responded Mr. Lincoln, thoughtfully, "it is only a dream, Mary. Let us say no more about it, and try to forget it."

This dream was so horrible, so real, and so in keeping with other dreams and threatening presentiments of his, that Mr. Lincoln was profoundly disturbed by it. During its recital he was grave, gloomy, and at times visibly pale, but perfectly calm. He spoke slowly, with measured accents and deep feeling. In conversation with me he referred to it afterward, closing one with this quotation from "Hamlet": "To sleep; perchance to dream! Ay, *there's the rub!*" with a strong accent on the last three words.

Once the President alluded to this terrible dream with some show of playful humor. "Hill," said he, "your apprehension of harm to me from some hidden enemy is downright foolishness. For a long time you have been trying to keep somebody — the Lord knows who — from killing me. Don't you see how it will turn out? In this dream it was not me, but some other fellow, that was killed. It seems that this ghostly assassin tried his hand on someone else. And this reminds me of an old farmer in Illinois whose family were made sick by eating greens. Some poisonous herb had got into the mess, and members of the family were in danger of dying. There was a half-witted boy in the family called Jake; and always afterward when they had greens the old man would say, 'Now, afore we risk these greens, let's try 'em on Jake. If he stands 'em, we're all right.' Just so with me. As long as this imaginary assassin continues to exercise himself on others I can stand it." He then became serious and said: "Well, let it go. I think the Lord in His own good time and way will work this out all right. God knows what is best."

These words he spoke with a sigh, and rather in a tone of soliloquy, as if hardly noting my presence.

Mr. Lincoln had another remarkable dream, which was repeated so frequently during his occupancy of the White House that he came to regard it as a welcome visitor. It was of a pleasing and promising character, having nothing in it of the horrible. It was always an omen of a Union victory, and came with unerring certainty just before every military or naval engagement where our arms were crowned with success. In this dream he saw a ship sailing away rapidly, badly damaged, and our victorious vessels in close pursuit. He saw, also, the close of a battle on land, the enemy routed, and our forces in possession of vantage ground of incalculable importance. Mr. Lincoln stated it as a fact that he had this dream just before the battles of Antietam, Gettysburg, and other signal engagements throughout the war.

The last time Mr. Lincoln had this dream was the night before his assassination. On the morning of that lamentable day there was a Cabinet meeting at which General Grant was present. During an interval of general discussion, the President asked General Grant if he had any news from

General Sherman, who was then confronting Johnston. The reply was in the negative, but the general added that he was in hourly expectation of a dispatch announcing Johnston's surrender. Mr. Lincoln then with great impressiveness said: "We shall hear very soon, and the news will be important." General Grant asked him why he thought so. "Because," said Mr. Lincoln, "I had a dream last night; and ever since this war began I have had the same dream just before every event of great national importance portends some important event that will happen very soon."

After this Mr. Lincoln became unusually cheerful. In the afternoon he ordered a carriage for a drive. Mrs. Lincoln asked him if he wished any one to accompany them. "No, Mary," said he, "I prefer that we ride by ourselves to-day."

Mrs. Lincoln said afterwards that she never saw him look happier than he did during that drive. In reply to a remark of hers to that effect, Mr. Lincoln said: "And well may I feel so, Mary; for I consider that this day the war has come to a close. Now, we must try to be more cheerful in the future; for between this terrible war and the loss of our darling son we have suffered much misery. Let us both try to be happy."

On the night of the fatal 14th of April, 1865, when the President was assassinated, Mrs. Lincoln's first exclamation was, "His dream was prophetic."

History will record no censure against Mr. Lincoln for believing, like the first Napoleon, that he was a man of destiny; for such he surely was, if the term is at all admissible in a philosophic sense. And our estimate of his greatness must be heightened by conceding the fact that he was a believer in certain phases of the supernatural. Assured as he undoubtedly was by omens which to his mind were conclusive that he would rise to greatness and power, he was as firmly convinced by the same tokens that he would be suddenly cut off at the height of his career and the fullness of his fame. He always believed that he would fall by the hand of an assassin; and yet with that appalling doom clouding his life, — a doom fixed and irreversible, as he was firmly convinced, — his courage never for a moment forsook him, even in the most trying emergencies. Can greatness, courage, constancy in the pursuit of exalted aims, be tried by a severer test? He believed with Tennyson that —

> Because right is right, to follow right
> Were wisdom in the scorn of consequence.

Concerning presentiments and dreams Mr. Lincoln had a philosophy of his own, which, strange as it may appear, was in perfect harmony with his character in all other respects. He was no dabbler in divination, — astrology, horoscopy, prophecy, ghostly lore, or witcheries of any sort. With Goethe, he held that "Nature cannot but do right eternally." Dreams and presentiments, in his judgment, are not of supernatural origin; that is, they proceed in a natural order, their essence being preternatural, but not *above* nature. The moving power of dreams and vision of an extraordinary character he ascribed, as did the Patriarchs of old, to the Almighty Intelligence that governs the universe, their processes conforming strictly to natural laws. "Nature," said he, "is the workmanship of the Almighty; and we form but links in the general chain of intellectual and material life."

Mr. Lincoln had this further idea. Dreams being natural occurrences, in the strictest sense, he held that their best interpreters are the common people; and this accounts in large measure of the profound respect he always had for the collective wisdom of plain people, — "the children of Nature," he called them, — touching matters belonging to the domain of psychical mysteries. There was some basis of truth, he believed, for whatever obtained general credence among these "children of Nature"; and as he esteemed himself one of their number, having passed the greater part of his life among them, we can easily account for the strength of his convictions on matters about which they and he were in cordial agreement.

The natural bent of Mr. Lincoln's mind, aided by early associations, inclined him to read books which tended to strengthen his early convictions on occult subjects. Byron's "Dream" was a favorite poem, and I have often heard him repeat the following lines: —

> Sleep hath its own world,
> A boundary between the things misnamed
> Death and existence: Sleep hath its own world
> And a wide realm of wild reality.
> And dreams in their development have breath,
> And tears and tortures, and the touch of joy;
> They leave a weight upon our waking thoughts,
> They take a weight from off our waking toils,
> They do divide our being.

He seemed strangely fascinated by the wonderful in history, — such as the fall of Geta by the hand of Caracalla, as foretold by Severus; the ghosts of Caracalla's father and murdered brother threatening and upbraiding him; and kindred passages. It is useless further to pursue this account of Mr. Lincoln's peculiar views concerning these interesting mysteries. Enough has been said to show that the more intense the light which is poured upon what may be regarded as Mr. Lincoln's weakest points, the greater and grander will his character appear.

Dorothy Lamon, ed., *Recollections of Abraham Lincoln: 1847–1865* (Chicago: A. C. McLure, 1895), 109–21.

"A Theatrical Manager's Reminiscences" (1895)

WILLIAM E. SINN

William E. Sinn (1834–1899) was born in Georgetown, D.C., but moved with his parents to Maryland soon after. With the commencement of the Civil War, he began a career as a theater manager. As a theater manager, owner, and political activist, he was the proprietor of the Canterbury Theater in Washington, where Abraham Lincoln frequented performances during the war years. Here Sinn recalls aspects of Lincoln's interest in drama, and writes of his intimate knowledge of John Wilkes Booth, the assassin of Lincoln with whom Sinn conversed just days before the murder.

THE YEAR AFTER the War broke out I was the proprietor of "Canterbury Hall," in Washington, where vaudeville entertainments were given. The same year I was associated with Mr. Leonard Grover in the management of the National Theatre. I remember that at the matinee performances at the "Canterbury" Mr. Lincoln's boys — particularly the young one, "Tad" — would often be sent down to see the performance. Mr. Lincoln himself was a frequent visitor at Grover & Sinn's National Theatre. He always gave us notice a day ahead, and we took care to have a private box reserved for him. From a business point of view, we were only too glad to have him visit the theatre, because it was a good advertisement, and we would have willingly given him complimentary tickets; but he would firmly decline them, invariably directing his secretary, or the messenger, to pay for the box.

One peculiar feature about Mr. Lincoln's theatre-going was that he never had the least desire (as many theatre-goers have) to go behind the scenes. He used to say that to do so would spoil the illusion surrounding the play. When very prominent actors appeared, however, in whom he was specially interested, Mr. Lincoln would invite them into his private box between the acts, and have a chat with them. He was a great admirer of the drama, and was particularly fond of comedy. When a good strong comedian appeared at our house, male or female, you would always find Mr. Lincoln present at the performance, unless sickness or extremely important business prevented his attendance. He came to the "Canterbury" vaudeville performance only once or twice, but often sent his boys there to the matinees in charge of some grown person. He was very democratic in his ways, always had a pleasant word if he happened to meet me at the entrance to the theatre, which he generally did, as I had charge of the front of the house. On one occasion he glanced over the auditorium, the theatre was crowded. "Ah!" he exclaimed, "I guess *this* business will pay."

At the time the President was assassinated I (or rather the firm of Grover & Sinn) was running the Chestnut Street Theatre in Philadelphia. Three or four days before the assassination, Wilkes Booth was in Philadelphia on his way to Washington to play for a benefit. I think the benefit of Miss Susan Denin. Through some misunderstanding the benefit was postponed. After the tragedy at Ford's Theatre, it was thought that on the occasion of Miss Denin's benefit, when the President was almost certain to be present, Booth would have attempted to assassinate the Chief Magistrate.

The last time I saw Wilkes Booth was at the stage door of the Chestnut Street Theatre, Philadelphia, at about ten o'clock at night. He was going to take the train in an hour for Washington. On that same afternoon I had seen him and been with him for fully three quarters of an hour, had walked down Chestnut Street with him, and left him to lunch with Miss Kate Pennoyer, an actress now retired from the stage. When I bade him good-bye he made a remark that I quickly recalled as soon as I heard of the assassination: "You will hear from me in Washington," he said. "I am going to make a hit." The term "hit" in theatrical parlance means a success. I said: "Good luck to you. You are a pretty good sort of an actor; I guess you will." The next thing I heard of Booth was the terrible news that he had killed President Lincoln.

Of course, after the assassination there was a close and careful examination as to Booth's antecedents and his movements just before the dreadful tragedy. It seems that during his few days' stay in Philadelphia he was seen a great deal in the company of Matt Canning (since deceased), at that time manager of Mme. Vestali, who was playing then at Mrs. John Drew's Arch Street Theatre. He stopped over in Baltimore on his way to Washington, and there he was often seen in the company of John T. Ford, then the manager of the Halliday Street Theatre, Baltimore, and of Ford's Theatre, Washington, the scene of the assassination. After the assassination Mr. Ford was arrested on the belief that, having been seen with Booth so shortly before the event, he might know something about it. But the fact was that he knew no more about it than a child. But he was arrested and incarcerated in the Old Capitol prison, Washington. Matt Canning was also arrested in Philadelphia. I was very much scared myself, for I had been seen with Booth on Chestnut Street, Philadelphia, and had been in his company much of the time during his stay in the city. I escaped arrest, however, but I passed several sleepless nights and days of worriment thinking over the matter. In fact, I tried to persuade myself that I did not know Booth. When questioned in regard to the subject my memory was blank. Mr. Ford and Mr. Canning were, of course, exonerated from any knowledge of the sad affair. I was spending the evening with some friends on the night of the assassination — Good Friday night. As I was returning home about twelve o'clock, walking down Chestnut Street, I saw signs of great excitement; crowds were running along the street. I thought there was a big fire; but I soon learned the news, that Abraham Lincoln had been assassinated, killed by Wilkes Booth, the man I had been chatting with pleasantly but a few days, you might say a few hours, before.

Within three or four days there was a great hue and cry raised against not only the actor, but actors and theatrical people in general. "An actor had assassinated the President!" I can truly say that I do not know of any class of people in the community at that time who were more greatly shocked or more deeply grieved than the members of the theatrical profession. Whatever the faults of actors may be (and they have their faults like the rest of the human race), they are not given to deeds of violence. So far from being predisposed to such crimes, they are brought up to an art which views the events of history only on their pathetic or their scenic side. They are philosophers of life, endeavoring to portray it, rather than to take part in the political or social struggles of the age. Many well-meaning, but narrow-minded persons, however, after the assassination, could not say anything too bad about actors and the theatre. They were particularly severe in their allusions to Edwin Booth, the distinguished tragedian, brother of the assassin, who probably suffered more mental torture from the cruel act of his unnatural relative than did any one else in the country, outside of the President's own family. Edwin Booth was so overcome that he retired from the stage temporarily, and it was many months before he appeared in a theatre before an audience.

Edwin Booth never played in Washington City from the time of the assassination until his death. Theatrical managers offered him the most fabulous prices to go there, but he had made a resolution that he would never play at the Capital of the nation, so intimately associated with his brother's terrible crime; and he kept this resolution until the day of his death.

But the honors shown Edwin Booth in his later years, and the esteem in which he was held by all classes of the community, did something to atone for the cruel and thoughtless treatment he received at the hands of some prejudiced and ignorant persons soon after the tragedy. Numerous rewards were promptly offered for the capture of Wilkes Booth. I added $500 to the reward that was offered in Philadelphia, and promptly did what I could to show that the members of the dramatic profession were not in sympathy with Wilkes Booth, and looked with horror upon his terrible crime.

The advertisement which I inserted in the Philadelphia newspapers was as follows:

> $500 REWARD. — The undersigned will add to the reward offered by the Government and municipal authorities the sum of FIVE HUNDRED DOLLARS for the arrest of John Wilkes Booth, the assassin of our late beloved President. I have no doubt but the sum of ten thousand dollars will be raised to further this really necessary object by the different Managers. In offering this reward I feel it my conscientious duty to aid to the utmost in bringing this atrocious murderer to justice. I feel convinced that every Manager in the land will second this object, and take the same view of the case. As this crime was committed in one of our principal theatres, we should endeavor to use our utmost ability in an object of so much importance to every American citizen.
>
> William E. Sinn, for Grover and Sinn

It was not long before theatrical people in all parts of the country put themselves before the public in their proper light, condemning the crime, both in public and in private, both in the North and in the South, showing that, so far as the members of their profession were concerned, there had been no collusion in the matter, and that the crime had been committed by John Wilkes Booth in a false and cruel spirit of devotion to the South.

I think the assassination of President Lincoln was the severest blow the South could have had. Certainly the act was not endorsed by the thinking men in the South. So far from its being a benefit to the South, it put back reconstruction fully ten or fifteen years.

Ward, *Abraham Lincoln*, 169–74.

From *The Great Funeral Oration on Abraham Lincoln* (1865)

EMMA HARDINGE

Emma Hardinge (1823–1899) was a key leader and historian of the spiritualist movement that sprang to life in the 1850s and remained firmly widespread for the rest of the century. Born in London, England, she arrived in America in 1856 and quickly was converted into the spiritualist camp through the teachings of Ada Hoyt and the "trance speaking" methods of the dazzling seventeen-year-old Cora Hatch. She later developed connections with famous spiritualists such as Andrew Jackson Davis, Amy Post, and others. Hardinge's books and speeches, especially *Modern American Spiritualism* (1870), would eventually become widely influential, making her a chief spokesperson for the movement whose main desire was to communicate with the departed spirits of the dead. Spiritualist enthusiasm even penetrated the White House, where Mary Lincoln was known to have conducted séances, seeking contact with her dead son Willie, and Lincoln himself attended at least one of these sessions.[1] Hardinge was already well known as a medium by the end of the 1850s, and during the Civil War her support of Lincoln's administration — and her passionate advocacy of his second presidential campaign — culminated in her famous speech, "The Coming Man; or the Next President of the United States," which led to a successful national lecturing tour. As a result, upon the news of Lincoln's death she received almost immediately an invitation from several influential citizens to deliver a eulogy for the slain leader. The invitation was accepted and, with little time for preparation, Hardinge's effort was largely extemporaneous. She was the first woman known to have given a eulogy in honor of Lincoln, and her words were widely disseminated to a grieving nation. The speech was delivered on April 16, 1865, at the Cooper Institute in New York City, before more than three thousand people.

IT SEEMS TO ME as if I heard a tone, borne on the wings of time and sounding through the corridors of space, sweeping the earth like a breeze, from the shores of the remotest East to this land of the distant West — a voice that for eighteen hundred years has pleaded before the throne of Almighty Justice in the only strain that can solve the dire and dreadful problem of red murder saying, "Father, forgive them, *they know not what they do.*" Friends, this voice most surely speaks, both to you and me, in this hour of awful grief. There seems no other utterance fit to explain its meaning, or able to pronounce sentence on the terrible cause, of pain that afflicts us in this most unparalleled and sublime national woe. I recall the page of history in vain to find any precedent (save the one which laid the foundations of your religion) for this foul and monstrous act of guilt which forms the record of this solemn hour. . . .

I cannot think it is out of place to-day to retrace "those shining footprints on the sands of time" which he we mourn has left behind him, although they are, as they justly should be, already household words among the people of his love. Now, will you deem it less in order that I should presume to be your memento of this sacred page? Month after month it has seemed my special inspiration to call upon the people, whom it was my privilege to address, to study out and comprehend the acts of him whom I felt and named as the true "PRESERVER OF HIS COUNTRY." . . .

What a retrospect of a splendid career developed, if not wholly fashioned, by the fostering sun of American republicanism, does our great chief magistrate's history present us with! Fifty-six years ago, and the low sigh of the breeze stirring the trees of old Kentucky, the song of the lonely woodbird, and the chirp of the tenants of the wildest solitudes were the natal songs that welcomed into life the child whose name has to reverberate through the earth in the clarion tones of a worldwide fame; born to the inheritance of stern poverty and rude toil, a log-cabin was his only shelter, the cathedral arches of the green forest his baptismal roof, and the lonely stars and voiceless flowers, the backwoodsman father and humble mother, his only friends and teachers; and yet we trace the germs of Nature's truest nobility unfolding themselves in every year of his faithful life; always the good and dutiful child, the industrious little aid of the toiling father, the willing little drudge of the patient mother.

At seven years he goes forth with the spelling-book, one of the three volumes that constitute the family library. At eight he learns the first dread lesson of slavery, namely, that free white labor has no chance in competition with captive black; that the condition of a poor white laborer in a slave State is more hopeless than the slave himself; and hence himself and little household endure the toil and hardship of a weary pioneer journey from Kentucky slavery and darkness, to, Indiana freedom and light. Remember, thus early, did Abraham Lincoln learn his first practical lessons of the corrupting and festering influences of slavery. At ten years old the little backwoodsman's boy, by industry and (for time and condition) most arduous study, had become the wonder of the scattered population in which he dwelt for his skill in reading, and his yet more astonishing faculty for writing, only equaled by the kindness which urged him to become the scribe of all who sought the good boy's service in this humble way. At nineteen he is the Mississippi boat-man, intrusted with wealth and others' welfare, honored and sought for himself and his honest manhood.

At twenty-one he first set foot in that Illinois whose proudest boast to-day is to call him hers. Here he makes his father's home, helps build his house, and fence his farm, and immortalized that humble form of labor which renders the title of the "rail-splitter" a patent of America's nobility. From this we trace him from his final exodus from the paternal roof, now the hired farm hand, the clerk in the petty store, the agent, buyer, scribe, postmaster, captain in the Black Hawk war, surveyor, lawyer, legislator, but ever the same, good, self-made, self-taught, toiling, honest, truthful, studious man. . . .

No one can fail to perceive, from the entire tenor of Mr. Lincoln's remarkable life, that he fully understood and completely loathed the monstrous blot that had crept into the national legislation in the form of legalized slavery.

He was its open and avowed enemy, ever voting in his place, whenever occasion served, against its extension in any form; the contest I have alluded to, enabled him to bring all the powers of his acute and logical mind and forcible nervous oratory, to bear on the monstrous evil of its extension into the Territories, or the perpetuation of the gigantic wrong in any form outside of its then existing State limits. . . .

One of the noblest State papers that the records of any nation can show is, to my thinking, to be found in Mr. Lincoln's first inaugural address to this nation. There the entire question of the Protean Problem — Slavery — in connection with its legalized existence in the States as guaranteed by the Constitution, is fairly and fully laid out, the suicidal character of secession unveiled, and the magnificent proportions of a united American republicanism grandly depicted. A mind capable of analyzing with such irresistible and clear deductions the entangled meshes of treason in which the nation's life was involved, never could fail in steering the ship of State through all the shoals and reefs in which she was subsequently to struggle for the port of safety. The prescient wisdom of the many great statesmen who had preceded him seemed to culminate in his simple yet lucid definition of the nation's situation, in a speech made by him, as early as 1858, on the occasion of his nomination as candidate for senator in Illinois, when he says: "A house divided against itself cannot stand; I believe this government cannot endure permanently half slave and half free. I do not expect the Union to be dissolved; I do not expect the house to fall; but I do expect it will cease to be divided. It will become all one thing or all the other." These and many other such utterances of his public life conclusively prove not only his perfect understanding of the vexed questions that were agitating the land, but also give the key to that policy which his opponents have so often and so rashly denounced as "time-serving," but which now looms up as the providential wisdom which not only foresees, but knows how to await the ripening of the proper time for action. And when that time came, was Mr. Lincoln slow, fearful, or disobedient to "the higher law" that ever ruled his life in availing himself of it? I allude to the enunciation of the immortal proclamation of emancipation, the deed which, beyond all others of his life, crowns him with eternal honor, and will hand his name down to an immortal glory through all posterity. Up to the end of the first three years of the war Mr. Lincoln had robbed the rebellious foe of every shadow of plea against his administration by a guard over the very rights they had forfeited, as jealous as themselves could have exercised, retaining by his wise policy the strength of the vacillating western and border States still attached to the Union.

Assailed by unwise friends and bitter foes, with taunts and revilings on every hand, still he moved not; but when the crisis came in which the nation's life was balanced against protective southern policy, how long did the noble statesman hesitate? The cry of the discontented and disloyal raised its accustomed wail against freedom and howled out "abolitionism"; but above the murmur of the storm arose in his ear the grand Mosaic cry of "Let my people go!" and although that voice has been thundering down the ages, and a burning bush and a fire-crowned Sinai has flashed before the eyes of despots in every century of time, whenever God's oppressed and captive people cried to Him for deliverance, three thousand years has seen that awful charge . . . disregarded, mocked, and spit upon, until good Abraham Lincoln, in 1863, proclaimed it in "Liberty throughout the land, to every inhabitant thereof!" God bless him for it!

I was present in San Francisco one year after this memorable deed, and, in company with the only other white orator who could be found to take part on such an occasion, helped the enfranchised race to honor the glorious anniversary.

The memory of the sable martyrs that had perished at Port Hudson and Fort Pillow was still green in memory; they told of the black regiments, formed of men whose ancestors' unpaid toil had made the country rich, whose backs were still seamed with lashes, and whose limbs still gashed with the mark of fetters, but whose freed lives were now devoted to the salvation of the land that had enslaved them. These pictures were vividly portrayed in their own peculiar, wild, and touching eloquence; but all was forgotten, all forgiven when the name of their modern Moses was pronounced, and then it was that a shout went up to God, chorused by four millions of glad, rejoicing voices, echoed by the white slaves of despotism and tyranny all over the world — a shout of "God bless Abraham Lincoln!" That cry will be a passport to his soul through the courts of heaven, in all eternity, did it stand alone as the only record of his pure and spotless life. . . .

Oh people of the land he blessed and saved! can I deal justly with his sacred name, unless I present it to your undivided admiration as your "Father Abraham Lincoln!" — a man whose page of history stands without a blemish, whose bright escutcheon will shine through all futurity without one single spot. My retrospect of this noble life is almost ended. It but remains in this place to remind you that if our Chief Magistrate was, in his own unassuming phrase, "too deficient in military experience to general the situation," he was amply supplied with that moral fitness for command which has made the world's most potent conquests and furnished in history its brightest wreaths of victory. From the very hour when he gave to the armies of the North, a moral watchword and the glorious war-cry "Liberty" the most genuine and unequivocal success has marked their every action. From point to point, their march has been a triumph. . . .

We have traced him as the incarnate spirit of true republicanism, the self-made boy, the unimpeachable youth, the noble man, the legislator, statesman, orator, chief magistrate, and father of a mighty people, their staff in the earthquake's shock, their anchor in the storm. What more remains than to contemplate him obeying the behests of his Almighty Father, killing the fatted calf to welcome back the returning prodigal, following the foot-steps of his Christian Master, returning good for evil, dispensing blessings for curses, and conquering foes more surely with his generous acts of mercy than all the armies of the earth could do with sword and cannon. . . .

"He, being dead, yet speaketh." Let the glorious voice of Freedom, calling in trumpet-tongue from the grave of Abraham Lincoln, and ascending, in the immortal proclamation of emancipation, to the very heavens with his marching soul—let this speak for you, and, in the name of the "higher law," God's law, and Abraham Lincoln's own most godlike act, decide your problem, and reconstruct your laws on the rock which death, nor hell, nor time, nor human trespass can ever touch with fingers of decay—the eternal rock of JUSTICE! You say you love your "Father Abraham"—prove it by swearing over his martyr-grave not to dishonor the grandest of his deeds by a base repudiation of its legality. That charter which will not sanction liberty in the land of the Stars and Stripes, and nullifies the brightest act of Abraham Lincoln's life, is itself the fittest subject in the land for the scalpel-knife of reconstruction. As for the rest, your duty's very simple. The first that presses home on every living creature in this land is a firm and devoted heart of loyalty tendered to your new President. Did not the enormous exigencies of his momentous situation appeal to every better feeling in man's nature for faithful service? Andy Johnson of Tennessee deserves it of you—another self-made man; another man of the people; another grand Republican ladder, on which the mudsills rise to the highest rounds of nature's loyalty; another living protest against the destroying influence of slavery on whites as well as blacks. . . .

Mourn for Abraham Lincoln with your hearts, but prove your love to him by taking up the burden he's laid down and finishing the noble purposes of his great life so untimely quenched. For you, his country, and the holy cause of patriotism, he perished. He spoke no word, he made no sign, nor left a single charge on mortal man; but, oh, if ever silence was most eloquent, if speechless, dying martyrdom pleads now, as in the days of "righteous Stephen," with an angel light upon its blood-stained brow, obey that dumb behest, and do his work, and break the last blood-crusted link of those iron bonds that have well-nigh killed the earth's last, best republic. . . . Follow his brave, strong footsteps in his great ascent of life; his noble words and pledges of good faith ere the nation's need had come, and be sure that God has sent him to our rescue, and your part is to give him added strength in a nation's united heart and faith. . . . Sooner or later, for us all, his summons will be ours. God only give us grace to follow him to the land of light and never-setting sun, to clasp his immortal band again in eternal fellowship in our own Easter resurrecting day, and hear the glorious greeting that, with the arisen sun of his bright eternity, has welcomed him to the home he's so justly earned: "Well done, thou good and faithful servant, enter thou into the joy of thy Lord."

Note

1. Ann Braude, *Radical Spirits: Spiritualism and Women's Rights in Nineteenth-Century America* (Boston: Beacon, 1989), 27.

Emma Hardinge, *The Great Funeral Oration on Abraham Lincoln* (New York, n.p., 1865).

From "Abraham Lincoln" (1865)

HENRY WARD BEECHER

> As he returned from the Fort Sumter flag raising of April 14, 1865, the Rev.
> Henry Ward Beecher (1813–1887), the most famous preacher in America and
> a solid defender of the Union cause, discovered the news of the president's
> assassination. The following Sunday, April 23, at the Plymouth Church in
> Brooklyn, Beecher gave this eulogy, one that illuminates the almost imme-
> diate desire among the religious citizenry to wrap the memory of the slain
> leader in sacred terms. The charisma of this brilliant orator is hard to cap-
> ture in such works, but Beecher was widely considered the great American
> preacher and orator of his lifetime. For instance, politician Chauncey Depew
> remembered him in these terms: "One of the greatest and most remarkable
> orators of his time was Henry Ward Beecher. I never met his equal in readi-
> ness and versatility. His vitality was infectious. He was a big, healthy, vigor-
> ous man with the physique of an athlete, and his intellectual fire and vigor
> corresponded with his physical strength."[1] Thus, Beecher's eulogy was one
> of the most widely read in the weeks after Lincoln's death.
>
> The central text, Deuteronomy 34:1–5, describes how Moses was led by
> the Lord to the top of Mount Pisgah, from where he could only view the
> promised land of Canaan, before his death there on the mountain—an allu-
> sion developed famously by the Rev. Martin Luther King Jr. a century later, in
> the last sermon King ever preached. Like their forebear Moses, neither King
> nor Lincoln was able to reach the land of promise in their own lifetimes.

THERE IS NO historic figure more noble than that of the Jewish lawgiver.
After so many thousand years the figure of Moses is not diminished but
stands up against the background of early days distinct and individual as if
he had lived but yesterday. There is scarcely another event in history more
touching than his death. He had borne the great burdens of state for forty
years, shaped the Jews to a nation, filled out their civil and religious polity,
administered their laws, guided their steps, or dealt with them in all their

journeyings in the wilderness; had mourned in their punishment, kept step with their march, and led them in wars until the end of their labours drew nigh. The last stage was reached. Jordan, only, lay between them and the "promised land." The Promised Land! O what yearnings had heaved his breast for that divinely foreshadowed place! He had dreamed of it by night, and mused by day; it was holy and endeared as God's favoured spot. It was to be the cradle of an illustrious history. All his long, laborious, and now weary life, he had aimed at this as the consummation of every desire, the reward of every toil and pain. Then came the word of the Lord to him: "Thou mayest not go over. Get thee up into the mountain; look upon it; and die!"

From that silent summit the hoary leader gazed to the north, to the south, to the west with hungry eyes. The dim outlines rose up. The hazy recesses spoke of quiet valleys between hills. With eager longing, with sad resignation, he looked upon the promised land. It was now to him a forbidden land. This was but a moment's anguish; he forgot his personal wants and drank in the vision of his people's home. His work was done. There lay God's promise fulfilled. There was the seat of coming Jerusalem; there the city of Judah's King; the sphere of judges and prophets; the Mount of sorrow and salvation; the nest whence were to fly blessings innumerable to all mankind. Joy chased sadness from every feature, and the prophet laid him down, and died. . . .

There has not been a poor drummer-boy in all this war that has fallen for whom the great heart of Lincoln would not have bled; there has not been one private soldier, without note or name, slain among thousands and hid in the pit among hundreds, without even the memorial of a separate burial, for whom the President would not have wept. He was a man from the common people who never forgot his kind. And now that he who might not bear the march, and the toil, and the battle with these humble citizens has been called to die by the bullet, as they were, do you not feel that there was a peculiar fitness to his nature and life that he should in death be joined with them in a final common experience to whom he had been joined in all his sympathies?

For myself, when any event is susceptible of a higher and nobler garnishing, I know not what that disposition is that should seek to drag it down to the depths of gloom, and write it all over with the scrawls of horror or fear.

I let the light of nobler thoughts fall upon his departure, and bless God that there is some argument of consolation in the matter and manner of his going as there was in the matter and manner of his staying.

Then again, this blow was but the expiring rebellion. As a miniature gives all the form and features of its subject, so, epitomized in this foul act, we find the whole nature and disposition of slavery. It begins in a wanton destruction of all human rights, and in a desecration of all the sanctities of heart and home; and it is the universal enemy of mankind, and of God, who made man. It can be maintained only at the sacrifice of every right moral feeling in its abettors and upholders. I deride him who points me to any one bred amid slavery, believing in it, and willingly practicing it, and tells me that he is a man. I shall find saints in perdition sooner than I shall find true manhood under the influences of so accursed a system as this. It is a two-edged sword, cutting both ways, violently destroying manhood in the oppressed, and insidiously destroying manhood in the oppressor. The problem is solved, the demonstration is completed in our land. Slavery wastes its victims, and it destroys the masters. It kills public morality, and the possibility of it. It corrupts manhood in its very centre and elements. Communities in which it exists are not to be trusted. They are rotten. Nor can you find timber grown in this accursed soil of iniquity that is fit to build our Ship of State, or lay the foundation of our households. The patriotism that grows up under this blight, when put to proof, is selfish and brittle; and he that leans upon it shall be pierced. The honour that grows up in the midst of slavery is not honour, but a bastard quality that usurps the place of its better, only to disgrace the name. And, as long as there is conscience, or reason, or Christianity, the honour that slavery begets will be a byword and a hissing. The whole moral nature of men reared to familiarity and connivance with slavery is death-smitten. The needless rebellion; the treachery of its leaders to oaths and solemn trusts; their violation of the commonest principles of fidelity, sitting in senates, in councils, in places of public confidence only to betray and to destroy; the long general, and unparallelled cruelty to prisoners, without provocation, and utterly without excuse; the unreasoning malignity and fierceness, — these all mark the symptoms of that disease of slavery, which is a deadly poison to soul and body.

I do not say that there are not single natures, here and there, scattered through the vast wilderness which is covered with this poisonous vine, who escaped the poison. There are; but they are not to be found among the men that believe in it, and that have been moulded by it. They are the exceptions. Slavery is itself barbarity. That nation which cherishes it is barbarous; and no outside tinsel or glitter can redeem it from the charge of barbarism. And it was fit that its expiring blow should be such as to take away from men the last forbearance, the last pity, and fire the soul with an invincible determination that the breeding-ground of such mischiefs and monsters shall be utterly and forever destroyed.

We needed not that he should put on paper that he believed in slavery, who, with treason, with murder, with cruelty infernal, hovered around that majestic man to destroy his life. He was himself but the long sting with which slavery struck at liberty; and he carried the poison that belonged to slavery. As long as this Nation lasts, it will never be forgotten that we have had one martyred President—never! Never, while time lasts, while heaven lasts, while hell rocks and groans, will it be forgotten that slavery, by its minions, slew him, and in slaying him made manifest its whole nature and tendency.

But another thing for us to remember is that this blow was aimed at the life of the Government and of the Nation. Lincoln was slain; America was meant. The man was cast down; the Government was smitten at. It was the president who was killed. It was national life, breathing freedom and meaning beneficence, that was sought. He, the man of Illinois, the private man, divested of robes and the insignia of authority, representing nothing but his personal self, might have been hated; but that would not have called forth the murderer's blow. It was because he stood in the place of Government, representing government and a government that represented right and liberty, that he was singled out.

This, then, is a crime against universal government. It is not a blow at the foundations of our Government, more than at the foundations of the English government, of the French government, of every compacted and well-organized government. It was a crime against mankind. The whole world will repudiate and stigmatize it as a deed without a shade of redeeming light. For this was not the oppressed, goaded to extremity, turning on his oppressor. Not even the shadow of a cloud of wrong has rested on the South, and they know it right well.

In a council held in the city of Charleston, just preceding the attack on Fort Sumter, two commissioners were appointed to go to Washington; one on the part of the army from Fort Sumter, and one on the part of the Confederates. The lieutenant that was designated to go for us said it seemed to him that it would be of little use for him to go, as his opinion was immovably fixed in favour of maintaining the government in whose service he was employed. Then Governor Pickens took him aside, detaining for an hour and a half the railroad train that was to convey them on their errand. He opened to him the whole plan and secrets of the Southern conspiracy, and said to him, distinctly and repeatedly (for it was needful, he said, to lay aside disguises), that the South had never been wronged, and that all their pretenses of grievance in the matter of tariffs, or anything else, were invalid. "But," said he, "we must carry the people with us and we allege these things as all statesmen do many things they do not believe because they are the only instruments by which the people can be managed." He then and there declared that it had simply come to this: that the two sections of country were so antagonistic in ideas and policies that they could not live together; that it was foreordained that on account of differences in ideas and policies, Northern and Southern men must keep apart. This is testimony which was given by one of the leaders in the Rebellion, and which will probably, ere long, be given under hand and seal to the public. So the South has never had wrongs visited upon it except by that which was inherent in it.

This was not, then, the avenging hand of one goaded by tyranny. It was not a despot turned on by his victim. It was the venomous hatred of liberty wielded by an avowed advocate of slavery. And, though there may have been cases of murder in which there were shades of palliation, yet this murder was without provocation, without temptation, without reason, sprung from the fury of a heart cankered to all that was just and good, and corrupted by all that was wicked and foul.

The blow, however, has signally failed. The cause is not stricken; it is strengthened. This Nation has dissolved—but in tears only. It stands, four-square, more solid, to-day, than any pyramid in Egypt. This people are neither wasted, nor daunted, nor disordered. Men hate slavery and love liberty with stronger hate and love to-day than ever before. The Government is not weakened, it is made stronger. How naturally and easily were the ranks closed! Another stepped forward, in the hour that the one fell, to take his place and his mantle; and I utter my trust that he will be found a man true to every instinct of liberty; true to the whole trust that is reposed in him; vigilant of the Constitution; careful of the laws; wise for liberty in that he himself, through his life, has known what it was to suffer from the stings of slavery, and to prize liberty from bitter personal experiences.

Where could the head of government in any monarchy be smitten down by the hand of an assassin, and the funds not quiver nor fall one half of one per cent? After a long period of national disturbance, after four years of drastic war, after tremendous drafts on the resources of the country, in the height and top of our burdens, the heart of this people is such that now, when the head of government is stricken down, the public funds do not waver, but stand as the granite ribs in our mountains. Republican institutions have been vindicated in this experience as they never were before; and the whole history of the last four years, rounded up by this cruel stroke, seems now in the providence of God to have been clothed with an illustration, with a sympathy, with an aptness, and with a significance, such as we never could have expected or imagined. God, I think, has said, by the voice of this event, to all nations of the earth, "Republican liberty, based upon true Christianity, is firm as the foundation of the globe."

Even he who now sleeps has, by this event, been clothed with new influence. Dead, he speaks to men who now willingly hear what before they refused to listen to. Now, his simple and weighty words will be gathered like those of Washington, and your children and your children's children shall be taught to ponder the simplicity and deep wisdom of utterances, which in their time, passed, in the party heat, as idle words. Men will receive a new impulse of patriotism for his sake, and will guard with zeal the whole country which he loved so well; I swear you, on the altar of his memory, to be more faithful to the country for which he has perished. Men will, as they follow his hearse, swear a new hatred to that slavery against which he warred, and which in vanquishing him has made him a martyr and a conqueror; I swear you, by the memory of this martyr, to hate slavery with an unappeasable hatred. Men will admire and imitate his unmoved firmness, his inflexible conscience for the right, and yet his gentleness, as tender as a woman's, his moderation of spirit, which not all the heat of party could inflame, nor all the jars and disturbances of this country shake out of its place; I swear you to an emulation of his justice, his moderation and his mercy.

You I can comfort; but how can I speak to that twilight million to whom his name was as the name of an angel of God? There will be wailing in places which no ministers shall be able to reach. When, in hovel and in cot, in wood and in wilderness, in the field throughout the South, the dusky children, who looked upon him as that Moses whom God sent before them to lead them out of the land of bondage, learn that he has fallen, who shall comfort them? Oh, Thou Shepherd of Israel, that didst comfort Thy people of old, to Thy care we commit the helpless, the long-wronged, and grieved!

And now the martyr is moving in triumphal march, mightier than when alive. The Nation rises up at every stage of his coming. Cities and States are his pallbearers, and the cannon beats the hours with solemn progression. Dead-dead-dead-he yet speaketh! Is Washington dead? Is Hampden dead? Is David dead? Is any man dead that ever was fit to live? Disenthralled of flesh, and risen to the unobstructed sphere where passion never comes, he begins his illimitable work. His life now is grafted upon the Infinite, and will be fruitful as no earthly life can be. Pass on, thou that hast overcome! Your sorrows, O people, are his peace! Your bells, and bands, and muffled drums sound triumph in his ear. Wail and weep here; God makes it echo joy and triumph there. Pass on, thou victor!

Four years ago, O Illinois, we took from your midst an untried man, and from among the people; we return him to you a mighty conqueror. Not thine any more, but the Nation's; not ours, but the world's. Give him place, ye prairies! In the midst of this great Continent his dust shall rest, a sacred treasure to myriads who shall make pilgrimage to that shrine to kindle anew their zeal and patriotism. Ye winds, that move over the mighty places of the West, chant his requiem! Ye people, behold a martyr, whose blood as so many articulate words, pleads for fidelity, for law, for liberty!

Note

1. Chauncey M. Depew, *My Memories of Eighty Years* (New York: Scribner's, 1922), 324.

Henry Ward Beecher, *Patriotic Addresses in America and England, from 1850 to 1885* (New York: Fords, Howard, and Hulbert, 1887), 701–12.

From "Abraham Lincoln" (1865)

Ralph Waldo Emerson

> Ralph Waldo Emerson (1803–1882), born and raised in the heart of New England literary culture, was the leading light of nineteenth-century American letters. Educated at Harvard, and then a Unitarian minister in Boston, he resigned his pastorate over controversies about church doctrine. His subsequent philosophical writings, beginning with *Nature* (1836) and followed by influential essays such as "Self-Reliance" and "The Poet," both from his *Essays: Second Series* (1844), made him the iconic leader of the transcendentalist movement, centered in his home of Concord, where his neighbors and friends included Henry Thoreau, Nathaniel Hawthorne, and Bronson Alcott, among others. He wrote excellent poetry to illustrate his theories of literature, founded the movement's organ, *The Dial*, in 1840, and influenced directly the lives of many of the century's greatest authors, including Margaret Fuller, Walt Whitman, Emily Dickinson, and the minister Theodore Parker, whose particular brand of transcendentalism sparked the imagination of Abraham Lincoln.
>
> Emerson's analysis here of Lincoln's character is from an address delivered at the funeral services in Concord on the 19th of April, 1865. His high esteem for Lincoln is clear, as the eulogy reflects Emerson's view from earlier writings such as his essay on the Emancipation Proclamation. There he conceded that, "great as the popularity of the President has been, we are beginning to think that we have underestimated the capacity and virtue which the Divine Providence has made an instrument of benefit so vast. He has been permitted to do more for America than any other American man."[1]

A PLAIN MAN of the people, an extraordinary fortune attended him. Lord Bacon says: "Manifest virtues procure reputation; occult ones, fortune." He offered no shining qualities at the first encounter; he did not offend by superiority. He had a face and manner which disarmed suspicion, which inspired confidence, which confirmed good will. He was a man without vices. He had a strong sense of duty, which it was very easy for him to obey. Then, he had what farmers call a long head; was excellent in working out the sum for himself; in arguing his case and convincing you fairly and firmly. Then, it turned out that he was a great worker; had a prodigious faculty of performance; worked easily. A good worker is so rare; everybody has some disabling quality. In a host of young men that start together, and promise so many brilliant leaders for the next age, each fails on trial; one by bad health, one by conceit; one by love of pleasure, or lethargy, or an ugly temper — each has some disqualifying fault that throws him out of the career. But this man was sound to the core, cheerful, persistent, all right for labor, and liked nothing so well.

Then, he had a vast good nature, which made him tolerant and accessible to all; fair minded, leaning to the claim of the petitioner; affable and not sensible to the affliction which the innumerable visits paid to him, when President, would have brought to any one else. And how this good nature became a noble humanity, in many a tragic case which the events of the war brought to him, every one will remember; and with what increasing tenderness he dealt, when a whole race was thrown on his compassion. The poor negro said of him, on an impressive occasion, "Massa Linkum am everywhere."

Then his broad good humor, running easily into jocular talk, in which he delighted and in which he excelled, was a rich gift to this wise man. It enabled him to keep his secret: to meet every kind man, and every rank of society; to take off the edge of the severest decisions; to mask his own purpose, and sound his companion; and to catch with true instinct the temper of every company he addressed. And, more than all, it is to a man of severe labor, in anxious and exhausting crises, the natural restorative, good as sleep, and is the protection of the overdriven brain against rancor and insanity.

He is the author of a multitude of good sayings, so disguised as pleasantries that it is certain they had no reputation at first but as jests; and only later, by the acceptance and adoption they find in the mouths of millions, turn out to be the wisdom of the hour. I am sure if this man had ruled in a period of less facility of printing, he would have become mythological in a very few years, like Aesop or Pilpay, or one of the Seven Wise Masters, by his fables and proverbs. But the weight and penetration of the many passages in his letters, messages and speeches, hidden now by the very closeness of their application to the moment, are designed hereafter to a wide fame. What pregnant definitions: what unerring common sense; what foresight and, on great occasions, what lofty, and more than national, what humane tone? His brief speech at Gettysburg will not easily be surpassed by words on any recorded occasion. This, and one other American Speech, that of John Brown to the court that tried him, and a part of Kossuth's speech at Birmingham, can only be compared, with each other, and with no fourth.

His occupying the chair of state was a triumph of the good sense of mankind, and of the public conscience. This middle-class country had got a middle-class President, at last. Yes, in manners and sympathies, but not in powers, for his powers were superior. This man grew according to the need. His mind mastered the problem of the day; and, as the problem grew, so did his comprehension of it. Rarely was man so fitted to the event. In the midst of fears and jealousies, in the Babel of counsels and parties, the man wrought incessantly with all his might and all his honesty, laboring to find what the people wanted, and how to obtain that. It cannot be said there is any exaggeration of his words. If ever a man was fairly tested, he was. There was no lack, of resistance, nor of slander, nor of ridicule. The times have allowed no state secrets, the nation has been in such ferment, such multitudes had to be trusted, that no secret could be kept. Every door was ajar and we knew all that befell.

Then, what an occasion was the whirlwind of the war. Here was place for no holiday magistrate, no fair-weather sailor; the new pilot was hurried to the helm in a tornado. In four years — four years of battle-days — his endurance, his fertility of resources, his magnanimity, were sorely tried and never found wanting. There, by his courage, his justice, his even temper, his fertile counsel, his humanity, he stood a heroic figure in the centre of a heroic epoch. He is the true history of the American people in his time. Step by step he walked before them; slow with their slowness, quickening his march by theirs; the true representative of this continent; an entirely public man; father of his country, the pulse of twenty millions throbbing in his heart, the thought of their minds articulated by his tongue.

Note

1. Ralph Waldo Emerson, "The Emancipation Proclamation," in *Complete Works*, vol. 11, *Miscellanies*, 316.

Ralph Waldo Emerson, *Complete Works*, vol. 11, *Miscellanies* (Cambridge, MA: Riverside, 1883), 305–15.

"Abraham Lincoln" (1865)

Philips Brooks

Honored for much of his lifetime as one of the foremost ministers of the northeastern states, Philips Brooks (1835–1893) was a prolific author and speaker who later was canonized in the Episcopal Church. A graduate of Harvard, he pastored for many years in Philadelphia, including throughout the Civil War, and then went on to become rector of Trinity Church in Boston beginning in 1870. On Sunday, April 23, 1865, while Lincoln's body lay in state nearby at Independence Hall in Philadelphia, the twenty-nine-year-old Brooks, already recognized as one of America's top clergymen, preached a memorial sermon at Holy Trinity Episcopal Church. Brooks saw in Lincoln a man who was the natural result of the frontier, or "the character of an American under the discipline of freedom." Brooks's framing of Lincoln as a quintessentially mythic American hearkens back to Emerson's idea of a "representative man"—even as it anticipates Frederick Jackson Turner's thesis that the frontier shaped American character and that the true Americans rose from the untamed wilderness of the continent. Brooks also captures the regnant view of the Civil War at its conclusion, held by many Americans in the North: a Manichean vision of Good triumphing over Evil, and Slavery as an abstraction symbolic of that Evil. Lincoln, says Brooks, succeeds in marrying head and heart, male and female, rationality and sympathy. A "union of the mental and moral" springs from Lincoln's frontier youth, and this union is the unique character of his genius. Indeed, it is the unique character of the Union as well.[1]

WHILE I SPEAK to you to-day, the body of the President who ruled this people, is lying, honored and loved, in our city. It is impossible with that sacred presence in our midst for me to stand and speak of ordinary topics which occupy the pulpit. I must speak of him to-day; and I therefore undertake to do what I had intended to do at some future time, to invite you to study with me the character of Abraham Lincoln, the impulses of his life and the causes of his death. I know how hard it is to do it worthily. But I shall speak with confidence, because I speak to those who love him, and whose ready love will fill out the deficiencies in a picture which my words will weakly try to draw.

We take it for granted, first of all, that there is an essential connection between Mr. Lincoln's character and his violent and bloody death. It is no accident, no arbitrary decree of Providence. He lived as he did, and he died as he did, because he was what he was. The more we see of events, the less we come to believe in any fate or destiny except the destiny of character. It will be our duty, then, to see what there was in the character of our great President that created the history of his life, and at last produced the catastrophe of his cruel death. After the first trembling horror, the first outburst of indignant sorrow, has grown calm, those are the questions which we are bound to ask and answer. . . .

It is the great boon of such characters as Mr. Lincoln's, that they reunite what God has joined together and man has put asunder. In him was vindicated the greatness of real goodness and the goodness of real greatness. The twain were one flesh. Not one of all the multitudes who stood and looked up to him for direction with such a loving and implicit trust can tell you to-day whether the wise judgments that he gave came most from a strong head or a sound heart. If you ask them, they are puzzled. There are men as good as he, but they do bad things. There are men as intelligent as he, but they do foolish things. In him goodness and intelligence combined and made their best result of wisdom. For perfect truth consists not merely in the right constituents of character, but in their right and intimate conjunction. This union of the mental and moral into a life of admirable simplicity is what we most admire in children; but in them it is unsettled and unpractical. But when it is preserved into manhood, deepened into reliability and maturity, it is that glorified childlikeness, that high and reverend simplicity, which shames and baffles the most accomplished astuteness and is chosen by God to fill his purposes when he needs a ruler for his people, of faithful and true heart, such as he had who was our President.

Another evident quality of such a character as this will be its freshness or newness, if we may so speak. Its freshness or readiness — call it what you will — its ability to take up new duties and do them in a new way, will result of necessity from its truth and clearness. The simple natures and forces will always be the most pliant ones. Water bends and shapes itself to any channel. Air folds and adapts itself to each new figure. They are the simplest and the most infinitely active things in nature. So this nature, in very virtue of its simplicity, must be also free, always fitting itself to each new need. It will always start from the most fundamental and eternal conditions, and work in the straightest even although they be the newest ways, to the present prescribed purpose. In one word, it must be broad and independent and radical. So that freedom and radicalness in the character of Abraham Lincoln were not separate qualities, but the necessary results of his simplicity and childlikeness and truth.

Here then we have some conception of the man. Out of this character came the life which we admire and the death which we lament to-day. He was called in that character to that life and death. It was just the nature, as you see, which a new nation such as ours ought to produce. All the conditions of his birth, his youth, his manhood, which made him what he was, were not irregular and exceptional, but were the normal conditions of a new and simple country. His pioneer home in Indiana was a type of the pioneer land in which he lived. If ever there was a man who was a part of the time and country he lived in, this was he. The same simple respect for labor won in the school of work and incorporated into blood and muscle; the same unassuming loyalty to the simple virtues of temperance and industry and integrity; the same sagacious judgment which had learned to be quick-eyed and quick-brained in the constant presence of emergency; the same direct and clear thought about things, social, political, and religious, that was in him supremely, was in the people he was sent to rule. Surely, with such a type-man for ruler, there would seem to be but a smooth and even road over which he might lead the people whose character he represented into the new region of national happiness and comfort and usefulness, for which that character had been designed.

But then we come to the beginning of all trouble. Abraham Lincoln was the type-man of the country, but not of the whole country. This character which we have been trying to describe was the character of an American under the discipline of freedom. There was another American character which had been developed under the influence of slavery. There was no one American character embracing the land. There were two characters, with impulses of irrepressible and deadly conflict. This citizen whom we have been honoring and praising represented one. The whole great scheme with which he was ultimately brought in conflict, and which has finally killed him, represented the other. Beside this nature, true and fresh and new, there was another nature, false and effete and old. The one nature found itself in a new world, and set itself to discover the new ways for the new duties that were given it. The other nature, full of the false pride of blood, set itself to reproduce in a new world the institutions and the spirit of the old, to build anew the structure of the feudalism which had been corrupt in its own day, and which had been left far behind by the advancing conscience and needs of the progressing race. The one nature magnified labor, the other nature depreciated and despised it. The one honored the laborer, and the other scorned him. The one was simple and direct; the other, complex, full of sophistries and self-excuses. The one was free to look all that claimed to be truth in the face, and separate the error from the truth that might be in it; the other did not dare to investigate, because its own established pride and systems were dearer to it than the truth itself, and so even truth went about in it doing the work of error. The one was ready to state broad principles, of the brotherhood of man, the universal fatherhood and justice of God, however imperfectly it might realize them in practice; the other denied even the principles, and so dug deep and laid below its special sins the broad foundation of a consistent, acknowledged sinfulness. In a word, one nature was full of the influences of Freedom, the other nature was full of the influences of Slavery. . . .

Here then we have the two. The history of our country for many years is the history of how these two elements of American life approached collision. They wrought their separate reactions on each other. Men debate and quarrel even now about the rise of Northern Abolitionism, about whether the Northern Abolitionists were right or wrong, whether they did harm or good. How vain the quarrel is! It was inevitable. It was inevitable in the nature of things that two such natures living here together should be set violently against each other. It is inevitable, till man be far more unfeeling and untrue to his convictions than he has always been, that a great wrong asserting itself vehemently should arouse to no less vehement assertion the opposing right. The only wonder is that there was not more of it. The only wonder is that so few were swept away to take by an impulse they could not resist their stand of hatred to the wicked institution. The only wonder is, that only one brave, reckless man came forth to cast himself, almost single-handed, with a hopeless hope, against the proud power that he hated, and trust to the influence of a soul marching on into the history of his countrymen to stir them to a vindication of the truth he loved. At any rate, whether the Abolitionists were wrong or right, there grew up about their violence, as there always will about the extremism of extreme reformers, a great mass of feeling, catching their spirit and asserting it firmly, though in more moderate degrees and methods. About the nucleus of Abolitionism grew up a great American Anti-Slavery determination, which at last gathered strength enough to take its stand to insist upon the checking and limiting the extension of the power of slavery, and to put the type-man, whom God had been preparing for the task, before the world, to do the work on which it had resolved. Then came discontent, secession, treason. The two American natures, long advancing to encounter, met at last, and a whole country, yet trembling with the shock, bears witness how terrible the meeting was.

Thus I have tried briefly to trace out the gradual course by which God brought the character which He designed to be the controlling character of this new world into distinct collision with the hostile character which it was to destroy and absorb, and set it in the person of its type-man in the seat of highest power. The character formed under the discipline of Freedom and the character formed under the discipline of Slavery developed all their difference and met in hostile conflict when this war began. Notice, it was not only in what he did and was towards the slave, it was in all he did and was everywhere that we accept Mr. Lincoln's character as the true result of our free life and institutions. . . .

Now it was in this character, rather than in any mere political position, that the fitness of Mr. Lincoln to stand forth in the struggle of the two American natures really lay. We are told that he did not come to the Presidential chair pledged to the abolition of Slavery. When will we learn that with all true men it is not what they intend to do, but it is what the qualities of their natures bind them to do, that determines their career! The President came to his power full of the blood, strong in the strength of Freedom. He came there free, and hating slavery. He came there, leaving on record words like these spoken three years before and never contradicted. He had said, "A house divided against itself cannot stand. I believe this Government cannot endure permanently, half slave and half free. I do not expect the Union to be dissolved; I do not expect the house to fall; but I expect it will cease to be divided. It will become all one thing or all the other." When the question came, he knew which thing he meant that it should be. His whole nature settled that question for him. Such a man must always live as he used to say he lived (and was blamed for saying it), "controlled by events, not controlling them." And with a reverent and clear mind, to be controlled by events means to be controlled by God. For such a man there was no hesitation when God brought him up face to face with Slavery and put the sword into his hand and said, "Strike it down dead." He was a willing servant then. If ever the face of a man writing solemn words glowed with a solemn joy, it must have been the face of Abraham Lincoln, as he bent over the page where the Emancipation Proclamation of 1863 was growing into shape, and giving manhood and freedom as he wrote it to hundreds of thousands of his fellow-men. Here was a work in which his whole nature could rejoice. Here was an act that crowned the whole culture of his life. All the past, the free boyhood in the woods, the free youth upon the farm, the free manhood in the honorable citizen's employments — all his freedom gathered and completed itself in this. And as the swarthy multitudes came in, ragged, and tired, and hungry, and ignorant, but free forever from anything but the memorial scars of the fetters and the whip, singing rude songs in which the new triumph of freedom struggled and heaved below the sad melody that had been shaped for bondage; as in their camps and hovels there grew up to their half-superstitious eyes the image of a great Father almost more than man, to whom they owed their freedom, — were they not half right? For it was not to one man, driven by stress of policy, or swept off by a whim of pity, that the noble act was due. It was to the American nature, long kept by God in his own intentions till his time should come, at last emerging into sight and power, and bound up and embodied in this best and most American of all Americans, to whom we and those poor frightened slaves at last might look up together and love to call him, with one voice, our Father. . . .

Solemnly, in the sight of God, I charge this murder where it belongs, on Slavery. I dare not stand here in His sight, and before Him or you speak doubtful and double-meaning words of vague repentance, as if we had killed our President. We have sins enough, but we have not done this sin, save as by weak concessions and timid compromises we have let the spirit of Slavery grow strong and ripe for such a deed. In the barbarism of Slavery the foul act and its foul method had their birth. By all the goodness that there was in him; by all the love we had for him (and who shall tell how great it was?), by all the sorrow that has burdened down this desolate and dreadful week, — I charge this murder where it belongs, on Slavery. I bid you to remember where the charge belongs, to write it on the door-posts of your mourning houses, to teach it to your wondering children, to give it to the history of these times, that all times to come may hate and dread the sin that killed our noblest President. . . .

He stood once on the battle-field of our own State, and said of the brave men who had saved it words as noble as any countryman of ours ever spoke. Let us stand in the country he has saved, and which is to be his grave and monument, and say of Abraham Lincoln what he said of the soldiers who had died at Gettysburg. He stood there with their graves before him, and these are the words he said: —

> We cannot dedicate, we cannot consecrate, we cannot hallow this ground. The brave men who struggled here have consecrated it far beyond our power to add or detract. The world will little note nor long remember what we say here, but it can never forget what they did here. It is for us the living rather to be dedicated to the unfinished work which they who fought here have thus far so nobly advanced. It is rather for us to be here dedicated to the great task remaining before us, that from these honored dead we take increased devotion to that cause for which they gave the last full measure of devotion; that we here highly resolve that these dead shall not have died in vain; and this nation, under God, shall have a new birth of freedom, and that government of the people, by the people, and for the people, shall not perish from the earth.

May God make us worthy of the memory of Abraham Lincoln.

Note

1. On this tension of opposites in the nineteenth century, see Garry Wills, *Head and Heart: American Christianities* (New York: Penguin, 2007).

Philips Brooks, *Addresses* (Boston: C. E. Brown, 1893), 140–65.

From "Death of Abraham Lincoln" (1879)

Walt Whitman

One of the iconic literary figures in American history, Walt Whitman (1819–1892) developed a unique poetic voice and authored *Leaves of Grass*, first issued in 1855 and then revised, expanded, and reissued for the rest of the poet's life. After Whitman went looking for his brother George, a Union soldier in northern Virginia, in late 1862, he settled in Washington, D.C., and began visiting wounded soldiers being cared for in the vast, filthy military hospitals located in the capital. While in Washington he held various jobs, including clerking in the Lincoln administration's Department of the Interior, and he developed a nearly obsessive emotional tie with the president though they evidently never met. "I think well of the President. He has a face like a hoosier Michael Angelo, so awful ugly it becomes beautiful," he wrote a friend.[1] Whitman composed a lengthy set of brilliant poems about the war called "Drum Taps," included in later editions of *Leaves of Grass*; these poems are some of the most moving depictions of the sufferings and experiences of the common soldier ever composed. He penned at least six separate poems commemorating Lincoln after his death, several of which — "Hushed Be the Camps To-day," "When Lilacs Last in the Dooryard Bloomed," and "O Captain! My Captain!" — are among the greatest elegies ever penned by an American. The "good gray poet" was one of the earliest observers to appreciate fully Lincoln's emerging mystical weightiness, as seen here in an excerpt from his famous speech, delivered on many occasions in the final years of Whitman's life, beginning in 1879. The speech's tone is perhaps best summed up in a line he scratched into his notebook in 1863: "I love the President personally."[2]

I SHALL NOT easily forget the first time I ever saw Abraham Lincoln. It must have been about the 18th or 19th of February, 1861. It was rather a pleasant afternoon, in New York city, as he arrived there from the West, to remain a few hours, and then pass on to Washington, to prepare for his inauguration. I saw him in Broadway, near the site of the present Post-office. He came down, I think from Canal street, to stop at the Astor House. The broad spaces, sidewalks, and street in the neighborhood, and for some distance, were crowded with solid masses of people, many thousands. The omnibuses and other vehicles had all been turned off, leaving an unusual hush in that busy part of the city. Presently two or three shabby hack barouches made their way with some difficulty through the crowd, and drew up at the Astor House entrance. A tall figure step'd out of the centre of these barouches, paus'd leisurely on the sidewalk, looked up at the granite walls and looming architecture of the grand old hotel — then, after a relieving stretch of arms and legs, turn'd round for over a minute to slowly and good-humoredly scan the appearance of the vast and silent crowds. There were no speeches — no compliments — no welcome — as far as I could hear, not a word said. Cautious persons had fear'd some mark'd insult or indignity to the President-elect — for he possess'd no personal popularity at all in New York city, and very little political. But it was evidently tacitly agreed that if the few political supporters of Mr. Lincoln present would entirely abstain from any demonstration on their side, the immense majority, who were any thing but supporters, would abstain on their side also. The result was a sulky, unbroken silence, such has certainly never before characterized so great a New York crowd.

Almost in the same neighborhood I distinctly remember'd seeing Lafayette on his visit to America in 1825. I had also personally seen and heard how Andrew Jackson, Clay, Webster, Hungarian Kossuth, Filibuster Walker, the Prince of Wales on his visit, and other celebres, native and foreign, had been welcom'd there, at various times — that indescribable human roar and magnetism, unlike any other sound in the universe — the glad exulting thunder-shouts of countless unloos'd throats of men! But on this occasion, not a welcoming voice — not a sound.

From the top of an omnibus, (driven up one side, close by, and block'd by the curbstone and the crowds,) I had, I say, a capital view of it all, and especially of Mr. Lincoln, his look and gait — his perfect composure and coolness — his unusual and uncouth height, his dress of complete black, stovepipe hat push'd back on the head, his dark-brown complexion, seam'd and wrinkled yet canny-looking face, his black, bushy head of hair, disproportionaly long neck, and his hands held behind as he stood observing the people. He look'd with curiosity upon that immense sea of faces, and the sea of faces return'd the look with similar curiosity. In both there was a dash of comedy, almost farce, such as Shakspere puts in his blackest tragedies. The crowd that hemm'd around consisted I should think of thirty to forty thousand men, not a single one his personal friend—while I have no doubt, (so frenzied were the ferments of the time,) many an assassin's knife and pistol lurked in hip or breast pocket there, ready, soon as break and riot came.

But no break or riot came. The tall figure gave another relieving stretch or two of arms and legs; then with moderate pace, and accompanied by a few unknown looking persons, ascended the portico-steps of the Astor House, disappeared through its broad entrance—and the dumb-show ended.

I saw Abraham Lincoln often the four years following that date. He changed much during his Presidency—but this scene and him in it, are indelibly stamped upon my recollection. As I sat on the top of my omnibus, and had a good view of him, the thought, dim and inchoate then, has since come out clear enough, that perhaps four sorts of genius—four mighty and primal hands, will be needed to the complete limning of this man's future portrait—the eyes and brains and finger-touch of Plutarch and Aeschylus and Michael Angelo, assisted by Rabelais.

And now—(Mr. Lincoln passing on from this scene to Washington, where he was inaugurated, amid armed cavalry, and sharpshooters at every point—the first instance of the kind in our history—and I hope it will be the last)—Now the rapid succession of well-known events,—the National Flag fired on at Sumter—the uprising on the North in paroxysms of astonishment and rage—the chaos of divided councils—the call for troops—the first Bull Run—the stunning cast-down, shock, and dismay of Unionism—And so in full flood the Secession War.—Four years of lurid, bleeding, murky, murderous war. Who paint those years, with all their scenes?—the hard-fought engagements—the defeats, plans, failures—the gloomy hours, days, when our Nationality seem'd hung in pall of doubt, perhaps death—the Mephistophelean sneers of foreign lands and attachés—the dreaded Scylla of European interference, and the Charybdis of the tremendously dangerous latent strata of secession sympathizers throughout the Free States, (far more numerous than is supposed,)—the long marches in summer—the hot sweat, and many a sunstroke, as on the rush to Gettysburg in '63—the night battles in the woods, as under Hooker at Chancellorsville, (a strange episode)—the camps in winter—the military prisons—the Hospitals—(alas! alas! the Hospitals).

[165]

The Secession War? Nay, let me call it the UNION WAR. Though whatever call'd, it is even yet too near us—too vast and too closely overshadowing—its branches unform'd yet, (but certain,) shooting too far into the future—and the most indicative and mightiest of them yet ungrown.

A great literature will yet arise out of the era of those four years, those scenes—Era compressing centuries of native passion, first-class pictures, tempests of life and death—an inexhaustible mine for the Histories, Drama, Romance, and even Philosophy, of people to come—indeed the Verteber of Poetry and Art, (of personal character too,) for all future America—more grand, in my opinion, to the hands capable of it, than Homer's siege of Troy, or the French wars to Shakspere.

But I must leave these speculations, and come to the theme I have assigned and limited myself to.

Of the actual murder of President Lincoln, though so much has been written, probably the facts are yet very indefinite in most persons' minds. I read from my Memoranda, mainly written at the time, on the spot, and revised frequently since.

—The day, April 14, 1865, seems to have been a pleasant one throughout the whole land—the moral atmosphere pleasant too—the long storm, so dark, so fratricidal, full of blood and doubt and gloom, over and ended at last by the sun-rise of such an absolute National victory, and utter breakdown of Secession—we almost doubted our own senses! Lee had capitulated beneath the apple-tree of Appomattax. The other armies, the flanges of the revolt, swiftly follow'd. . . . And could it really be, then? Out of all the affairs of this world of woe and failure and disorder, was there really come the unerring sign of plan, like a shaft of pure light—of rightful rule—of God?. . . So the day, as I say, was propitious. Early herbage, early flowers, were out. (I remember where I was stopping at the time, the season being advanced, there were many lilacs in full bloom. By one of those caprices that enter and give tinge to events without being at all a part of them, I find myself always reminded of the great tragedy of that day by the sight and odor of these blossoms. It never fails.)

But I must not dwell on accessories. The deed hastens. The popular afternoon paper of Washington, the little *Evening Star*, had spatter'd all over its third page, divided among the advertisements in a sensational manner in a hundred different places, *The President and his Lady will be at the The-*

atre this evening. . . . (Lincoln was fond of the theatre. I have myself seen him there several times. I remember thinking how funny it was that He, in some respects, the leading actor in the stormiest drama known to real history's stage, through centuries, should sit there and be so completely interested and absorb'd in those imaginary doings.)

On this occasion the theatre was crowded, many ladies in rich and gay costumes, officers in their uniforms, many well known citizens, young folks, the usual clusters of gas-lights, the usual magnetism of so many people, cheerful, with perfumes, music of violins and flutes — (and over all, and saturating all, that vast vague yet realistic wonder, *Victory*, the Nation's Victory, the triumph of the Union, filling the air, the thought, the sense, with exhilaration more than all music and perfumes).

The President came betimes, and, with his wife, witness'd the play, from the large stage-boxes of the second tier, two thrown into one, and profusely draped with the National flag. The acts and scenes of the piece — one of those singularly written compositions which have at least the merit of giving entire relief to an audience engaged in mental action or business excitements and cares during the day, as it makes not the slightest call on either the moral, emotional, esthetic, or spiritual nature — a piece, ('Our American Cousin,') in which, among other characters, so call'd, a Yankee, certainly such a one as was never seen, or the least like it ever seen, in North America, is introduced in England, with a varied fol-de-rol of talk, plot, scenery, and such phantasmagoria as goes to make up a modern popular drama — had progress'd through perhaps a couple of its acts, when in the midst of this comedy, or tragedy, or nonesuch, or whatever it is to be call'd, and to off-set it or finish it out, as if in Nature's and the Great Muse's mockery of those poor mimes, comes interpolated that Scene, not really or exactly to be described at all, (for on the many hundreds who were there it seems to this hour to have left little but a passing blur, a dream, a blotch) — and yet partially to be described as I now proceed to give it. . . .

There is a scene in the play representing a modern parlor, in which two English ladies are inform'd by the unprecedented and impossible Yankee that he is not a man of fortune, and therefore undesirable for marriage-catching purposes; after which, the comments being finish'd, the dramatic trio make exit, leaving the stage clear for a moment. At this period came the murder of Abraham Lincoln. Great as that was, with all its manifold train, circling round it, and stretching into the future for many a century, in the politics, history, art, &c., of the New World, in point of fact the main thing, the actual murder, transpired with the quiet and simplicity of any common-est occurrence—the bursting of a bud or pod in the growth of vegetation, for instance. Through the general hum following the stage pause, with the change of positions, came the muffled sound of a pistol shot, which not one hundredth part of the audience heard at the time—and yet a moment's hush—somehow, surely a vague startled thrill—and then, through the or-namented, starr'd and striped space-way of the President's box, a sudden figure, a man raises himself with hands and feet, stands a moment on the railing, leaps below to the stage, (a distance of perhaps fourteen or fifteen feet,) falls out of position, catching his boot-heel in the copious drapery, (the American flag,) falls on one knee, quickly recovers himself, rises as if nothing had happen'd, (he really sprains his ankle, but unfelt then,)—and so the figure, Booth, the murderer, dress'd in plain black broadcloth, bare-headed, with full glossy, raven hair, and his eyes like some mad animal's flashing with light and resolution, yet with a certain calmness, holds aloft in one hand a large knife—walks along not much back from the foot-lights—turns fully toward the audience his face of statuesque beauty, lit by those basilisk eyes, flashing with desperation, perhaps insanity—launches out in a firm and steady voice the words, *Sic semper tyrannis*—and then walks with neither slow nor very rapid pace diagonally across to the back of the stage, and disappears. . . . (Had not all this terrible scene—making the mimic ones preposterous—had it not all been rehears'd, in blank, by Booth, beforehand?)

A moment's hush,—a scream—the cry of *Murder*—Mrs. Lincoln leaning out of the box, with ashy cheeks and lips, with involuntary cry, pointing to the retreating figure, *He has kill'd the President.* . . . And still a moment's strange, incredulous suspense—and then deluge!—then that mixture of horror, noises, uncertainty—(the sound, somewhere back, of a horse's hoofs clattering with speed)—the people burst through chairs and railings, and break them up—there is inextricable confusion and ter-ror—women faint—quite feeble persons fall, and are trampled on—many cries of agony are heard—the broad stage suddenly fills to suffocation with a dense and motley crowd, like some horrible carnival—the audience rush generally upon it—at least the strong men do—the actors and actresses are all there in their play-costumes and painted faces, with mortal fright show-ing through the rouge—the screams and calls, confused talk—redoubled, trebled—two or three manage to pass up water from the stage to the President's box—others try to clamber up—&c., &c.

In the midst of all this, the soldiers of the President's Guard, with others, suddenly drawn to the scene, burst in—(some two hundred altogether)—they storm the house, through all the tiers, especially the upper ones, inflamed with fury, literally charging the audience with fix'd bayonets, muskets and pistols, shouting *Clear out! clear out! you sons of—*. . . . Such the wild scene, or a suggestion of it rather, inside the play-house that night.

Outside, too, in the atmosphere of shock and craze, crowds of people, fill'd with frenzy, ready to seize any outlet for it, come near committing murder several times on innocent individuals. One such case was especially exciting. The infuriated crowd, through some chance, got started against one man, either for words he utter'd, or perhaps without any cause at all, and were proceeding at once to actually hang him on a neighboring lamp post, when he was rescued by a few heroic policemen, who placed him in their midst and fought their way slowly and amid great peril toward the Station House. . . . It was a fitting episode of the whole affair and I give it to you, indeed, as a sample-drop of the surrounding ocean. The crowd rushing and eddying to and fro—the night, the yells, the pale faces, many frighten'd people trying in vain to extricate themselves—the attack'd man, not yet freed from the jaws of death, looking like a corpse—the silent resolute half-dozen policemen, with no weapons but their little clubs, yet stern and steady through all those eddying swarms—made this side-scene to the grand tragedy of the murder. . . . They gain'd the Station House with the protected man, whom they placed in security for the night, and discharged him in the morning.

And in the midst of that pandemonium, infuriated soldiers, the audience and the crowd—the stage, and all its actors and actresses, its paint-pots, spangles, and gas-lights—the life-blood from those veins, the best and sweetest of the land, drips slowly down, and death's ooze already begins its little bubbles on the lips. . . . Such, hurriedly sketch'd, were the accompaniments of the death of President Lincoln. So suddenly and in murder and horror unsurpass'd he was taken from us.

Thus the visible incidents and surroundings of President Lincoln's murder, as they really occur'd. Thus ended the Attempted Secession of These States. Thus the four years' war. But the main things come subtly and invisibly afterward, perhaps long afterward—neither military, political, nor (great as those are) historical. I say, certain secondary and indirect results, out of this Death, are, in my opinion, greatest. Not the event of the murder itself. Not that Mr. Lincoln strung the principal points and personages of the period, like beads, upon the single string of his career. Not that his idiosyncracy, in its sudden appearance and disappearance, stamps this Republic with a stamp more mark'd and enduring than any yet given by any one man—(more even than Washington's;)—But, join'd with these, the immeasurable value and meaning of that whole tragedy lies, to me, in senses finally dearest to a Nation, (and here all our own)—the permeating imaginative and the artistic senses—the literary and the dramatic ones. Not in any common or low meaning of those terms, but a meaning precious to the race, and to every age. A long and varied series of contradictory events arrives at last at its highest poetic, single, central, pictorial denouement. The whole involved, baffling, multiform whirl of the Secession period comes to a head, and is gather'd in one brief flash of lightening-illumination—one simple, fierce deed. Its sharp culmination, and as it were solution, of so many bloody and angry problems, illustrates those climax-moments on the stage of universal Time, where the Historic Muse at one entrance, and the Tragic Muse at the other, suddenly ringing down the curtain, close an immense act in the long drama of creative thought, and give it radiation, tableau, stranger than fiction. Fit radiation—fit close! How the imagination—how the student loves these things! America, too, is to have them. For not in all great deaths—not Caesar in the Roman Senate-house, or Napoleon passing away in the wild night-storm at St. Helena—Not Paleolagus, falling, desperately fighting, piled over dozens deep with Grecian corpses—Not calm old Socrates, drinking the hemlock—outvies that terminus of the Secession War, in one man's life, here in our midst, in our own time—that seal of the emancipation of three million slaves—that parturition and delivery of our at last really free Republic, henceforth to commence its career of genuine homogeneous Union, compact, born again, consistent with itself.

Nor will ever future American Patriots and Unionists, indifferently over the whole land, or North or South, find a better seal to their lesson. All serves the true spirit, the true development of America. Life serves, and death also—even the death of the sweetest and wisest. Crumbled and wordless now lie his remains long buried there in his prairie-grave—aside from cities, and all the din of wealth-making and politics and all contention and doubt. The storm is long over. The battle, the anguish, the uncertainty whom to trust, are over, the slur, the envenom'd bullet and the slug of many a traitor's tongue and pen, are over. With the first breath of a [the?] great historic triumph, and in murder and horror unsurpassed, Abraham Lincoln died. But not only the incalculable value he gave the New World in life survives for ever, but the incalculable value of his death survives forever. The final use of the greatest men of a Nation is not with reference to their deeds in themselves, or their direct bearing on their times or lands. The final use of a heroic-eminent life — especially of a heroic-eminent death — is its indirect filtering into the nation and the race, and to give, often at many removes, but unerringly, color and fibre to the Personalism of the youth and maturity of that age, and all ages, of mankind. Then there is a cement to the whole People, subtler, more underlying, than any thing in written Constitution, or courts or armies — namely, the cement of a first-class tragic incident thoroughly identified with that People, at its head, and for its sake. Strange, (is it not?) that battles, martyrs, blood, even assassination, should so condense — perhaps only really, lastingly condense — a Nationality.

I repeat it — the grand deaths of the race — the dramatic deaths of every Nationality — are its most important inheritance-value — in some respects, beyond its literature and art — (as the hero is beyond his finest portrait, and the battle itself beyond its choicest song or epic.) Is not here indeed the point underlying all tragedy? the famous pieces of the Grecian Masters — and all Masters? Why, if the old Greeks had had this man, what trilogies of plays — what epics — would have been made out of him! How the rhapsodes would have recited him! How quickly that quaint tall form would have entered into the region where men vitalize gods, and gods divinify men! But Lincoln, his times, his death — great, emotional, eventful, as any, any age — belong altogether to our own, and are autochthonic. Sometimes indeed I think our American days, our own stage — the actors we know and have shaken hands, or talk'd with — more fateful than any thing in Eschylus — more heroic than the fighters around Troy: afford kings of men, prouder than Agamemnon — models of character cute and hardy as Ulysses — deaths more pitiful than Priam's — Afford too, (as all history for future us is resolv'd into persons,) central figures, illustrators, in whom our whirling periods shall concentrate — the best future Art and Poetry find themes — and around which the whole congeries of time shall turn.

[171]

Thus my friends I draw to a finish the duty I spoke of and to which I have invited you—turning aside a moment from all our business and pleasure—from the rush of streets and crowds and din and talk—to give a commemorative moment, this twenty-fifth anniversary to the dead President—and in his name, and truly radiating his spirit, to all the dead soldiers of the war—all indeed all—I feel myself to say, to faithfully fervently invested, or lost or won, or South, or North.

When, centuries hence, (as it must, in my opinion, be centuries hence before the Life of These States, or of Democracy, can be really written and illustrated,) the historians and dramatists seek for some special event, incisive enough to mark with deepest cut, and mnemonize, this turbulent Nineteenth Century of ours, (not only These States but all over the political and social world)—something, perhaps, to close that gorgeous procession of European Feudalism, with all its pomp and caste-prejudices, (of whose long train we in American are yet so inextricably the heirs)—Something to identify with terrible identification, by far the greatest revolutionary step in the history of The United States, (perhaps the greatest of the world, our century)—the absolute extirpation and erasure of Slavery the last, general underpinning and lingering result of feudalism from The States—those historians will seek in vain for any point to serve more thoroughly their purpose, than Abraham Lincoln's death.

Dear to the Muse—thrice dear to Nationality—to the whole human race—Precious to this Union—precious to Democracy—unspeakably and forever precious—their first great Martyr Chief.

Notes

1. Quoted in Daniel Mark Epstein, *Lincoln and Whitman: Parallel Lives in Civil War Washington* (New York: Ballantine, 2004), 133.

2. Walt Whitman, *Notebooks and Unpublished Prose Manuscripts*, ed. Edward F. Grier (New York: New York UP, 1984), 2:539.

Walt Whitman, *Complete Prose Works* (Philadelphia: David McKay, 1892), 1–14.

"Lincoln's Imagination" (1879)

Noah Brooks

The journalist Noah Brooks (1830–1903) met Lincoln for the first time in Illinois during John Fremont's campaign for the presidency in 1856. After some time spent in California, and following the death of his wife, Brooks became the Washington correspondent for the *Sacramento Daily Union* in 1862 and soon grew familiar with the White House. He composed several well-known pieces about his intimate times with Lincoln, including a book-length collection based on his wartime postings called *Mr. Lincoln's Washington* (1895). Perhaps less well known, yet valuable in terms of understanding Lincoln's literary temperament, is the following essay published in 1879.

CONSIDERING THE affectionate curiosity with which the American people dwell on the traits of Lincoln's character, it is unfortunate that so much prominence has been given to his humor, his jokes and his little stories. Lincoln undoubtedly took great delight in a good story, and his sense of humor was quick and responsive. During his life-time, however, he was compelled to protest that many anecdotes and quaint sayings were unwarrantedly attributed to him; and, now that he is gone, the last of the Lincoln stories is yet to be invented. I have sometimes wondered how many of those who seize with delight on every reminiscence of Lincoln, ready to break into laughter, remember that he had many pleasant traits of character which do not strongly appear in Lincoln the statesman and politician, or Lincoln the story-teller of the White House.

It does not seem that Lincoln had a nimble fancy; his imagination was not fertile; if it was, he took pains to keep it under; but there was a vein of poetic sentiment which appears in many of his earlier writings and speeches. When the poetical tastes of Lincoln are mentioned, immediately there comes to mind that depressing and bilious poem, "Oh, why should the spirit of mortal be proud?" Those verses, with their lugubrious and sentimental refrain, undoubtedly affected Lincoln strongly on the tragic side of his nature; but they have received a somewhat fictitious value as the expression of his literary taste. It is true, however, that he inclined toward the poetry which dwells on sad and pathetic themes. It has been said that this was a sort of prophetic indication of the tragical ending of his own life; and some have thought that they detected in "the far-away look of his eyes" the gaze of one who was destined to a violent death. It is not likely that such thoughts occurred to any of us while he was yet alive; they are, however, the most natural of afterthoughts.

Like many men who have a keen sense of humor, Lincoln was easily moved by the pathos which is so nearly allied to jocularity. This is the reason, I suppose, why he liked best the minor poems of Thomas Hood and Oliver Wendell Holmes. Of the latter's works, "The Last Leaf" was one of his special favorites, and it readily can be understood how the subtly mingled pathos and humor of those verses should captivate the fancy of one of Lincoln's peculiar temperament. Few men ever passed from grave to gay with the facility that characterized him. He liked, too, sad and pensive songs. I remember that, one night at the White House, when a few ladies were with the family, singing at the piano-forte, he asked for a little song in which the writer describes his sensations when revisiting the scenes of his boyhood, dwelling mournfully on the vanished joys and the delightful associations of forty years ago. It is not likely that there was anything in Lincoln's lost youth that he would wish to recall; but there was a certain melancholy and half-morbid strain in that song which struck a responsive chord in his heart. The lines sunk into his memory, and I remember that he quoted them, as if to himself, long afterward. His powers of memory were very great. It was no evidence of his special delight in any poem, or bit of prose, that he was able to repeat it from memory without having the words before him. He once recited to me a long and doleful ballad, something like "Vilikins and his Dinah," the production of a rural Kentucky bard, and, when he had finished, he added, with a laugh, "I don't believe I have thought of that before for forty years."

Lincoln's reading, it would seem, was discursive. He could not have pursued any systematic course of study except that of the law; but, with a fine sense of fitness, he picked up whatever came in his way, reserving that which suited his purpose and leaving the rest. He never seemed to lose his hold upon what he liked in literature; when a young man he studied Shakspere, and some parts of the plays he involuntarily committed to memory;

these he repeated with surprising verbal accuracy. It is related of him that, spending a few days at Fortress Monroe, he took up a volume of Shakspere and read aloud to General Wool's aid, who chanced to be near him, several passages from "Hamlet" and "Macbeth"; then, after reading from the third act of "King John," he closed the book and recalled the lament of *Constance* for her boy, beginning:

> And, father cardinal, I have heard you say
> That we shall see and know our friends in heaven:
> If that be true, I shall see my boy again.

These words, he said, with deep emotion, reminded him of hours when he seemed to be holding communion with his lost boy, Willie, yet knowing, the while, that this was only a vision. Consider the pathos of this incident. The worn and grief-burdened President was waiting for the results of a movement against Norfolk, then in possession of the enemy; and it was thus he beguiled the heavy hours.

Lincoln seldom quoted poetry in his letters or speeches, although in conversation he often made an allusion to something which he had read, always with the air of one who deprecated the imputation that he might be advertising his erudition. Occasionally, as in his farewell speech to his neighbors and friends in Springfield, he employed a commonplace quotation, with due credit to the unknown author. In that address he said, "Let us believe, as some poet has expressed it, 'Behind the cloud the sun is still shining.'" In a speech in Congress, on so unpromising a theme as internal improvements, then one of the issues of the time, he quoted Robert Herrick's lines:

> Attempt the end, and never stand to doubt;
> Nothing's so hard but search will find it out.

Another example occurs in an address made to a delegation of colored men who had waited on him to obtain an expression of opinion on the subject of colonization. The President spoke at great length, and concluded by saying that he hoped that his visitors would consider the matter seriously, not for themselves alone, nor for the present generation, but for the good of mankind, and he added:

> From age to age descends the lay
> To millions yet to be,

Till far its echoes roll away
Into eternity.

Amid all his labors, Lincoln found time to read the newspapers, or, as he sometimes expressed it, "to skirmish" with them. From their ephemeral pages he rescued many a choice bit of verse, which he carried with him until he was quite familiar with it. I am bound to say that some of these waifs would not receive the hospitality of a severe literary critic; but it was noticeable that they were almost invariably referable to his tender sympathy with humanity, its hopes and its sorrows. I recall one of these extracts, which he took out of his pocket one afternoon, as we were riding out to the Soldiers' Home. It began:

A weaver sat at his loom
Flinging his shuttle fast,
And a thread that should wear till the hour of doom
Was added at every cast.

The idea was that men weave in their own lives the garment which they must wear in the world to come. I do not know who wrote the verses; but the opening lines were fixed in my mind by their frequent repetition by the President, who seemed to be strongly impressed by them. During the evening, he murmured them to himself, once or twice, as if in a soliloquy.

I think it was early in the war that some public speaker sent Lincoln a newspaper report of a speech delivered in New York. The President, apparently, did not pay much attention to the speech, but a few lines of verse at the close caught his eye. These were the closing stanzas of Longfellow's "Building of the Ship," beginning with:

Thou too, sail on, O Ship of State!
Sail on, O Union, strong and great!

To my surprise, he seemed to have read the lines for the first time. Knowing the whole poem as one of my early exercises in recitation, I began, at his request, with the description of the launch of the ship, and repeated it to the end. As he listened to the last lines:

Our hearts, our hopes, our prayers, our tears,
Our faith triumphant o'er our fears, etc.,

his eyes filled with tears, and his cheeks were wet. He did not speak for some minutes, but finally said, with simplicity: "It is a wonderful gift to be able to stir men like that." It is quite possible that he had read the poem long before the war for the Union gave to the closing portion that depth of meaning which it now holds for us.

Though Lincoln does not appear to have used much imagery in his letters and speeches, his innumerable good sayings were pregnant with meaning; as Emerson has said, his fables were so wise that in an earlier time he would have been a mythological character, like Aesop. His parables were similes. His figures of speech, used sparingly, were homely and vigorous, the offspring of an uncultivated imagination, rather than of a mind stored with the thoughts of the great men of all ages. The simplest incidents of every-day life furnished him with similes. In one of his speeches in the famous campaign with Douglas, he said, referring to the suppression of political debate, "These popular sovereigns are at their work, blowing out the moral lights around us." This figure of blowing out the lights is not only a simple one, but highly suggestive of the homely incident which was in the mind of the speaker; an affected or fastidious person, would have weakly said, "extinguishing." In the same way, Lincoln insisted on retaining in his first annual message to Congress the phrase "sugar-coated pills"; and when remonstrated with by the printer, who was a personal friend, he defended his use of the figure by declaring that the time would never come when the American people would not know what a sugar-coated pill was. In like manner, too, representing the incipient stages of reconstruction in the lately rebellious states as an egg which might be crushed, but which should be hatched, he adhered to his homely illustration, in spite of all criticism. Such sayings as these became, in time, incorporated into the current speech of the people.

Lincoln's earlier addresses showed, perhaps, more imagination than did his later ones. Criticising that part of President Polk's message which referred to the Mexican War, Lincoln, then a representative in Congress, compared it to "the half-insane mumbling of a fever-dream." In the same speech he described military glory as "the attractive rainbow that rises in showers of blood; the serpent's eye that charms to destroy." I do not now recall a more striking picture, drawn by Lincoln, than this description of the helpless state of the American slave in 1857: "They have him in his prison-house," said he. "They have searched his person and have left no prying instrument with him. One after another, they have closed the heavy iron doors upon him, and now they have him, as it were, bolted in with a lock of a hundred keys, which can never be unlocked without the concurrence of every key; the keys in the hands of a hundred different men, and they scattered to a hundred different and distant places; and they stand musing as to what invention, in all the dominions of mind and matter, can be produced to make the impossibility of his escape more complete than it is."

Lincoln was a close observer of nature, as well as of men. He used natural objects to complete his similes. Into the wonderful alembic of his mind everything was received, to be brought forth again as aphorism, parable, or trenchant saying. In woodcraft, for example, he was deeply skilled, his habit of close observation leading him to detect curious facts which escaped the notice of most men. Riding through a wood in Virginia, he observed a vine which wrapped a tree in its luxuriant growth. "Yes," he said, "that is very beautiful; but that vine is like certain habits of men; it decorates the ruin that it makes." At another time, when we were in Virginia together, just after a fall of snow, I found him standing on the stump of a tree, looking out over the landscape. He called attention to various subtle features of the view, and said, among other things, that he liked the trees best when they were not in leaf, as their anatomy could then be studied. And he bade me look at the delicate yet firm outline of the leafless tree against the sky. Then, pointing to the fine net-work of shadows cast on the snow by the branches and twigs, he said that that was the profile of the tree. The very next day, somebody was discussing with him the difference between character and reputation, when he said, — with a look at me, as if to remind me of what he had been talking about the day before, — perhaps a man's character was like a tree, and his reputation like its shadow; the shadow is what we think of it; the tree is the real thing. The President was at that time weighed down with anxieties; it was a few weeks before General Hooker's crossing of the Rappahannock, at Fredericksburg; and he was daily expecting to hear of an attack on Charleston. I remember that it seemed to me a marvelous thing that he could unfix his mind from all these great cares long enough to consider such trifling things.

In his letter declining an invitation to attend the Illinois Republican Convention, in 1863, Lincoln made use of two or three striking figures. Reviewing the military events of the past year, which had been favorable to the cause of the Union, he said: "The Father of waters again goes unvexed to the sea." And, referring to the fact that Southern Unionists and ex-slaves had done something to help on the good work, he said: "On the spot, their part of the history is dotted down in black and white." There was something in the phrase "dotted down in black and white" which mightily tickled the popular fancy. At the time, however, criticism was provoked by this odd figure employed by the President: "Nor must Uncle Sam's web-feet be forgotten. At all the watery margins they have been present not only on the deep sea, the broad bay, the rapid river, but also up the narrow, muddy bayous, and wherever the ground was a little damp, they have been and made their tracks." Lincoln was amused by the discussion in the newspapers to which the use of the phrase "Uncle Sam's web-feet" gave rise. He explained that the remarkable feats performed by the gun-boats, in making their way through sloughs and bayous, heretofore considered unnavigable, reminded him of the stealthy passage of water-fowl. The pleasantry concerning light-draught steamers going where "the ground is a little damp" is familiar to everybody.

It will be a long time before our people will forget Lincoln's homely simile of "elder-squirts charged with rose-water," as applied to the conservative programme for prosecuting the war. This was used in a letter addressed to Cuthbert Bullitt, of New Orleans, in which letter he also said that the conservatives were like complaining passengers on a ship — "The mutineers must go untouched, lest one of these sacred passengers should receive an accidental wound." His imagination was powerfully stimulated by any reference to the history of the republic. His address at Gettysburg, now one of the great historical speeches of the world, suggests, rather than expresses, a crowd of images. To Lincoln's mind, apparently, American history was filled with noble and pathetic figures. In some of the loftier flights of his eloquence may be found traces of a strong poetic fancy — an imagination fired by love of country, and inspired by the contemplation of the stirring events that have marked its history. No more striking example of this can be found anywhere than in the memorable words which closed his first inaugural address:

"The mystic chords of memory, stretching from every battle-field and patriot grave to every living heart and hearth-stone, all over this broad land, will yet swell the chorus of the Union, when again touched, as surely they will be, by the better angels of our nature."

Noah Brooks, "Lincoln's Imagination," *Scribner's Monthly*, August 1879, 584–87.

From "Abraham Lincoln: A Speech" (1865)

FREDERICK DOUGLASS

Frederick Douglass (1817–1895) was a former slave who rose to the most prominent position among all African Americans of his lifetime, as orator, abolitionist, and editor. He became a well-known cultural figure through his first autobiographical account of his enslavement, rebellion, and escape, known as the *Narrative* and published in 1845, and by his subsequent lecturing with the most famous abolitionist of all, William Lloyd Garrison. Douglass would end up publishing two more detailed autobiographies, editing several newspapers, and presenting numerous famous orations throughout a very busy and productive public career. Although his views of Lincoln changed dramatically over time, they shared much in common and, as James Oakes has recently argued, in many ways needed each other. Their lives "converged at the most dramatic moment in American history," as Oakes puts it, and they "reveal what can happen in American democracy when progressive reformers and savvy politicians make common cause."[1]

Although at first he was hesitant in his support of Lincoln, in the end Douglass greatly admired the president and he visited with Lincoln at the White House no less than three times. His much more famous speech on Lincoln is certainly the "Oration . . . Delivered on the Occasion of the Unveiling of the Freedman's Monument in Memory of Abraham Lincoln" (1876), a widely available lecture that was controversial for its depiction of Lincoln as the white man's president. Published here, evidently for the first time, is another fine meditation on the slain president that has remained until very recently unavailable and unknown to most readers.

THE PRESENT YEAR will long be remembered for two very important and instructive events in American history: one of which brought unspeakable joy and hope to the national heart, for it was the sudden collapse and downfall of a stubborn, protracted, fierce and languishing [?] rebellion, undertaken and prosecuted, for no other earthly object, than to perpetuate a privileged class in the Southern states and to make slavery perpetual on this continent. The other event to which I refer, and which will mainly occupy our attention this Evening, filled the national heart with the bitterest anguish it ever knew, for it was, the [assassination] of Abraham Lincoln, one of the best men that ever presided over the destinies of this or any other country. This eventful year is now drawing to a close. But a few days of it remain to us — for good or for evil: Yet judging now the ominous clouds that hang on the political sky, this [?] year of ours which has borne so many marked features, is fated to bear still another. One which shall be more striking, and revolting than either rebellion or assassination. . . .

The American people have experienced many shocks during the last four years: some of these have been heavy and terrible in the extreme causing the very pillars of the state to tremble and the boldest to quake [?] in view of the possible fate of the Republic: but the shock caused by the assassination of Abraham Lincoln was the heaviest of all and should never be forgotten.

It was as if some grand convulsion in nature had occurred; for had the solid earth opened and swallowed up one our chief towns or cities — had the tombs burst beneath our feet and the sheeted dead risen from the dust of ages and stalked through our streets in open day the sensation of horror could not have been more profound than when this terrible crime was first announced: A hush fell upon the land as though each man in it heard a voice from Heaven, an uninterrupted sound from the sky and had paused to learn its meaning.

The calamity was so sudden, so out of joint with the prevailing sense of security, involved such a transition from one extreme of feeling to another, now the wildest joy and exultation of victory to the very dust and ashes of sorrow and mourning that few could at first believe it.

As at no time before during all the war, the loyal people were rejoicing in great and decisive victories. The rebel capital so long besieged and so desperately defended had fallen. General Lee with his boasted invincible army composed of the elite of Virginia had surrendered to General Grant. Mobile and Wilmington had capitulated. Loyal Black troops were timing their high footsteps to the tune of Old John Brown in the city of Charleston, the very nest of the rebellion. The rebel army was everywhere beaten in the field — scattered like the dust before the north wind, and the end of the rebellion seemed at the door.

The great North was even then beginning to soften down its justly kindled wrath, and to exhibit unexampled magnanimity — in its clemency and forgiveness towards the rebels. The tone of our public journals was rapidly assuming that sickly sentimental character which so disgusted earnest men during the first two years of the war.

Southern Generals were becoming decidedly popular at the north. Lee was spoken of with only a little less respect than General Grant. Men seemed as thankful to General Lee for surrendering as to General Grant for making him surrender. The South was no longer our deadly foe but our erring brother. It was at such a time as this when the nation was weary of war — sick of blood, gladly laying off its armour, meditating mercy — it was when the whole southern horizon so long dark and grim with clouds of war, was fringed with the golden dawn of peace, that slavery dealt us its heaviest blow and committed its most stupendous crime.

I do not intend to treat you to a lecture entirely devoted to the life and character of Abraham Lincoln. That is already a well-trodden field. It has been gleaned from centre to circumference. The press, the pulpit, the platform, poetry and song, art and skill in all their departments have been busily employed in illustrating his character and commending his many virtues. All, therefore, that I can do in what I have to say of him, will be to give back in some humble measure to my audience their own thoughts and feelings.

The function of the orator is high, but it is seldom higher or nobler than this. Where most successful, he resembles his audience as the wave the ocean. His weight and volume, his strength and beauty, are borrowed from the sea out of which he rises.

There is a charm about the life and character of the illustrious deceased which will never lose its power.

A thousand years hence, where even the solid marble that shades his honored dust shall have crumbled, when the great names of military heroes which are now every where greeted with a shout shall cease to dazzle and shall be forgotten by the masses, when even the harrowing details of the late rebellion shall have faded from the page of history, and when the tremendous war which filled the eye of the civilized world during four years, shall seem but as a speck upon the immense distance of time, the name of Abraham Lincoln like that of Dear Old John Brown, will still hold its place in the memories of men, and find eloquent tongues to discourse of his virtues and hold up his character for admiration and imitation. For whenever men love good Government and abhor treason; Whenever simple manhood commands respect, and kindness of heart awakens love; Whenever freedom has an advocate, the oppressed a friend and the tyrant a foe, the name of Abraham Lincoln, will be honored, venerated, loved.

His life requires a book rather than a lecture. More history that will *live* has been made in connection with his name, than with that of any other American, not excepting Washington. The position he occupied as the head of the American Government, the grandest of the continent and which may ever yet be the grandest of the globe; the social depression from which he rose to eminence and greatness illustrating in his character the best peculiarities of his country, and the benignest tendencies of free institutions; the mighty perils through which he successfully conducted the country; the singular purity of his life, and the tragic manner of his death, afford matter for volumes.

One great charm of his life is that he was indebted to himself for himself. He was the architect of his own fortune, a self made man, a flat boat captain, a splitter of rails; a man of toil—one who travelled far but made the road on which he travelled—one who ascended high, but with hard hands and honest work built the ladder on which he climbed. Flung upon the sea of life in the midnight storm, without oars or life preservers he bravely buffetted the billows—and with sinewy arms swam in safety, where other men despair and sink.

You all know his life by heart: All know of his excellent temper which no indolence could disturb his good natured anicdotes—so humble and yet so wise; all know of his caution, his vigelence, his firmness, his industry, and his honest devotion to his duties as the chief magistrate of the Republic, and are familiar with the leading qualities of the man.

Why then do I make him the subject of discourse on this occasion? The answer is ready—The assassination of Abraham Lincoln, is an instructive and convenient medium through which we may survey to some extent the dangers, and learn the solemn duties of this hour.

We are indebted to our enemies here as elsewhere. They have given us in this, as in many other instances during the last thirty years the events which have been most efficacious in the overthrow of slavery and the slave power.

They annexed Texas twenty years ago and swelled the vote for freedom—from seven thousand to seventy; They repealed the Missouri Compromise, and thereby unmasked their revolting designs to nationalize slavery; They thronged the virgin soul of Kansas with border ruffians and thereby roused the loyal north to make Kansas a free state; they enacted a fugitive slave bill, and each slave caught made a thousand abolitionists. They hanged John Brown, and thereby kindled the wrath of the civilized world against slavery, and placed his name with those of saints and heroes.

Had Abraham Lincoln died from any of the numerous ills, that flesh is heir to, and by which men are ordinarily removed from the busy scenes of life; had he reached that good old age of which his excellent constitution and his equally excellent temperate habits gave promise, ~~had~~ the curtain of death falling gradually around him, we should have followed him sadly enough to his honored grave: placing him side by side with our most honored dead, — but without any special distinction, and without the manefestation of those unusual sighs of National bereavement for which his funeral will be ever memorable.

But dying as he did die, for a cause that takes hold of human nature; Dying as he did die, by the red hand of violence; Dying as he did die at a moment when evincing his greatest trust in the people, — going among them freely like a common man without a guard when he was Commander in Chief of a million of armed men — Snatched suddenly away from his work without warning — killed, murdered, assassinated not because of any personal hate which any malice in him provoked, for no man who knew Abraham Lincoln could hate him.

No man ever defined his character better, than himself, where he said — as in his last inaugural — he had malice towards none but charity towards all; but he died as I have said for a cause. He died for the country — for loyalty as against Treason, for — Republican Government baised upon Liberty and Equal rights — as against a proud and selfish class Government based upon the enslavement of millions of their fellowmen.

Dying thus, his name becomes a text from which to preach that Liberty, and that human Equality, to strike down which he was ruthlessly murdered.

The name of Abraham Lincoln pleads today with all the eloquence of Martyrdom, for the utter extinction, of every root, and fibre, not merely of slavery, but of the insolent, aggressive, and Malignent oligarchy — or privileged class founded upon it.

Since his death, every man who gives his voice or his vote, in a way to uphold this privileged class as the South stamps upon the grave of Abraham Lincoln, insults his memory, and commends the ~~Myrt~~ Martyr a fresh. He will shrink from all those manly enterprizes which require strength and develop energy. The same is true of a nation. The weak man depends upon cunning. He conceals his opinion if he dares to have one, for fear of inability to defend it: He is ever ready for a compromise when resisted. He does not dare to espause the cause of the weak against the strong — but folds his hands and talks about the wisdom of minding his own business — and leaving other people to manage their own affairs. The couragious, the noble and heroic, do not exist for him. Self preservation becomes his constant and all controlling thought.

Now it cannot be denied that our Nationality under the name of the Union has leaned very much towards the ignoble attitude of the weak man. Under the predecessor of our Martyred President the union was too weak to defend itself from treason. The preservation of the Union was with all parties a few years ago — as the very end of the Law for Righteousness. The clear old union was always sick just before an Election and the leader of the people insisted that if certain things were done, or certain things were left undone the union would ~~disolve~~ dissolve. We were kept constantly in a state of alarm. The general aim was not to *do* — but to be. The opinion formed of our National Government by European Statesmen and Political Philosophers was not calculated to increase our faith in free institutions. They warned us that though well enough in a calm the ship of state was too weak for stormy weather — that though beautiful to the eye, strong to the touch and swift upon the waves — where the skies come bright and the wind fair — ~~The We Should go dow~~ She would go down in the first great storm. With them there was nothing stable but thrones, nothing powerful but standing armies — nothing authorative, unsupported by the pretension of devine right. It is not strange that men educated in distrust of the wisdom and ~~very~~ virtue of the people should entertain such opinions. We should waste no indignation on those foreigners of little faith. It was natural for them to see, ~~in~~ as they did see, at the beginning of the slaveholders rebellion the certain downfall of the American Republic.

The same thing was felt at home and if thus in the *Green tree*, of vigourous democratic institutions, what else could have been expected in the dried up mummyfied, king craft and priest craft Government of the old world.

Nor was doubt of free popular Government confined to unfriendly thinkers at home or abroad. Many of the most patriotic men of this country shared in that doubt. Thomas Jefferson saw the conflict coming and trembled for his country. Many of the Fathers of the Republic argued in favor of a strong and against the union on the ground of its weakness. Well, the trial has come. The experiment has been tried. The strength of the Republic has been tested — tried by treason, by rebellion and by the assassination of its chief; tried as few forms of Government were ever tried before.

What is the result? This it is, the country was never stronger than to-day. Certainty has taken the place of death. Strength has taken the place of weakness — and men now talk of principles where they once dreamed only of compromise. A solid nation takes the place of a deceptive union — and the national *will* dictates the Law instead of an insolent oligarchy composed of the traffickers in human flesh. We no longer tremble for the safety of the Ship of State. There is a feeling of security and repose among all on board except those of the crew who attempted to convert our gallant bark into a pirate.

Happily too, this general confidence is not confined to the limits of our own country. Over the seas, and distant continents it has gone: He never awed by his silence, nor silenced by the volubility or authority of his speech: Willing always to give, he was ever, equally willing to receive. He managed to leave his visitor not only free to utter his opinions, but by a wise reserve in the manner of insisting upon his own, he got even a little more from his visitor than his visitor got from him.

From the first moment of my interview with him I seemed to myself to have been acquainted with him for years — for while he was among the most solid men I ever met he was among the most transparent.

What Mr Lincoln was when in company with white men, of course I cannot tell. I saw him mostly alone; but this much I can say of him; he was one of the very few ~~white men~~ Americans, who could entertain a negro and converse with ~~a negro~~ him without in anywise reminding him of the unpopularity of his color.

If you will pardon the egotism, I will mention a fact or two in further illustration of his friendly feeling for the colored race. On one occasion, I remember while conversing with him, his messenger twice announced as in an adjoining room and as wishing to see him Governor ~~Buke~~ Buckingham of Connecticut. Tell the Governor to wait, said President Lincoln — I wish to have a long talk with my friend Douglass. I remained a full hour after this, while the Governor of Connecticut waited without for an interview.

The last days of Mr Lincoln were his best days. If he did not control events he had the wisdom to be instructed by them. When he could no longer withstand current he swam with it. What he said on the steps of the capital four years ago did not determine what the same lips should utter four years afterward. No two papers are in stronger contrast than his first and his last Inaugural addresses. The first was intended to reconcile the rebels to the Government by argument and persuasion, the second was a recognition of the operation of inevitable and universal laws. ~~As old as eternity~~. In this he was willing to let justice have its course. You all remember with what solemn emphasis he expressed this on the fourth of March — six weeks before his assassination:

> Fondly do we hope, fervently do we pray that this mighty Scourge of war shall soon pass away. Yet if God wills it continue till all the treasure piled by two hundred ~~af~~ and fifty years of the bondman's unrequited toil shall have been wasted. Each drop of blood drawn by the lash shall have been paid for by one drawn by the sword, we must still say, as was said three thousand years ago — the judgements of the Lord are true and righteous altogether.

Had Mr Lincoln lived, we might have looked for still greater progress. Learning wisdom by war he would have learned more from Peace. Already he had expressed himself in favor of extending the right of suffrage to two classes, machinery which moves the world on the plane of advancement and civilization.

Our work was prepared before hand. We had amongst us a gigantic system of bondage, an offense against the enlightened judgment of mankind, one which we were required by our relations to the outside world — to put out of the way — or give up the experiment of free Government. We have decided to do the former.

While thus serving ourselves as a nation, we have done other and greater service to mankind. To the grand [slew?] of human knowledge as to what men will do — what great States and nations will do where great interests are involved and powerful human passions are stirred we have added, ~~the~~ our special and peculiar experience a contribution such as no other nation could make.

During this tremendous struggle for national life, so fierce, so sanguinary, so long protracted and so desperate, we have illustrated both extremes of human possibilities—exemplifying the noblest qualities which can distinguish human nature, as well as those which most disgrace it.

Perhaps, the history of our war—in order to its full effect upon ourselves and the world required some such termination as that of the colored men, first to the brave colored soldiers who had fought under our flag—and second to the very intelligent part of the colored population south. This declaration on his part though it seemed to mean but little meant a great deal. It was like Abraham Lincoln. He never shocked prejudices unnecessarily. Having learned statesmanship while splitting rails, he ~~allays~~ always used the thin edge of the wedge first—and the fact that he used this ~~wa~~ at all—meant that he would if need be, use that thick as well as the thin. He saw the absurdity of asking men to fight for a Government which should degrade them—and the meanness of enfranchising enemies and disfranchising friends—He was a progressive man, a humane man, an honorable man, and at heart an antislavery man. He had exhausted the resources of conciliation upon rebels and slaveholders and now looked to the principles of liberty and justice, for the peace, security happiness and prosperity of his country. I assume therefore, had Abraham Lincoln been spared to see this day—the negro of the south would have more than a hope of enfranchisement and no rebels could hold the ~~reig~~ reins of Government in any one of the late rebellious states. Whosoever else, have cause to mourn the loss of Abraham Lincoln, to the colored people of the country—his death is an unspeakable calamity.

Note

1. James Oakes, *The Radical and the Republican: Frederick Douglass, Abraham Lincoln, and the Triumph of Antislavery Politics* (New York: Norton, 2007), xix–xx.

Frederick Douglass, "Abraham Lincoln: A Speech" (unpublished manuscript 1865), Library of Congress holograph.

"Lincoln's Philosophy of Life" (1886)

WILLIAM HENRY HERNDON

For more than a decade after Lincoln's death in 1865, William Herndon—discussed in an earlier headnote—could find little direction for his life. At first he was driven to collect information about Lincoln, primarily through interviews of people in Illinois, Indiana, and Kentucky who had known the assassinated president. He proposed to several publishers a full-length biography based on a series of lectures he gave in 1865 and 1866, the fourth of which provoked a torrent of criticism in its claim that Lincoln had loved only one woman in his life, Ann Rutledge. Herndon became notorious for many of his opinions about Lincoln, such as his argument that Rutledge's death drove Lincoln into a suicidal depression and a lifelong struggle with melancholy. Herndon insisted that his version was a truth that he told to protect Lincoln from inappropriate hagiography. But the hostile reaction to his lectures prompted Herndon to lose interest in the biography for more than two decades.

Similarly, Herndon reported that Lincoln was not an orthodox Christian, and often even a scoffer at religion, a position that received extensive criticism, such as the following remarks of Noah Brooks in 1872: "There is no possible reason to suppose that Mr. Lincoln would ever deceive me as to his religious sentiments. In many conversations with him, I absorbed the firm conviction that Mr. Lincoln was at heart a Christian man, believed in the Savior, and was seriously considering the step which would formally connect him with the visible church on earth. Certainly, any suggestion as to Mr. Lincoln's skepticism or Infidelity, to me who knew him intimately from 1862 till the time of his death, is a monstrous fiction—a shocking perversion."[1]

The following is one of many of essays written by Herndon regarding Lincoln's beliefs, in this case as a letter to a friend in 1886. Decades later (1933), it was privately printed as a six-page pamphlet with this introduction by the publisher, H. E. Barker.

> This letter of Herndon's, addressed to his "Friend Fowler," was written three years before he published his now famous "Herndon's Lincoln," and strange to say, its matter is nowhere incorporated in that extended work.

It is an analysis of Lincoln's philosophy of life such as could have been written only by Herndon. His long and intimate association with Lincoln enabled him to build it, bit by bit, from daily happenings at the office and on the circuit. It is a careful study, well thought out and skillfully phrased, and yet—is it possible to reconcile this attitude attributed to the Lincoln of earlier days, with the President's well known habit of special and daily prayer?

Springfield, Ills.
Febry 18th, 1886

Friend Fowler:

It may help you to understand Lincoln somewhat thoroughly by stating to you his philosophy. My Lincoln believed that what was to be would be, and no prayers of ours could arrest or reverse the decree; he was a thorough fatalist, and thought the fates ruled the world; he believed that the conditions made the man—does make the man; he believed that general, universal and eternal laws governed both matter and mind, always and everywhere.

This philosophy as a whole will account for much of the facts and laws of his splendid life. Things that were to be, *would* be, and hence he patiently waited on events; His charity for men—their feelings—thoughts—willings—and acts sprang out of his philosophy, that conditions made them; his want of malice sprang out of the same. Lincoln neither hated nor did he love; he never but once or twice eulogized men, nor did he ever curse them. Men were mere tools in the hands of fate—were made as they are made, by conditions; and to praise or blame men was pure folly. Men were not entitled to credit for what they were or did—what they thought or said—how they felt or acted. The thing was to be and no prayers of ours could arrest or avert the decree; men are made by conditions that surround them—that have somewhat existed for a hundred thousand years or more.

Man is compelled to feel—think—will and act by virtue and force of these conditions; he is a mere child moved and governed by this vast world machine, forever working in grooves—and moving in deep cut channels; and now what is man? He is simply a simple tool—a cog—a part and parcel of this vast iron machine that strikes and cuts and mashes all things that resist it. The fates had decreed it and what they decreed is irresistible and inevitable. Here human prayers are blank absurdities. What a man is, he is because of the world's eternal conditions, and is entitled to no credit for virtue nor should he be blamed for vice. "With malice toward none and charity for all" — I live for men — was Lincoln's feelings — thoughts — wills and acts. Man does but what is commanded by his superiors.

Lincoln used to quote Shakespeare's philosophy:

> There is a divinity that shapes our ends
> Rough hew them how we will.

If a man did him an injury — or grievous wrong, the man was a mere tool and obeyed the powers; and if the man did him a great good — blessed him and made him happy, still he but obeyed orders, and he was not to be censured for the wrong nor praised for the right. Everything, everywhere, is doomed for all time. If a man was good or bad — small or great — and if virtue or vice prevailed it was so doomed. If bloody war — deathly famine and cruel pestilence stalked over the land, it was to be and *had come*, and to mourn for this — to regret it — to resist it, would only be flying in the face of the inevitable.

Lincoln was patient and calmly waited on events; he knew that they would come in their own good and appointed time; he was not surprised at their coming nor astonished at their extent, nor depth, nor fury. The fates and the conditions were *the* powers. Laws ruled everything, everywhere, both matter and mind from the beginning to the end, if there was a beginning and an end.

Such was Lincoln's philosophy; he was in religion a *Liberal* — naturally and logically so. Do not misunderstand me — probably Lincoln *did not* believe that Brutus was specially made and ordered to kill Caesar with a dagger in the Senate Chamber; and yet he fully believed that Brutus and Caesar stood in the line of the rush of the forces of nature let loose millions of years ago and let go at full play.

I hope that these remarks will assist you in finding Lincoln — the real man as he lived among us.

You spoke in your eloquent letter of Emerson and Lincoln; they differed widely. Emerson had the genius of the Spiritual and ideal. Lincoln had the genius of the real and the practical. Emerson lived high among the stars — Lincoln lived low among men. Emerson dreamed, Lincoln acted. Emerson was intuitional, Lincoln reflective. Both were Liberals in religion and were great men.

Your friend,
W. H. Herndon

Note

1. James A. Reed, "The Later Life and Religious Sentiments of Abraham Lincoln," *Scribner's Monthly*, July 1873, 339.

William Henry Herndon, *Lincoln's Philosophy of Life* (Los Angeles: privately printed by H. E. Barker, 1933).

From "Abraham Lincoln" (1895)

ROBERT G. INGERSOLL

> Known in his day as one of the flashiest and most brilliant American ora-
> tors, Robert G. Ingersoll (1833–1899) was born in upstate New York to a Pres-
> byterian father who occasionally filled the pulpit for the firebrand evangelist
> and abolitionist Charles G. Finney. Ingersoll grew up in Illinois and served
> heroically in the Civil War, where he attained the rank of colonel. His color-
> ful speechifying on a plethora of radical topics made him one of the most
> popular and well-liked public speakers of his age. Americans as different as
> Walt Whitman and Mark Twain both agreed on this view. In particular he
> championed Free Thought, a view of religion and morality that led to mod-
> ern agnosticism and often led to charges of blasphemy. It may seem ironic,
> given Ingersoll's status as America's leading free-thinker and agnostic, that
> in his speeches he commonly made broad, metaphysical assertions about
> the meaning and purpose of the Civil War and the Union. Catherine Albanese
> explains that for the generation of free-thinking leaders who guided America
> through its near dissolution, "the Civil War . . . represent[ed] a new and more
> intensive valorization for them of the civil religion" upon which America was
> founded.[1] In addition, Ingersoll is one of few speakers to note that Lincoln
> was born on the same day as Charles Darwin, a connection that might have
> offended deeply religious Americans. As a religious and political thinker, In-
> gersoll considered Lincoln to be the preeminent philosophical example of all
> that was pure, possible, and sweet about America, as this ravishing account
> documents.

ON THE 12TH of February, 1809, two babes were born—one in the woods
of Kentucky, amid the hardships and poverty of pioneers; one in England,
surrounded by wealth and culture. One was educated in the University of
Nature, the other at Cambridge. One associated his name with the enfranchisement of labor, with the emancipation of millions, with the salvation of
the Republic. He is known to us as Abraham Lincoln. The other broke the
chains of superstition and filled the world with intellectual light, and he is
known as Charles Darwin.

Nothing is grander than to break chains from the bodies of men — nothing nobler than to destroy the phantoms of the soul.

Because of these two men the nineteenth century is illustrious. A few men and women make a nation glorious — Shakespeare made England immortal, Voltaire civilized and humanized France; Goethe, Schiller and Humboldt lifted Germany into the light. Angelo, Raphael, Galileo and Bruno crowned with fadeless laurel the Italian brow, and now the most precious treasure of the Great Republic is the memory of Abraham Lincoln.

Every generation has its heroes, its iconoclasts, its pioneers, its ideals. The people always have been and still are divided, at least into classes — the many, who with their backs to the sunrise worship the past, and the few, who keep their faces toward the dawn — the many, who are satisfied with the world as it is; the few, who labor and suffer for the future, for those to be, and who seek to rescue the oppressed, to destroy the cruel distinctions of caste, and to civilize mankind.

Yet it sometimes happens that the liberator of one age becomes the oppressor of the next. His reputation becomes so great — he is so revered and worshiped — that his followers, in his name, attack the hero who endeavors to take another step in advance.

The heroes of the Revolution, forgetting the justice for which they fought, put chains upon the limbs of others, and in their names the lovers of liberty were denounced as ingrates and traitors.

During the Revolution our fathers to justify their rebellion dug down to the bed-rock of human rights and planted their standard there. They declared that all men were entitled to liberty and that government derived its power from the consent of the governed. But when victory came, the great principles were forgotten and chains were put upon the limbs of men. Both of the great political parties were controlled by greed and selfishness. Both were the defenders and protectors of slavery. For nearly three-quarters of a century these parties had control of the Republic. The principal object of both parties was the protection of the infamous institution. Both were eager to secure the Southern vote and both sacrificed principle and honor upon the altar of success. . . .

When Lincoln was a child his parents removed from Kentucky to Indiana. A few trees were felled — a log hut open to the south, no floor, no window, was built — a little land plowed and here the Lincolns lived. Here the patient, thoughtful, silent, loving mother died — died in the wide forest as a leaf dies, leaving nothing to her son but the memory of her love.

In a few years the family moved to Illinois. Lincoln then almost grown, clad in skins, with no woven stitch upon his body — walking and driving the cattle. Another farm was opened — a few acres subdued and enough raised to keep the wolf from the door. Lincoln quit the farm — went down the Ohio and Mississippi as a hand on a flat-boat — afterward clerked in a country store — then in partnership with another bought the store — failed. Nothing left but a few debts — learned the art of surveying — made about half a living and paid something on the debts — read law — admitted to the bar — tried a few small cases — nominated for the Legislature and made a speech. . . .

Lincoln was educated in the University of Nature — educated by cloud and star — by field and winding stream — by billowed plains and solemn forests — by morning's birth and death of day — by storm and night — by the ever eager Spring — by Summer's wealth of leaf and vine and flower — the sad and transient glories of the Autumn woods — and Winter, builder of home and fireside, and whose storms without, created the social warmth within.

He was perfectly acquainted with the political questions of the day — heard them discussed at taverns and country stores, at voting places and courts and on the stump. He knew all the arguments for and against, and no man of his time was better equipped for intellectual conflict. He knew the average mind — the thoughts of the people, the hopes and prejudices of his fellow-men. He had the power of accurate statement. He was logical, candid and sincere. In addition, he had the "touch of nature that makes the whole world kin." . . .

In 1831, Lincoln went down the Mississippi on a flat-boat. He received the extravagant salary of ten dollars a month. When he reached New Orleans, he and some of his companions went about the city.

Among other places, they visited a slave market, where men and women were being sold at auction. A young colored girl was on the block. Lincoln heard the brutal words of the auctioneer — the savage remarks of bidders. The scene filled his soul with indignation and horror.

Turning to his companions, he said, "Boys, if I ever get a chance to hit slavery, by God I'll hit it hard!"

The helpless girl, unconsciously, had planted in a great heart the seeds of the Proclamation.

Thirty-one years afterward the chance came, the oath was kept, and to four millions of slaves, of men, women and children, was restored liberty, the jewel of the soul.

In the history, in the fiction of the world, there is nothing more intensely dramatic than this.

Lincoln held within his brain the grandest truths, and he held them as unconsciously, as easily, as naturally, as a waveless pool holds within its stainless breast a thousand stars. . . .

The soldiers thought of him as a father. All who had lost their sons in battle felt that they had his sympathy — felt that his face was as sad as theirs. They knew that Lincoln was actuated by one motive, and that his energies were bent to the attainment of one end — the salvation of the Republic.

They knew that he was kind, sincere and merciful. They knew that in his veins there was no drop of tyrants' blood. They knew that he used his power to protect the innocent, to save reputation and life — that he had the brain of a philosopher — the heart of a mother. . . .

What he did was worth living for, worth dying for. He lived until he stood in the midst of universal joy, beneath the outstretched wings of Peace — the foremost man in all the world.

And then the horror came. Night fell on noon. The Savior of the Republic, the breaker of chains, the liberator of millions, he who had "assured freedom to the free," was dead.

Upon his brow Fame placed the immortal wreath, and for the first time in the history of the world a Nation bowed and wept. The memory of Lincoln is the strongest, tenderest tie that binds all hearts together now, and holds all States beneath a Nation's flag. . . .

Hundreds of people are now engaged in smoothing out the lines of Lincoln's face — forcing all features to the common mould — so that he may be known, not as he really was, but, according to their poor standard, as he should have been.

Lincoln was not a type. He stands alone — no ancestors, no fellows, and no successors.

He had the advantage of living in a new country, of social equality, of personal freedom, of seeing in the horizon of his future the perpetual star of hope. He preserved his individuality and his self-respect. He knew and mingled with men of every kind; and, after all, men are the best books. He became acquainted with the ambitions and hopes of the heart, the means used to accomplish ends, the springs of action and the seeds of thought. He was familiar with nature, with actual things, with common facts. He loved and appreciated the poem of the year, the drama of the seasons. . . .

In the country is the idea of home. There you see the rising and setting sun; you become acquainted with the stars and clouds. The constellations are your friends. You hear the rain on the roof and listen to the rhythmic sighing of the winds.

You are thrilled by the resurrection called Spring, touched and sad-dened by Autumn — the grace and poetry of death. Every field is a picture, a landscape; every landscape a poem; every flower a tender thought, and every forest a fairy-land. In the country you preserve your identity — your personality. There you are an aggregation of atoms, but in the city you are only an atom of an aggregation.

In the country you keep your cheek close to the breast of Nature. You are calmed and ennobled by the space, the amplitude and scope of earth and sky — by the constancy of the stars.

Lincoln never finished his education. To the night of his death he was a pupil, a learner, an inquirer, a seeker after knowledge. You have no idea how many men are spoiled by what is called education. For the most part, colleges are places where pebbles are polished and diamonds are dimmed. If Shakespeare had graduated at Oxford, he might have been a quibbling attorney, or a hypocritical parson. . . .

He was an orator — clear, sincere, natural. He did not pretend. He did not say what he thought others thought, but what he thought.

If you wish to be sublime you must be natural, you must keep close to the grass. You must sit by the fireside of the heart; above the clouds it is too cold. You must be simple in your speech; too much polish suggests insincerity.

The great orator idealizes the real, transfigures the common, makes even the inanimate throb and thrill, fills the gallery of the imagination with stat-ues and pictures perfect in form and color, brings to light the gold hoarded by memory the miser, shows the glittering coin to the spendthrift hope, en-riches the brain, ennobles the heart, and quickens the conscience. Between his lips words bud and blossom.

If you wish to know the difference between an orator and an elocutionist—between what is felt and what is said—between what the heart and brain can do together and what the brain can do alone—read Lincoln's wondrous speech at Gettysburg, and then the oration of Edward Everett.

The speech of Lincoln will never be forgotten. It will live until languages are dead and lips are dust. The oration of Everett will never be read.

The elocutionists believe in the virtue of voice, the sublimity of syntax, the majesty of long sentences, and the genius of gesture.

The orator loves the real, the simple, the natural. He places the thought above all. He knows that the greatest ideas should be expressed in the shortest words—that the greatest statues need the least drapery. . . .

He had the unconscious naturalness of Nature's self. He built upon the rock. The foundation was secure and broad. The structure was a pyramid, narrowing as it rose. Through days and nights of sorrow, through years of grief and pain, with unswerving purpose, "with malice towards none, with charity for all," with infinite patience, with unclouded vision, he hoped and toiled. Stone after stone was laid, until at last the Proclamation found its place. On that the Goddess stands. . . . .

Note

1. Catherine L. Albanese, *Sons of the Fathers: The Civil Religion of the American Revolution* (Philadelphia: Temple UP, 1976), 16; see also Harold K. Bush and Joe Webb, "'Transfigured by Oratory': 'Thomas Paine, Robert Ingersoll, Mark Twain, and the Roots of American Civil Religion," *The Mark Twain Annual* 7.1 (2009), 79–101.

The Works of Robert G. Ingersoll, Vol. 3 (New York: Farrell, 1900), 123–73.

From *Abraham Lincoln: The Evolution of His Literary Style* (1900)

Daniel K. Dodge

Daniel K. Dodge (1863–1933), after studying at Columbia College, became chair of English literature at the University of Illinois in 1892, and rapidly became one of the nation's experts on Lincoln. Dodge published the first serious academic study of Lincoln's literary and rhetorical styles in 1900. This long excerpt is important as it brings together in one source almost everything that was known at the turn of the century about Lincoln's early reading, his frontier education in letters, and his extensive engagement with literary culture of all kinds.

THE STORY OF Abraham Lincoln's early education in Kentucky and Indiana has been so often told and the different accounts agree so closely, that we need not dwell upon it here. All the important facts can be obtained from Nicolay and Hay's *Life*. His schooling "amounted to less than a year in all." "His last school days were passed with one Swaney in 1826, when he was seventeen years old, who taught at a distance of four and a half miles from the Lincoln cabin." No one was more conscious of the shortcomings of his education than Lincoln himself. In the Dictionary of Congress he describes his education as "defective," and in the Short Autobiography he writes: "He regrets his want of education, and does what he can to supply the want." A chief difficulty at the beginning of his career was the mastery of English grammar. In 1831, when he was twenty-two years old, he studied Kirkham's English Grammar. According to Nicolay and Hay, "he seemed surprised at the . . . ease with which it yielded all there was to it to the student." In the Autobiography Lincoln says: "He studied grammar — imperfectly, of course, but so as to speak and write as well as he now does."

. . .

According to Herndon, the school books used by Lincoln were Webster's Spelling Book, the American Speller, Pike's Arithmetic, and probably Murray's English Reader. In addition to these books, Lincoln read with eagerness the Bible, Pilgrim's Progress, Robinson Crusoe, Aesop's Fables, Weems' [not Weem's, as in Nicolay and Hay] Life of Washington, and a History of the United States. It would be hard to find better models of a pure English style than the Bible, Bunyan, and DeFoe, while the deep impression made upon Lincoln by Aesop can be seen in his love of illustrative anecdotes, and perhaps in the epigrammatic quality of his style.

It is impossible to follow in detail the course of Lincoln's reading, but some hints as to its general direction in the early Illinois days can be gathered, the chief source of this information being Herndon's "Life." Writing of the New Salem period of 1833, Herndon says:

"Meanwhile he was reading not only law books, but natural philosophy and other scientific subjects. He was a careful and patient reader of newspapers . . . He paid a less degree of attention to historical works, although he read Rollin and Gibbon . . . He had a more pronounced fondness for fictitious literature, and read with evident relish Mrs. Lee Hentz's novels, which were very popular books in that day, and which were kindly loaned him by his friend A. Y. Ellis . . . He [Ellis] says that Lincoln was fond of short, spicy stories one or two columns long . . . He remembered everything he read, and could afterwards without apparent difficulty relate it."

This account is of special interest for several reasons. In the first place, it brings out clearly Lincoln's early habit of newspaper reading, which was kept up even after the duties of his presidential office made it necessary for him to obtain most of the news of the day by deputy. The reference, too, to his fondness for newspaper stories is important. We shall several times have occasion to mention his equal fondness for the poets' corner and the use he made of it. Of far greater importance is the negative reference to Lincoln's historical reading. A possible clue to his apparent lack of interest in this class of literature is furnished by the following criticism, as reported by Herndon, of a life of Burke: "In 1856 I purchased in York a Life of Edmund Burke. I have forgotten now who the author was . . . One morning Lincoln came into the office and, seeing the book in my hands, enquired what I was reading . . . Taking it in his hand he threw himself down on the office sofa and hastily ran over its pages, reading a little here and there. At last he closed and threw it on table with the exclamation, 'No, I've read enough of it. It's like all the others. Biographies as generally written are not only misleading, but false. The author of this life of Burke makes a wonderful hero out of his subject. He magnifies his perfections — if he had any — and suppresses his imperfections. He is so faithful in his zeal and so lavish in praise of his every act that one is almost driven to believe that Burke never made a mistake or a failure in his life . . . History is not history unless it is the truth.'" Lincoln's lack of interest would seem to be not in history, but in histories as he found them.

A third element of interest found in the quotation from which the criticism of Burke has led us, is the information it gives of Lincoln's early attitude toward prose fiction. In spite of Herndon's statement, however, it would appear that Lincoln's taste for imaginative literature inclined far more toward poetry than prose. He once remarked: "It may seem somewhat strange to say, but I never read an entire novel in my life . . . I once commenced 'Ivanhoe,' but never finished it." In this same conversation Mr. Lincoln said to Carpenter: "'Who wrote the play?' [Richelieu, which was to be performed by Forrest.] 'Bulwer,' I replied. 'Ah!' he rejoined. 'Well, I knew Bulwer wrote novels, but I did not know he was a playwriter also.'" This is not quoted in order to expose Mr. Lincoln's ignorance of the authorship of Richelieu, which is not at all strange, but as being one of the very few references to novels made by him. In Reuben E. Fenton's article a conversation is reported in which Mr. Lincoln mentioned Dickens. But these later references to fiction prove only that Lincoln did not care for Scott, not that he had read either Bulwer or Dickens. So we must leave to Mrs. Lee Hentz the one distinction of which she can now boast, of being the only novelist that Lincoln is known to have enjoyed.

Finally, we have in Herndon's account one of the many references to Lincoln's phenomenal memory, a memory apparently of very much the same character as Macaulay's. A careful examination of the facts, however, seems to bring out contradictions in the claims made by some of Lincoln's friends. Herndon says: "No one had a more retentive memory. If he ever read or heard a good thing it never escaped him." In the same strain Noah Brooks says: "The truth was, that anything he heard or read fastened itself into his mind, if it tickled his fancy." And General Viele states that he had "a memory so wonderful that he could repeat, almost word for word, whatever he had read." On the other hand, Lincoln himself once said: "My mind is like a piece of steel, — very hard to scratch anything on it, almost impossible after you get it there to rub it out." But it is probable that Lincoln referred here to the slowness with which he received ideas rather than to the impression made on his mind by the language in which they were expressed. Unconscious testimony is given by Noah Brooks in his account of Lincoln's acquaintance with Longfellow's "Birds of Killingworth," "which he picked up somewhere in a newspaper, cut out and carried in his vest pocket until it was committed to memory." If Lincoln had had the memory so often attributed to him, one reading of the piece would have done away with the necessity of carrying it in his pocket for later reference. An examination of the list of quotations will justify General Viele's limitation, for several of them are far from being "word for word."

While Herndon's statements of facts are invaluable, his expressions of opinion must often be taken with a generous pinch of salt. It is certainly going too far to say that "beyond a limited acquaintance with Shakespeare, Byron and Burns, Mr. Lincoln, comparatively speaking, had no knowledge of literature." This statement probably reflects more severely upon Mr. Herndon's appreciation of Mr. Lincoln, than upon the latter's knowledge of literature. This much may be said, however, in extenuation, that Lincoln's powers of literary criticism do not seem to have found frequent expression until during the last four years of his life, when they were brought out by the congenial atmosphere of Washington. The volume of critical opinion by Lincoln, preserved from those four years, far exceeds that of the whole of his preceding life.

But before considering Lincoln's critical powers it will be well to present the facts gleaned with regard to his reading. Herndon gives a list of the newspapers and books that were read by Lincoln and him during the years immediately preceding the Lincoln-Douglas debates of 1858. The books included "the latest utterances of Giddings, Phillips, Sumner, Seward, and one whom I considered grander than all others, — Theodore Parker." It is interesting to note, though it has no direct bearing on the question of his literary taste and development, that at that time Lincoln regularly read two of the leading Southern pro-slavery journals, The Charleston Mercury and The Richmond Enquirer, and that he read, also with Herndon, "all the leading histories of the slavery movement, and other works which treated on that subject."

Of special interest in connection with the study of Lincoln's public speaking is the question of what public speakers he himself read and admired. Disregarding here the contemporary debaters of the slavery question, whose works would be read by Lincoln for the arguments they presented, and without any necessary reference to their literary qualities, we find the following important statement by Lincoln's intimate friend Isaac N. Arnold: "Patrick Henry had always been his ideal orator." He also admired Clay, whom he called his "beau ideal of a statesman," Calhoun, and, of course, Webster, whose reply to Hayne "he read when he lived at New Salem, and which he always regarded as the grandest specimen of American oratory." This last does not contradict Arnold's statement as to Patrick Henry, as it refers to the single oration, not to the orator. In a conversation with Noah Brooks Mr. Lincoln once said: "Now, do you know, I think Edward Everett was very much overrated." With the exception of the reference to the life of Burke, no mention of Burke's name has been discovered, and it is not at all improbable that Lincoln was not acquainted even with his speeches on the colonies.

While Lincoln's admiration of Byron is often referred to, only two of his works are specifically mentioned as having been read by him. Lamon says: "Byron's 'Dream' was a favorite poem, and I have often heard him repeat the following lines:

> Sleep hath its own world,
> A boundary between the things misnamed
> Death and existence: Sleep hath its own world,
> And a wide realm of wild reality!, etc.

The second reference, taken from Whitney, is far more important. "Closely allied with this sad trait was an inherent belief in his destiny; perhaps the specific destiny was not very clearly indicated, but that, somehow, the Genius, whom we hail as destiny, had touched him with her wand, and marked him for her own.

"Apropos of this, I recollect that in the fall of 1854, Mr. Lincoln, with other lawyers from abroad, drove over from Urbana, the county seat, to West Urbana (now Champaign), to see the embryo town, and, while there, stopped at my law office, which had been improvised in the dining-room of my father's house. I had no law library to speak of, but made a display of miscellaneous books to fill up, and render less inviting the appearance of the cupboard shelves. Lincoln took down a well-worn copy of Byron (which no boy's library at that time was without) and, readily turning to the third canto of Childe Harold, read aloud from the 34th verse [stanza], commencing: "There is a very life in our despair," etc. to and including the 45th verse,

> He who ascends to mountain tops shall find
> Those loftiest peaks most wrapped in clouds and snow:
> He who surpasses or subdues mankind
> Must look down on the hate of those below;
> Though high above, the sun of glory glow,
> And far beneath, the Earth and Ocean spread,
> Round him are icy rocks, and loudly blow
> Contending tempests on his naked head,
> And thus reward the toils which to those summits lead.

"This poetry was very familiar to him evidently; he looked specifically for, and found it with no hesitation, and read it with a fluency that indicated that he had read it oftentimes before. I think I am justified in saying that he read it sadly and earnestly, if not, indeed, reverently."

The references to Burns are of an even more unsatisfactory character. Carpenter is certainly wrong when he names Burns as Lincoln's favorite poet. Arnold says more reasonably: "Next to Shakespeare among the poets was Burns. There was a lecture of his upon Burns full of favorite quotations and sound criticism. He sympathized thoroughly with the poem 'A Man's a Man for a' that.'" and again, "He could repeat nearly all the poems of Burns." Though Noah Brooks does not mention Burns in connection with the President's reading, he refers to his fondness for "plaintive Scotch songs." And yet in spite of this strong evidence of Lincoln's admiration of Burns, not a single quotation from the Scotch poet occurs in either his speeches or conversation, and no trace of the lecture on Burns is to be found in his Works. Between Herndon's statement of "a limited acquaintance with Burns," and Arnold's claim that "he could repeat nearly all the poems of Burns," there is a middle ground of conjecture on which the critic is at liberty to disport himself to his heart's content. . . .

Much interesting information as to Lincoln's preference for single poems is given by Herndon, Whitney, Lamon and Noah Brooks. Lincoln preferred what he called "little sad songs." Brooks characterizes his taste as extending especially toward "all songs which had for their theme the rapid flight of time, decay, the recollections of early days." Among his favorites may be mentioned "Twenty Years Ago," "Ben Bolt," "The Sword of Bunker Hill," "The Lament of the Irish Emigrant," and Holmes' "The Last Leaf." Lincoln once said to Carpenter of the last: "There are some quaint, queer verses, written, I think, by Oliver Wendell Holmes, entitled, 'The Last Leaf,' one of which is to me inexpressibly touching." He then repeated these also from memory . . . As he finished this verse "The mossy marbles rest," he said, in his most emphatic way, "For pure pathos, in my judgment, there is nothing finer than those six lines in the English language." After Mr. Lincoln's death a copy of Charles Mackay's "The Enquiry" was found in an envelope marked in his handwriting, "Poem. I like this."

Lamon gives the titles of several comic songs that were enjoyed by Mr. Lincoln and mentions his fondness for negro melodies, but to judge by the example submitted, these latter were not of the genuine plantation growth, but were inferior minstrel exotics.

Special mention should be made of the poem that became so closely associated with Lincoln that its authorship was often attributed to him. This is "Immortality," or "Oh! why should the spirit of mortal be proud?" According to Herndon the poem was first given to Lincoln by Dr. Jason Duncan in 1842, shortly after the death of a friend, Bowlin Greene, by whom Lincoln had been helped in the trying months succeeding the death of his first love, Ann Rutledge. The poem seems to have been associated in his mind with that earlier grief. Mr. Lincoln himself said to Carpenter: "The poem was first shown to me by a young man named Jason Duncan, many years ago." Were it not for these explicit statements it would be natural to suppose that "Immortality" is the poem referred to in the following extract from a letter to _____ Johnston, dated April 18, 1846:

"I think you ask me who is the author of the piece I sent to you, and that you do so as to indicate a slight suspicion that I myself am the author. I would give all I am worth, and go in debt, to be able to write so fine a piece as I think that is. Neither do I know who is the author. I met it in a straggling form in a newspaper last summer, and I remember to have seen it once before, about fifteen years ago, and that is all I know about it."

Indeed, the references to this poem resemble so closely Lincoln's estimate of "Immortality" that one is tempted to disregard the slight contradictions of the three accounts.

The principal authorities for Lincoln's later reading, besides those already quoted, are the writers in the Reminiscences and General Viele. The last named gives the only reference that has been discovered to Lincoln's knowledge of Browning.

"With a mind well stored with the grandest and most beautiful in English literature . . . he would sit for hours during the trip repeating the finest passages of Shakespere's best plays, page after page of Browning and whole cantos of Byron. He was as familiar with *belles lettres* as many men who make much more pretension to 'culture.'"

One cannot help wondering what pages of Browning were repeated by so unexpected an admirer. It would be interesting also to learn what parts of Byron were included. If the phrase "whole cantos" is correctly used, the extracts must have been from one or more of the long poems. In the interview with McDonough three poets, not elsewhere mentioned, are connected with Lincoln's reading, but the statement is so general that it need not be taken too literally. "He interspersed his remarks with extracts striking from their similarity to, or contrast with, something of Shakespere's, from Byron, Rogers, Campbell, Moore and other poets."

Brooks speaks of Lincoln's fondness for Hood and Holmes, which we should expect. "Of the former author he liked best the last part of 'Miss Kilmansegg and her Golden Leg,' 'Faithless Sally Brown,' and one or two others not generally so popular as those which are called Hood's best. Holmes' 'September Gale,' 'Last Leaf,' 'Chambered Nautilus,' and 'Ballad of an Oysterman' were among his very few favorite poems. Longfellow's 'Psalm of Life' and 'Birds of Killingworth' were the only productions of that author he ever mentioned with praise . . . James Russell Lowell he only knew as 'Hosea Biglow,' every one of whose effusions he knew." . . . He once said that originality and daring impudence were sublimed in this stanza of Lowell's:

> Ef you take a sword and dror it,
> An' stick a feller creetur thru,
> Gov'ment hain't to answer for it,
> God'll send the bill to you.

On one occasion Noah Brooks repeated Longfellow's "The Building of the Ship," a quotation from which had attracted the President. "As he listened to the lines:

> Our hearts, our hopes, our prayers, our tears,
> Our faith triumphant o'er our fears.

his eyes filled . . . and his cheeks were wet. He did not speak for some minutes, but finally said, with simplicity: 'It is a wonderful gift to be able to stir men like that.'" N. P. Willis once told Carpenter that "he was taken by surprise on a certain occasion when he was riding with the President . . . by Mr. Lincoln of his own accord referring to and quoting several lines from his poem entitled 'Parrhasius [and the Captive].'"

The humorous prose writers from whom Mr. Lincoln so often quoted were David R. Locke (author of the Nasby Letters), Orpheus C. Kerr, Artemus Ward, Joe Miller, and Baldwin (author of "Flush Times in Alabama"). In his introduction to the "Nasby Letters," published in 1872, Charles Sumner gives a very interesting account of the book and its relations to Mr. Lincoln. He says: "Of publications during the war none had such charm for Abraham Lincoln. He read every letter as it appeared and kept them all within reach for refreshment . . . He then repeated with enthusiasm the message he had sent to the author: 'For the genius to write these things I would gladly give up my office.'" David R. Locke, in his article on Lincoln, states: "Lincoln also seized eagerly upon everything that Orpheus C. Kerr wrote, and knew it all by heart." Whitney furnishes the following testimony to Lincoln's acquaintance with one of the humorous classics: "Judge Treat told me that he once lent Lincoln a copy of 'Joe Miller,' and Lincoln kept it for a while and evidently learned its entire contents, for he found Lincoln narrating the stories therein around the Circuit, but very much embellished and changed, evidently by Lincoln himself."

Although Mr. Lincoln's later reading consisted for the most part of poetry and humorous prose, he was also "a lover of many philosophical works, and particularly liked Butler's Analogy of Religion, [John] Stuart Mill on Liberty, and he always hoped to get at President Edwards on the Memory." The only work at all belonging to this class that we know that Lincoln had read while living in Illinois is a book called "Vestiges of [the Natural History of] Creation," "which interested him so much that he read it through." In the same passage Herndon gives the negative testimony that Lincoln found the "works of Spencer, Darwin, and the utterances of other English scientists . . . entirely too heavy for an ordinary mind to digest." On a preceding page Herndon states: "Investigation into first causes, abstruse mental phenomena, the science of being, he brushed aside as trash — mere scientific absurdities." This view of Lincoln's mind is borne out by Joseph Gillespie in a letter of 1866. It is possible that Lincoln's taste for Butler and

Mill developed in the last years of his life, as the result of a broader mental outlook. In the lecture on Inventions, Lincoln quotes from Plato, but there is no proof that he had ever read the Greek Philosopher. Herndon states that Mr. Lincoln read Volney's "Ruins" and Paine's "Age of Reason."

Of special interest in connection with the study of Lincoln's style is his love of the Bible. Disregarding as irrelevant here the question of Lincoln's religious belief, concerning which his different biographers show such wide divergence of opinion, we are straightway impressed by the fact that at all stages of his development Lincoln refers to or quotes from the Bible, both in his conversation and in his writings. Indeed, he shows a familiarity with the Scriptures that almost justifies Arnold's statement: "He knew the Bible by heart. There was not a clergyman to be found so familiar with it as he." His knowledge of the Bible seems to have been as accurate as it was extensive. "He would sometimes correct a misquotation of Scripture, giving generally the chapter and verse where it could be found." In the same passage Brooks states, but unfortunately without furnishing proof, that Mr. Lincoln "liked the Old Testament best." He adds that "whole chapters of Isaiah, the New Testament and the Psalms were fixed in his memory." Lincoln's familiarity with the Psalms may be taken in connection with Ruskin's acknowledgment of his indebtedness to that book in the formation of his style. Lincoln's love of the Bible and Shakspere suggests Sir Henry Irving's reply to a request that he furnish a list of what he regarded as the hundred best books: "Before a hundred books commend me first to the study of two, — the Bible and Shakespeare."

Daniel K. Dodge, *Abraham Lincoln: The Evolution of His Literary Style* (Urbana: U of Illinois P, 1900), 3–35.

"A Lincoln Memorial" (1907)

MARK TWAIN

Born Samuel Langhorne Clemens in northern Missouri, Mark Twain (1835–
1910) was the pen name of arguably the most famous American author,
worldwide, in our entire national literature. During his lifetime he became
famous as a platform lecturer and also as the author of numerous novels
and travelogues, including *Innocents Abroad, Life on the Mississippi, Adventures of Huckleberry Finn, A Connecticut Yankee in King Arthur's Court*, and
many others. Throughout his career he maintained a keen interest in politics
and issues of social justice, especially in his final decade, when he became
America's most prominent anti-imperialist. After the turn of the century,
Twain penned some of his most memorable political essays such as "To the
Person Sitting in Darkness," "Concerning the Jews," "My First Lie and How I
Got Out of It," "United States of Lyncherdom," "The War Prayer," and "King
Leopold's Soliloquy."

    In a gala celebration of Lincoln's birthday in 1901, Twain was a featured
speaker on the program at New York's Carnegie Hall. By now Twain had
come to appreciate not only Lincoln's genius, but the intriguing traits that
he and Lincoln shared. Both of them, for instance, were from border states,
and both agreed that God's will is not so easy to discern—and that some
humility in claiming to know it would be proper.[1] That night he stated, "The
hearts of this whole nation, North and South, were in the war. We of the
South were not ashamed of the part we took. We believed in those days we
were fighting for the right—and it was a noble fight, for we were fighting for
our sweethearts, our homes, and our lives. Today we no longer regret the
result, today we are glad that it came out as it did, but we of the South are
not ashamed that we made an endeavor. . . . The old wounds are healed, and
you of the North and we of the South are brothers yet. We consider it to be
an honor to be of the soldiers who fought for the Lost Cause, and now we
consider it a high privilege to be here tonight and assist in laying our humble
homage at the feet of Abraham Lincoln. And we do not forget that you of the
North and we of the South, one-time enemies, can now unite in singing that
great hymn, 'America.'"[2] The brief piece below is Twain's fervent plea that the
Lincoln birthplace be saved for the sake of posterity.

THERE IS A natural human instinct that is gratified by the sight of anything hallowed by association with a great man or with great deeds. So many people make pilgrimages to the town whose streets were once trodden by Shakespeare, and Hartford guarded her Charter Oak for centuries because it had once had a hole in it that helped to save the liberties of a Colony. But in most cases the connection between the great man or the great event and the relic we revere is accidental. Shakespeare might have lived in any other town as well as in Stratford, and Connecticut's charter might have been hidden in a woodchuck hole as well as in the Charter Oak. But it was no accident that planted Lincoln on a Kentucky farm, half way between the lakes and the Gulf. The association there had substance in it. Lincoln belonged just where he was put. If the Union was to be saved, it had to be a man of such an origin that should save it. No wintry New England Brahmin could have done it, or any torrid cotton planter, regarding the distant Yankee as a species of obnoxious foreigner. It needed a man of the border, where civil war meant the grapple of brother and brother and disunion a raw and gaping wound. It needed one who knew slavery not from books only, but as a living thing, knew the good that was mixed with its evil, and knew the evil not merely as it affected the negroes, but in its hardly less baneful influence upon the poor whites. It needed one who knew how human all the parties to the quarrel were, how much alike they were at bottom, who saw them all reflected in himself, and felt their dissensions like the tearing apart of his own soul. When the war came Georgia sent an army in gray and Massachusetts an army in blue, but Kentucky raised armies for both sides. And this man, sprung from Southern poor whites, born on a Kentucky farm and transplanted to an Illinois village, this man, in whose heart knowledge and charity had left no room for malice, was marked by Providence as the one to "bind up the Nation's wounds." His birthplace is worth saving.

Notes

1. Harold K. Bush, *Mark Twain and the Spiritual Crisis of His Age* (Tuscaloosa: U of Alabama P, 2007), 222–33.

2. "Blue and Gray Pay Tribute to Lincoln," *New York Times*, February 12, 1901.

Mark Twain, *New York Times*, January 13, 1907.

"Lincoln as an Orator" (1909)

William Jennings Bryan

William Jennings Bryan (1860–1925), accomplished orator, Democratic party leader, and frequent presidential nominee, first garnered national attention in Lincoln, Nebraska, where in 1890 he was elected to the U.S. House of Representatives. By the 1896 Democratic convention, Bryan's "Cross of Gold" speech made him a national star and ultimately gave him the presidential nomination. War with Spain in 1898 presented new political issues when Bryan sought the presidency a second time in 1900. Bryan's platform condemned imperialism, promised independence to the Philippines, attacked big business, and reaffirmed his support for silver. Twice defeated by William McKinley, Bryan nonetheless remained the party's most significant national voice, wielding a rare level of popular support and speaking frequently throughout the country on behalf of Democratic candidates. Bryan launched a third presidential campaign in 1908, losing once again, this time to William Howard Taft. Soon after the results were known, Bryan announced he would not seek another presidential nomination, and he kept his word.

But Bryan's sonorous voice continued to be an influential one in American mainstream culture, as this speech documents. On the one-hundredth birthday of its most famous resident, the citizens of Springfield, Illinois, held an all-day celebration to honor Lincoln. A keynote address for the day was provided, ironically enough, by one of America's most famous Democrats, William Jennings Bryan, the bête noire to Republican heavyweights and recent candidate for president. Bryan focused on Lincoln's "merits as a public speaker," his legendary concreteness and simplicity, not speaking "over the heads of his hearers"—and his frequent citations of the King James version of the Bible, on which Bryan himself was a notable expert.

LINCOLN'S FAME AS A statesman and as the Nation's Chief Executive during its most crucial period has so overshadowed his fame as an orator that his merits as a public speaker have not been sufficiently emphasized. When it is remembered that his nomination was directly due to the prominence which he won upon the stump; that in a remarkable series of debates he

held his own against one of the most brilliant orators America has produced; and that to his speeches, more than to the arguments of any other
one man, or, in fact, of all other public men combined, was due the success
of his party—when all these facts are borne in mind, it will appear plain,
even to the casual observer, that too little attention has been given to the
extraordinary power which he exercised as a speaker. That his nomination was due to the effect that his speeches produced, cannot be disputed.
When he began his fight against slavery in 1858, he was but little known
outside of the counties in which he attended court. It is true that he had
been a member of Congress some years before, but that time he was not
stirred by any great emotion connected with the discussion of any important theme, and he made but little impression upon national politics. The
threatened extension of slavery, however, aroused him, and with a cause
which justified his best efforts, he threw his whole soul into the fight. The
debates with Douglas have never had a parallel in this, or, so far as history
shows, in any other country.

In engaging in this contest with Douglas, he met a foeman worthy of his
steel, for Douglas had gained a deserved reputation as a great debater, and
recognized that his future depended upon the success with which he met
the attacks of Lincoln. On one side, an institution supported by history and
tradition; and on the other, a growing sentiment against the holding of a
human being in bondage—these presented a supreme issue. Douglas won
the senatorial seat for which the two at that time had contested, but Lincoln
won a larger victory—he helped to mold the sentiment that was dividing
parties and rearranging the political map of the country. When the debates
were concluded, every one recognized him as the leader of the cause which
he had espoused, and it was a recognition of this leadership which he had
secured through his public speeches that enabled him, a western man, to
be nominated over the eastern candidates—not only a western man, but
a man lacking in book learning and the polish of the schools. No other
American President has ever so clearly owed his elevation to his oratory.
Washington, Jefferson, and Jackson, the Presidents usually mentioned in
connection with him, were all poor speakers.

In analyzing Lincoln's characteristics as a speaker, one is impressed with
the completeness of his equipment. He possessed the two things that are
absolutely essential to effective speaking—namely, information and earnestness. If one can be called eloquent who knows what he is talking about

and means what he says — and I know of no better definition — Lincoln's speeches were eloquent. He was thoroughly informed upon the subject; he was prepared to meet his opponent upon the general proposition discussed, and upon any deductions which could be drawn from it. There was no un-explored field into which his adversary could lead him; he had carefully examined every foot of the ground, and was not afraid of pitfall or ambush, and what was equally important, he spoke from his own heart to the hearts of those who listened. While the printed page cannot fully reproduce the impressions made by a voice trembling with emotion or tender with pathos one cannot read the reports of the debates without feeling that Lincoln re-garded the subject as far transcending the ambitions of the personal inter-ests of the debaters. It was of little moment, he said, whether they voted him or Judge Douglas up or down, but it was tremendously important that the question should be decided rightly. His reputation may have suffered in the opinion of some, because he made them think so deeply upon what he said that they, for the moment, forgot him altogether, and yet, is this not the very perfection of speech? It is the purpose of the orator to persuade, and to do this he presents, not himself, but his subjects. Someone, in describ-ing the difference between Demosthenes and Cicero, said that "When Ci-cero spoke, people said, 'How well Cicero speaks'; but when Demosthenes spoke, they said, 'Let us go against Philip!'" In proportion as one can forget himself and become wholly absorbed in the cause which he is presenting does he measure up to the requirements of oratory.

In addition to the two essentials, Lincoln possessed what may be called the secondary aids to oratory. He was a master of statement. Few have equalled him in the ability to strip a truth of surplus verbiage and present it in its naked strength. In the Declaration of Independence we read that there are certain self-evident truths, which are therein enumerated. If I were go-ing to amend the proposition, I would say that all truth is self-evident. Not that any truth will be universally accepted, for not all are in a position or in an attitude to accept any given truth. In the interpretation of the parable of the sower, we are told that "the cares of this world and the deceitfulness of riches choke the truth," and it must be acknowledged that every truth has these or other difficulties to contend with [Matt. 13:22]. But a truth may be so clearly stated that it will commend itself to anyone who has not some special reason for rejecting it.

No one has more clearly stated the fundamental objections to slavery than Lincoln stated them, and he had a great advantage over his opponent in being able to state those objections frankly, for Judge Douglas neither denounced nor defended slavery as an institution—his plan embodied a compromise, and he could not discuss slavery upon its merits without alienating either the slave owner or the abolitionist.

"Brevity is the soul of wit," and a part of Lincoln's reputation for wit lies in his ability to condense a great deal into a few words. He was epigrammatic. A molder of thought is not necessarily an originator of the thought molded. Just as lead molded into the form of bullets has its effectiveness increased, so thought may have its propagating power enormously increased by being molded into a form that the eye catches and the memory holds. Lincoln was the spokesman of his party—he gave felicitous expression to the thoughts of his followers.

His Gettysburg speech is not surpassed, if equalled, in beauty, simplicity, force, and appropriateness by any speech of the same length of any language. It is the world's model of eloquence, elegance, and condensation. He might safely rest his reputation as an orator on that speech alone.

He was apt in illustration—no one more so. A simple story or simile drawn from everyday life flashed before his hearers the argument that he wanted to present. He did not speak over the heads of his hearers, and yet his language was never commonplace. There is strength in simplicity, and Lincoln's style was simplicity itself.

He understood the power of the interrogatory, for some of his most powerful arguments were condensed into questions. Of all those who discussed the evils of separation and the advantages to be derived from the preservation of the Union, no one ever put the matter more forcibly than Lincoln did when, referring to the possibility of war and the certainty of peace sometime, even if the Union was divided, he called attention to the fact that the same question would have to be dealt with, and then asked, "Can enemies [aliens] make treaties easier than friends can make laws?" [First Inaugural Address, Mar. 4, 1861].

He made frequent use of Bible language and of illustrations drawn from Holy Writ. It is said that when he was preparing his Springfield speech of 1858, he spent hours trying to find language that would express the idea that dominated his entire career—namely, that a republic could not permanently endure half free and half slave, and that finally a Bible passage flashed through his mind and he exclaimed, "I have found it! 'A house divided against itself cannot stand.'" And probably no other Bible passage ever exerted as much influence as this one in the settlement of a great controversy.

I have enumerated some, not all—but the more important—of his characteristics as an orator, and on this day I venture for the moment to turn the thoughts of this audience away from the great work that he accomplished as a patriot, away from his achievements in the line of statecraft, to the means employed by him to bring before the public the ideas which attracted attention to him. His power as a public speaker was the foundation of his success, and while it is obscured by the superstructure that was reared upon it, it cannot be entirely overlooked as the returning anniversary of his birth calls increasing attention to the widening influence of his work. With no military career to dazzle the eye or excite the imagination; with no public service to make his name familiar to the reading public, his elevation to the presidency would have been impossible without his oratory. The eloquency of Demosthenes and Cicero were no more necessary to their work, and Lincoln deserved to have his name written on the scroll with theirs.

William Jennings Bryan, *Speeches of William Jennings Bryan* (New York: Funk and Wagnalls, 1909), 2:419–25.

From "My Tribute to the Great Emancipator" (1909)

Booker T. Washington

On February 12, 1909, at the Republican Club in New York City, a black man was invited to deliver an address commemorating the one-hundred-year anniversary of the birth of Abraham Lincoln. That man was Booker T. Washington (1856–1915), born a slave in Virginia, son of a white man and a slave mother, and now the most prominent spokesperson of his race. Washington had risen to great prominence as founder and president of the Tuskegee Institute, and had written several popular volumes expressing his theory of racial uplift, including his best-selling autobiography *Up from Slavery* (1901). He was supported by many of America's most influential and wealthy benefactors, including John D. Rockefeller, Henry Rogers, and even Mark Twain, who sat in the audience at the presentation of this important lecture, in which an African American was given the honor of speaking to the legacy of the martyred president.

YOU ASK THAT WHICH he found a piece of property and turned into a free American citizen to speak to you tonight on Abraham Lincoln. I am not fitted by ancestry or training to be your teacher tonight for, as I have stated, I was born a slave.

My first knowledge of Abraham Lincoln came in this way: I was awakened early one morning before the dawn of day, as I lay wrapped in a bundle of rags on the dirt floor of our slave cabin, by the prayers of my mother, just before leaving for her day's work, as she was kneeling over my body earnestly praying that Abraham Lincoln might succeed, and that one day she and her boy might be free. You give me the opportunity here this evening to celebrate with you and the nation the answer to that prayer.

Says the Great Book somewhere, "Though a man die, yet shall he live" [John 11:25]. If this is true of the ordinary man, how much more true is it of the hero of the hour and the hero of the century—Abraham Lincoln! One hundred years of the life and influence of Lincoln is the story of the struggles, the trials, ambitions, and triumphs of the people of our complex American civilization. Interwoven into the warp and woof of this human complexity is the moving story of men and women of nearly every race and color in their progress from slavery to freedom, from poverty to wealth, from weakness to power, from ignorance to intelligence. Knit into the life of Abraham Lincoln is the story and success of the nation in the blending of all tongues, religions, colors, races into one composite nation, leaving each group and race free to live its own separate social life, and yet all a part of the great whole.

If a man die, shall he live? Answering this question as applied to our martyred President, perhaps you expect me to confine my words of appreciation to the great boon which, through him, was conferred upon my race. My undying gratitude and that of ten millions of my race for this and yet more! To have been the instrument used by Providence through which four millions of slaves, now grown into ten millions of free citizens, were made free would bring eternal fame within itself, but this is not the only claim that Lincoln has upon our sense of gratitude and appreciation.

By the side of [Samuel Chapman] Armstrong, and [William Lloyd] Garrison, Lincoln lives today. In the very highest sense he lives in the present more potently than fifty years ago; for that which is seen is temporal, that which is unseen is eternal. He lives in the 32,000 young men and women of the Negro race learning trades and useful occupations; in the 200,000 farms acquired by those he freed; in the more than 400,000 homes built; in the forty-six banks established and 10,000 stores owned; in the $550,000,000 worth of taxable property in hand; in the 28,000 public schools existing, with 30,000 teachers; in the 170 industrial schools and colleges; in the 23,000 ministers and 26,000 churches.

But, above all this, he lives in the steady and unalterable determination of ten millions of black citizens to continue to climb year by year the ladder of the highest usefulness and to perfect themselves in strong, robust character. For making all this possible, Lincoln lives.

But, again, for a higher reason he lives tonight in every corner of the republic. To set the physical man free is much. To set the spiritual man free is more. So often the keeper is on the inside of the prison bars and the prisoner on the outside.

As an individual, grateful as I am to Lincoln for freedom of body, my gratitude is still greater for freedom of soul—the liberty which permits one to live up in that atmosphere where he refuses to permit sectional or racial hatred to drag down, to warp and narrow his soul.

The signing of the Emancipation Proclamation was a great event, and yet it was but the symbol of another, still greater and more momentous. We who celebrate this anniversary should not forget that the same pen that gave freedom to four millions of African slaves at the same time struck the shackles from the souls of twenty-seven millions of Americans of another color.

In any country, regardless of what its laws say, wherever people act upon the idea that the disadvantage of one man is the good of another, there slavery exists. Wherever in any country the whole people feel that the happiness of all is dependent upon the happiness of the weakest, there freedom exists.

In abolishing slavery, Lincoln proclaimed the principle that, even in the case of the humblest and weakest of mankind, the welfare of each is still the good of all. In reestablishing in this country the principle that, at bottom, the interests of humanity and of the individual are one, he freed men's souls from spiritual bondage; he freed them to mutual helpfulness. Henceforth no man of any race, either in the North or in the South, need feel constrained to fear or hate his brother.

By the same token that Lincoln made America free, he pushed back the boundaries of freedom everywhere, gave the spirit of liberty a wider influence throughout the world, and reestablished the dignity of man as man.

By the same act that freed my race, he said to the civilized and uncivilized world that man everywhere must be free, and that man everywhere must be enlightened, and the Lincoln spirit of freedom and fair play will never cease to spread and grow in power till throughout the world all men shall know the truth, and the truth shall make them free.

Lincoln in his day was wise enough to recognize that which is true in the present and for all time: that in a state of slavery and ignorance man renders the lowest and most costly form of service to his fellows. In a state of freedom and enlightenment he renders the highest and most helpful form of service.

The world is fast learning that of all forms of slavery there is none that is so harmful and degrading as that form of slavery which tempts one human being to hate another by reason of his race or color. One man cannot hold another man down in the ditch without remaining down in the ditch with him. One who goes through life with his eyes closed against all that is good in another race is weakened and circumscribed, as one who fights in a battle with one hand tied behind him. Lincoln was in the truest sense great because he unfettered himself. He climbed up out of the valley, where his vision was narrowed and weakened by the fog and miasma, onto the mountain top, where in a pure and unclouded atmosphere he could see the truth which enabled him to rate all men at their true worth. Growing out of this anniversary season and atmosphere, may there crystallize a resolve throughout the nation that on such a mountain the American people will strive to live.

We owe, then, to Lincoln physical freedom, moral freedom, and yet this is not all. There is a debt of gratitude which we as individuals, no matter of what race or nation, must recognize as due Abraham Lincoln — not for what he did as chief executive of the nation, but for what he did as a man. In his rise from the most abject poverty and ignorance to a position of high usefulness and power, he taught the world one of the greatest of all lessons. In fighting his own battle up from obscurity and squalor, he fought the battle of every other individual and race that is down, and so helped to pull up every other human who was down. People so often forget that by every inch that the lowest man crawls up he makes it easier for every other man to get up. Today, throughout the world, because Lincoln lived, struggled, and triumphed, every boy who is ignorant, is in poverty, is despised or discouraged, holds his head a little higher. His heart beats a little faster, his ambition to do something and be something is a little stronger, because Lincoln blazed the way.

To my race, the life of Abraham Lincoln has its special lesson at this point in our career. In so far as his life emphasizes patience, long suffering, sincerity, naturalness, dogged determination, and courage — courage to avoid the superficial, courage to persistently seek the substance instead of the shadow — it points the road for my people to travel.

As a race we are learning, I believe, in an increasing degree that the best way for us to honor the memory of our Emancipator is by seeking to imitate him. . . .

Lincoln also was a Southern man by birth, but he was one of those white men, of whom there is a large and growing class, who resented the idea that in order to assert and maintain the superiority of the Anglo-Saxon race it was necessary that another group of humanity should be kept in ignorance.

Lincoln was not afraid or ashamed to come into contact with the lowly of all races. His reputation and social position were not of such a transitory and transparent kind that he was afraid that he would lose them by being just and kind, even to a man of dark skin. I always pity from the bottom of my heart any man who feels that somebody else must be kept down or in ignorance in order that he may appear great by comparison. It requires no courage for a strong man to kick a weak one down.

Lincoln lives today because he had the courage which made him refuse to hate the man at the South or the man at the North when they did not agree with him. He had the courage as well as the patience and foresight to suffer in silence, to be misunderstood, to be abused, to refuse to revile when reviled. For he knew that, if he was right, the ridicule of today would be the applause of tomorrow. He knew, too, that at some time in the distant future our nation would repent of the folly of cursing our public servants while they live and blessing them only when they die. In this connection I cannot refrain from suggesting the question to the millions of voices raised today in his praise: "Why did you not say it yesterday?" Yesterday, when one word of approval and gratitude would have meant so much to him in strengthening his hand and heart.

As we recall tonight his deeds and words, we can do so with grateful hearts and strong faith in the future for the spread of righteousness. The civilization of the world is going forward, not backward. Here and there for a little season the progress of mankind may seem to halt or tarry by the wayside, or even appear to slide backward, but the trend is ever onward and upward, and will be until someone can invent and enforce a law to stop the progress of civilization. In goodness and liberality the world moves forward. It goes forward beneficently, but it moves forward relentlessly. In the last analysis the forces of nature are behind the moral progress of the world, and these forces will crush into powder any group of humanity that resists this progress.

As we gather here, brothers all, in common joy and thanksgiving for the life of Lincoln, may I not ask that you, the worthy representatives of seventy millions of white Americans, join heart and hand with the ten millions of black Americans — these ten millions who speak your tongue, profess your religion—who have never lifted their voices or hands except in defense of their country's honor and their country's flag—and swear eternal fealty to the memory and the traditions of the sainted Lincoln? I repeat, may we not join with your race, and let all of us here highly resolve that justice, good will, and peace shall be the motto of our lives? If this be true, in the highest sense Lincoln shall not have lived and died in vain. . . .

Ernest Davidson Washington, ed., *Selected Speeches of Booker T. Washington* (Garden City, NY: Doubleday, 1932), 190–99.

"The Supreme Vision of Abraham Lincoln" (1909)

Theodore Roosevelt

Theodore Roosevelt (1858–1919), twenty-sixth president of the United States, was frail, asthmatic, and nearsighted when he entered Harvard College in 1876, but before long he had became a competent horseman, boxer, and marksman. He entered New York state politics as an assemblyman for three years, beginning in 1881. His wife's death in 1884 forced him into a kind of voluntary exile in the Badlands of the Dakota Territory, where he became a passionate hunter and ardent advocate of what he later famously termed the "strenuous life" of the outdoorsman.

The advent of the Spanish-American War in the late 1890s, which Roosevelt passionately supported, changed his political fortunes forever, as he put together the First U.S. Volunteer Cavalry, dubbed the "Rough Riders." In a fierce battle for Kettle Hill (commonly misremembered as San Juan Hill), Roosevelt and his "Rough Riders" rode into popular American history with a victory over the Spanish. Not long after leaving the cavalry, Roosevelt was elected in 1898 the Republican governor of New York, and two years later became the nominee for vice president, winning election in a Republican landslide. He became president on 14 September 1901, the day after William McKinley died of an assassin's bullet, and just a month shy of his forty-third birthday, making him the youngest chief executive in the nation's history. He served as president nearly eight years, deciding that he would not run for re-election in 1908. Although we remember him mainly as commander in chief during some difficult times (and winner of the Nobel Peace Prize in 1906 for negotiating a peace between Russia and Japan), he also became an accomplished man of letters, producing an amazing number of books and published essays and articles that far exceeds the output of any other president.

In this speech commemorative of the centenary celebration of Lincoln's birth, Roosevelt's invocation of the Lincoln image included an appeal for reconciliation at a time when national unity was still a work in progress. Given in Kentucky, where divisions still lingered, Roosevelt reminded his Southern listeners that Lincoln "saw clearly that the same high qualities, the same courage, and willingness for self-sacrifice, and devotion to the right . . . belonged both to the men of the North and to the men of the South." Roosevelt brought his memorial speech to an exhilarating conclusion, calling Lincoln "the mightiest of the mighty men who mastered the mighty days." His account was sincere and moving, certainly capturing as well as anyone the heart of what most Americans thought of the slain leader at the time. As the editor of *Harper's Weekly* opined of Roosevelt's remarks: "So many speeches were made on the one hundredth anniversary of Lincoln's birthday that few found their way into print, but of those we have read that of President Roosevelt was incomparably the best . . . and will, in our judgment, stand out as the most satisfying effort Mr. Roosevelt has yet made."[1]

WE HAVE MET HERE to celebrate the hundredth anniversary of the birth of one of the two greatest Americans; of one of the two or three greatest men of the nineteenth century; of one of the greatest men in the world's history. This rail-splitter, this boy who passed his ungainly youth in the dire poverty of the poorest of the frontier folk, whose rise was by weary and painful labor, lived to lead his people through the burning flames of a struggle from which the nation emerged, purified as by fire, born anew to a loftier life. After long years of iron effort, and of failure that came more often than victory, he at last rose to the leadership of the Republic, at the moment when that leadership had become the stupendous world-task of the time. He grew to know greatness, but never ease. Success came to him, but never happiness, save that which springs from doing well a painful and a vital task. Power was his, but not pleasure. The furrows deepened on his brow, but his eyes were undimmed by either hate or fear. His gaunt shoulders were bowed, but his steel thews never faltered as he bore for a burden the destinies of his people. His great and tender heart shrank from giving pain; and the task allotted him was to pour out like water the life-blood of the young men, and to feel in his every fibre the sorrow of the women. Disaster saddened but never dismayed him. As the red years of war went by they found him ever doing his duty in the present, ever facing the future with fearless front, high of heart, and dauntless of soul. Unbroken by hatred, unshaken by scorn, he worked and suffered for the people. Triumph was his at the last; and barely had he tasted it before murder found him, and the kindly, patient, fearless eyes were closed forever.

As a people we are indeed beyond measure fortunate in the characters of the two greatest of our public men, Washington and Lincoln. Widely though they differed in externals, the Virginia landed gentleman and the Kentucky backwoodsman, they were alike in essentials, they were alike in the great qualities which made each able to render service to his nation and to all mankind such as no other man of his generation could or did render. Each had lofty ideals, but each in striving to attain these lofty ideals was guided by the soundest common sense. Each possessed inflexible courage in adversity, and a soul wholly unspoiled by prosperity. Each possessed all the gentler virtues commonly exhibited by good men who lack rugged strength of character. Each possessed also all the strong qualities commonly exhibited by those towering masters of mankind who have too often shown themselves devoid of so much as the understanding of the words by which we signify the qualities of duty, of mercy, of devotion to the right, of lofty disinterestedness in battling for the good of others. There have been other men as great and other men as good; but in all the history of mankind there are no other two great men as good as these, no other two good men as great. Widely though the problems of to-day differ from the problems set for solution to Washington when he founded this nation, to Lincoln when he saved it and freed the slaves, yet the qualities they showed in meeting these problems are exactly the same as those we should show in doing our work to-day.

Lincoln saw into the future with the prophetic imagination usually vouchsafed only to the poet and the seer. He had in him all the lift toward greatness of the visionary, without any of the visionary's fanaticism or egotism, without any of the visionary's narrow jealousy of the practical man and inability to strive in practical fashion for the realization of an ideal. He had the practical man's hard common sense and willingness to adapt means to ends; but there was in him none of that morbid growth of mind and soul which blinds so many practical men to the higher things of life. No more practical man ever lived than this homely backwoods idealist; but he had nothing in common with those practical men whose consciences are warped until they fail to distinguish between good and evil, fail to understand that strength, ability, shrewdness, whether in the world of business or of politics, only serve to make their possessor a more noxious, a more evil member of the community, if they are not guided and controlled by a fine and high moral sense.

We of this day must try to solve many social and industrial problems, requiring to an especial degree the combination of indomitable resolution with cool-headed sanity. We can profit by the way in which Lincoln used both these traits as he strove for reform. We can learn much of value from the very attacks which following that course brought upon his head, attacks alike by the extremists of revolution and by the extremists of reaction. He never wavered in devotion to his principles, in his love for the Union, and in his abhorrence of slavery. Timid and lukewarm people were always denouncing him because he was too extreme; but as a matter of fact he never went to extremes, he worked step by step; and because of this the extremists hated and denounced him with a fervor which now seems to us fantastic in its deification of the unreal and the impossible. At the very time when one side was holding him up as the apostle of social revolution because he was against slavery, the leading abolitionist denounced him as the "slave hound of Illinois." When he was the second time candidate for President, the majority of his opponents attacked him because of what they termed his extreme radicalism, while a minority threatened to bolt his nomination because he was not radical enough. He had continually to check those who wished to go forward too fast, at the very time that he overrode the opposition of those who wished not to go forward at all. The goal was never dim before his vision; but he picked his way cautiously, without either halt or hurry, as he strode toward it, through such a morass of difficulty that no man of less courage would have attempted it, while it would surely have overwhelmed any man of judgment less serene.

Yet perhaps the most wonderful thing of all, and, from the standpoint of the America of to-day and of the future, the most vitally important, was the extraordinary way in which Lincoln could fight valiantly against what he deemed wrong and yet preserve undiminished his love and respect for the brother from whom he differed. In the hour of a triumph that would have turned any weaker man's head, in the heat of a struggle which spurred many a good man to dreadful vindictiveness, he said truthfully that so long as he had been in his office he had never willingly planted a thorn in any man's bosom, and besought his supporters to study the incidents of the trial through which they were passing as philosophy from which to learn wisdom and not as wrongs to be avenged; ending with the solemn exhortation that, as the strife was over, all should reunite in a common effort to save their common country.

He lived in days that were great and terrible, when brother fought against brother for what each sincerely deemed to be the right. In a contest so grim the strong men who alone can carry it through are rarely able to do justice to the deep convictions of those with whom they grapple in moral strife. At such times men see through a glass darkly; to only the rarest and loftiest spirits is vouchsafed that clear vision which gradually comes to all, even to the lesser, as the struggle fades into distance, and wounds are forgotten, and peace creeps back to the hearts that were hurt. But to Lincoln was given this supreme vision. He did not hate the man from whom he differed. Weakness was as foreign as wickedness to his strong, gentle nature; but his courage was of a quality so high that it needed no bolstering of dark passion. He saw clearly that the same high qualities, the same courage, and willingness for self-sacrifice, and devotion to the right as it was given them to see the right, belonged both to the men of the North and to the men of the South. As the years roll by, and as all of us, wherever we dwell, grow to feel an equal pride in the valor and self-devotion, alike of the men who wore the blue and the men who wore the gray, so this whole nation will grow to feel a peculiar sense of pride in the man whose blood was shed for the union of his people and for the freedom of a race; the lover of his country and of all mankind; the mightiest of the mighty men who mastered the mighty days: Abraham Lincoln.

Note

1. Quoted in Braden, *Building the Myth*, 162.

Waldo Braden, ed., *Building the Myth: Selected Speeches Memorializing Abraham Lincoln* (Urbana: U of Illinois P, 1990), 164–67.

From "Abraham Lincoln: An Appreciation" (1913)

CHARLES CHESNUTT

One of the great African American writers of his time, Charles Chesnutt (1858–1932) was born in Ohio to parents who were both freed slaves, his father being the son of a white slavemaster. His books, including *The House Behind the Cedars* (1900) and *The Marrow of Tradition* (1901), are now recognized as among the most important African American novels prior to World War I. After 1901 he became involved with racial reform movements spearheaded by the likes of Booker T. Washington and W. E. B. DuBois, and he emerged as a prophetic voice whose musings on the legacy of Lincoln were among the most important at the beginning of the twentieth century. Chesnutt's rhetorical flourishes would be echoed later in works by DuBois and Martin Luther King Jr., assuring that an African American voice on the meaning of Lincoln would survive Jim Crow and continue to influence the nation into the civil rights era.

One of Chesnutt's enduring themes was his cagey recognition of Lincoln as Southerner: "Though Lincoln hated slavery, combatted its extension at every point, and ultimately destroyed it, he never hated the South or Southerners. He was of their blood; he had been brought up in a State largely settled by them." Chesnutt's fixation on matters of race and social justice in his fiction fits well with one critic's description of the literary period in general as marked by a "humanitarian realism" out to "affect the public mind . . . in relation to Human Rights."[1] In this excerpt, Chesnutt laments the ignoring of questions of race in the centennial celebrations of Lincoln's birth in 1909, a phenomenon related to what David Blight has called the nation's preference for themes of reunion between North and South as opposed to racial reconciliation.[2] Writers like Booker T. Washington and Chesnutt insisted that the nation not forget Lincoln's hatred of slavery, nor his powerful desire for racial rapprochement and equality as the most significant outcomes of the Civil War.

THE GREATEST ACHIEVEMENT of Lincoln was the abolition of slavery. In the modern era of harmony and good feeling, as the result of which no painting of a Civil War battle is allowed in the National Capitol, this service of Lincoln for humanity has been minimized and sometimes slurred. It was pitiable how little was said, in the late Lincoln Centennial celebration, about Lincoln the Emancipator. Perhaps this was inevitable, because to give emancipation its proper importance it would be necessary to properly characterize slavery, and to do this would, by implication, to criticize the slave-holder, and in our time this is not considered good taste. So warm has become the *rapprochement* between North and South, that slavery is almost regarded in some quarters as a beneficent patriarchal institution, which *Uncle Tom's Cabin* grossly slandered, and which, but for its influence on free labor, it might have been well to perpetuate indefinitely. It is conceivable that the people of the United States might have been well governed if divided into two nations. An equal expanse of territory in Europe, with a proportional aggregate of population, is divided into many nations and governments. The New England abolitionists advocated, academically, the reformation of the North & South. They preferred to live in a free country, if one only half as large; just as the secessionists preferred a wholly slave country to one which was partly free. The white people of the Confederacy, had it succeeded in establishing itself, would doubtless have been governed to their own liking, which is always the best form of government, or at least the most satisfactory to the governed, and the slaves would have been at least no worse off than they were before. But by suppressing the rebellion Lincoln not only preserved the Union for all its white inhabitants, but admitted its black inhabitants to the blessings of freedom and citizenship.

It is a common thing to hear it said that Lincoln freed the slaves purely as a war measure, to embarrass and cripple the enemy. And there were not wanting ardent abolitionists, Seward and Sumner and others, who found the President unduly cautious and fearful. But Lincoln was working toward a tremendous goal. We all know his feelings toward this twin relic of barbarism; how he himself related that having witnessed on one occasion a slave auction in New Orleans, he made up his mind that God helping him, if he ever had an opportunity he would scotch that snake. We know how, in his earlier professional days he had defended runaway slaves and unfortunate Negroes who had got into difficulties from one cause or another. But he was president of the entire nation. He had sworn to support the Constitution and laws of the United States. The Constitution and laws of the United States recognized and had fostered slavery. Slavery and slavocracy had dominated the politics and statesmanship of the Union for a generation. The United States might almost be said to have rested on slavery, which Robert Toombs declares to be the cornerstone of the Confederacy. Many of the slaveholders in the border states were loyal men who had supported and fought for the Union. Lincoln wanted to destroy slavery, he welcomed the military necessity which made it possible for him to do so; but he wanted to do it lawfully, and in a manner which would respect the rights of the loyal slave-holders and disarm criticism among the fair minded. Hence his preliminary proclamation, warning the seceding states of what they must expect unless they laid down their arms. But when the crucial moment came, Lincoln affixed his signature to the Emancipation Proclamation, the world held its breath for a moment, and then liberty-loving people all over the globe raised their voices in acclamation, while the Southern Confederacy, with its foundation stone removed, toppled to its fall. This demanded a high order of courage. For Charles Sumner or William H. Seward to have abolished slavery would have been by no means so great an act. Sumner was a New Englander, trained in traditions of liberty and human equality. Negroes had always been citizens in Massachusetts, had always had the right to vote, when properly qualified. Seward was also of Northern abolition blood and training. But Lincoln, it must be remembered was of Southern birth, born in Kentucky, reared in Southern Illinois, which was settled by Southerners and within the sweep of Southern sentiment and Southern prejudice. It is something like a Northern and a Southern white man eating at the same table with a Negro. To one it is a simple matter, other things being equal he would have no objection to dining at the same board with any man, if he were clean, well dressed and well behaved. To the other it is a tremendous thing, almost like a convulsion of nature, so tremendous an event that when a president of the United States invited a distinguished mulatto to lunch with him, it seemed as though it might almost precipitate a second rebellion. Not that Lincoln shared this feeling, but if he had at any time, he undoubtedly felt that freedom carried with it certain privileges, for, after the emancipation, as Frederick Douglass relates in his *Life and Times*, Lincoln invited that distinguished orator to dinner on one occasion, and Mr. Douglass, as he also said, never ceased to regret that he permitted a previous speaking engagement to deprive him of that pleasure and that wonderful opportunity. But for a man of Lincoln's antecedents, the Emancipation Proclamation was a tremendous achievement.

But apart from what he accomplished for the nation and for humanity, I think the world loves Lincoln best for his personality. Not that he was particularly pleasing to look at; he was tall, ungainly, homely in his appearance, especially in the hideous garb which gentlemen wore in the sixties. But in the lines of his rugged countenance may be read the index of a great soul, a soul attuned to the love of humanity in whatever form.

He loved the poor man, for he himself had been born and brought up for many years as that despised creature, in the Southern states a poor white man. His family was quite obscure, and his enemies even claimed that his birth was irregular, but this is historically disproved. . . .

Notes

1. Augusta Rohrbach, *Truth Stranger than Fiction: Race, Realism, and the U.S. Literary Marketplace* (New York: Palgrave, 2002), xiv–xv.

2. David W. Blight, *Race and Reunion: The Civil War in American Memory* (Cambridge, MA: Belknap Press of Harvard UP, 2001).

Charles W. Chesnutt, "Abraham Lincoln: An Appreciation," in *Essays and Speeches*, ed. Joseph R. McElrath Jr., Robert C. Leitz III, and Jesse S. Crisler (Stanford: Stanford UP, 1999): 349–52.

Selected Bibliography

Albanese, Catherine L. *Sons of the Fathers: The Civil Religion of the American Revolution*. Philadelphia: Temple UP, 1976. Print.

Angle, Paul M., ed. *The Lincoln Reader*. 1947. New York: Da Capo, 1990. Print.

Bacevich, Andrew J. *American Empire: The Realities and Consequences of U.S. Diplomacy*. Cambridge, MA: Harvard UP, 2002. Print.

Basler, Roy P., ed. *The Collected Works of Abraham Lincoln*. 8 vols. New Brunswick, NJ: Rutgers UP, 1953. Print.

——, and Christian Basler, eds. *The Collected Works of Abraham Lincoln. Second Supplement, 1845-1865*. New Brunswick, NJ: Rutgers UP, 1990. Print.

Becker, Carl. *The Declaration of Independence: A Study in the History of Political Ideas*. New York: Vintage, 1958. Print.

Beecher, Henry Ward. *Patriotic Addresses in America and England, from 1850 to 1885*. New York: Fords, Howard, and Hulbert, 1887. Print.

Belasco, Susan, ed. *Stowe in Her Own Time: A Biographical Chronicle of His Life Drawn from Recollections, Interviews, and Memoirs by Family, Friends, and Associates*. Iowa City: U of Iowa P, 2009. Print.

Bellah, Robert N. "Civil Religion in America." *Daedalus* 96.1 (1967): 1–21. Print.

Benner, Martha L., and Cullom Davis, eds. *The Law Practice of Abraham Lincoln: The Complete Documentary Edition*. Ver. 1.0.5. Urbana: U of Illinois P, 2000. CD-ROM.

Bennett, Lerone, Jr. *Forced into Glory: Abraham Lincoln's White Dream*. Chicago: Johnson, 2000. Print.

Bercovitch, Sacvan. *American Jeremiad*. Madison: U of Wisconsin P, 1978. Print.

Beveridge, Albert J. *Abraham Lincoln, 1809-1858*. 2 vols. Boston: Houghton Mifflin, 1928. Print.

Blight, David W. *Race and Reunion: The Civil War in American Memory*. Cambridge, MA: Belknap Press of Harvard UP, 2001. Print.

Bloch, Ruth. *Visionary Republic*. Cambridge: Cambridge UP, 1985. Print.

"Blue and Gray Pay Tribute to Lincoln." *New York Times*, February 12, 1901, 1.

Boritt, Gabor. *The Gettysburg Gospel: The Lincoln Speech That Nobody Knows*. New York: Simon and Schuster, 2006. Print.

Braden, Waldo. *Abraham Lincoln: Public Speaker*. Baton Rouge: Louisiana State UP, 1988. Print.

———, ed. *Building the Myth: Selected Speeches Memorializing Abraham Lincoln*. Urbana: U of Illinois P, 1990. Print.

Braude, Ann. *Radical Spirits: Spiritualism and Women's Rights in Nineteenth-Century America*. Boston: Beacon, 1989. Print.

Bray, Robert. "What Abraham Lincoln Read—An Evaluative and Annotated List." *Journal of the Abraham Lincoln Association* 28.2 (Summer 2007): 28–81. Print.

Brooks, Noah. "Lincoln's Imagination." *Scribner's Monthly*, August 1879, 584–87.

Brooks, Philips. *Addresses*. Boston: C. E. Brown, 1893. Print.

Bryan, William Jennings. *Speeches of William Jennings Bryan*. Vol. 2. New York: Funk and Wagnalls, 1909. Print.

Burlingame, Michael. *Abraham Lincoln: A Life*. Baltimore: Johns Hopkins UP, 2008. Print.

———. *The Inner World of Abraham Lincoln*. Urbana: U of Illinois P, 1994. Print.

———. *An Oral History of Abraham Lincoln: John G. Nicolay's Interviews and Essays*. Carbondale: Southern Illinois UP, 1996. Print.

———. "The Trouble with the Bixby Letter." *American Heritage* 50.4 (1999): 64–67. Print.

———, ed. *With Lincoln in the White House: Letters, Memoranda, and Other Writings of John G. Nicolay*. Carbondale: Southern Illinois UP, 2000. Print.

———, and John R. Turner Ettlinger, eds. *Inside Lincoln's White House: The Complete Civil War Diary of John Hay*. Carbondale: Southern Illinois UP, 1997. Print.

Bush, Harold K. *American Declarations: Rebellion and Repentance in American Cultural History*. Urbana: U of Illinois P, 1999. Print.

———. *Mark Twain and the Spiritual Crisis of His Age*. Tuscaloosa: U of Alabama P, 2007. Print.

———, and Joe Webb. "'Transfigured by Oratory': Thomas Paine, Robert Ingersoll, Mark Twain, and the Roots of American Civil Religion." *The Mark Twain Annual* 7.1 (2009): 79–101. Print.

Carpenter, Francis B. *The Inner Life of Abraham Lincoln: Six Months at the White House.* New York: Hurd and Houghton, 1867. Print.

Carr, Clark E. *Lincoln at Gettysburg: An Address.* Chicago: A. C. McClure, 1906. Print.

Carwardine, Richard. *Lincoln: A Life of Purpose and Power.* New York: Knopf, 2008. Print.

Chapman, Ervin, ed. *Latest Light on Abraham Lincoln and War-Time Memories.* New York: Fleming H. Revell, 1917. Print.

Chesnutt, Charles W. *Essays and Speeches.* Ed. Joseph R. McElrath Jr., Robert C. Leitz, III, and Jesse S. Crisler. Stanford: Stanford UP, 1999. Print.

Concerning Mr. Lincoln. Compiled by Harry Pratt. Springfield, IL: Abraham Lincoln Association, 1944. Print.

Cox, Lawanda. *Lincoln and Black Freedom.* Columbia: U of South Carolina P, 1981. Print.

Current, Richard N. *The Lincoln Nobody Knows.* 1958. New York: Hill and Wang, 1963. Print.

——, ed. *The Political Thought of Abraham Lincoln.* Indianapolis: Bobbs-Merrill, 1967. Print.

Davis, Cullom, ed. *The Public and the Private Lincoln: Contemporary Perspectives.* Carbondale: Southern Illinois UP, 1979. Print.

Delbanco, Andrew. *The Real American Dream: A Meditation on Hope.* Cambridge, MA: Harvard UP, 1999. Print.

Dennett, Tyler, ed. *Lincoln and the Civil War in the Diaries and Letters of John Hay.* New York: Dodd, Mead, 1939. Print.

Depew, Chauncey M. *My Memories of Eighty Years.* New York: Scribner's, 1922. Print.

Dicey, Edward. "Nathaniel Hawthorne." *Hawthorne in His Own Time: A Biographical Chronicle of His Life, Drawn from Recollections, Interviews, and Memoirs by Family, Friends, and Associates.* Ed. Ronald A. Bosco and Jillmarie Murphy. Iowa City: U of Iowa P, 2007. 115–23. Print.

Diggins, John P. *On Hallowed Ground: Abraham Lincoln and the Foundations of American History.* New Haven: Yale UP, 2000. Print.

DiLorenzo, Thomas J. *Lincoln Unmasked: What You're Not Supposed to Know about Dishonest Abe.* New York: Three Rivers, 2006. Print.

——. *The Real Lincoln: A New Look at Abraham Lincoln, His Agenda, and an Unnecessary War.* New York: Three Rivers, 2003. Print.

Dodge, Daniel K. *Abraham Lincoln: The Evolution of His Literary Style.* Urbana: U of Illinois P, 1900. Print.

Donald, David Herbert. *Lincoln.* New York: Simon & Schuster, 1995. Print.

———. *Lincoln's Herndon: A Biography*. 1948. New York: Da Capo, 1988. Print.

———. *"We Are Lincoln Men": Abraham Lincoln and His Friends*. New York: Simon and Schuster, 2003. Print.

Emerson, Ralph Waldo. *Complete Works. Vol. 11, Miscellanies*. Cambridge, MA: Riverside, 1883. Print.

Epstein, Daniel Mark. *Lincoln and Whitman: Parallel Lives in Civil War Washington*. New York: Ballantine, 2004. Print.

Fehrenbacher, Don E., ed. *Abraham Lincoln, 1832–1858: Speeches, Letters, and Miscellaneous Writings, the Lincoln-Douglas Debates*. New York: Library of America, 1989. Print.

———, ed. *Abraham Lincoln: Speeches and Writings, 1859–1865*. New York: Library of America, 1989. Print.

———. *The Changing Image of Lincoln in American Historiography*. Oxford: Clarendon, 1968. Print.

———, ed. *Lincoln in Text and Context: Collected Essays*. Stanford: Stanford UP, 1987. Print.

———. *Prelude to Greatness: Lincoln in the 1850's*. Stanford: Stanford UP, 1962. Print.

———, and Virginia Fehrenbacher, eds. *Recollected Words of Abraham Lincoln*. Stanford: Stanford UP, 1996. Print.

Feiler, Bruce. *America's Prophet: Moses and the American Story*. New York: Morrow, 2009. Print.

Fields, James T. "Our Whispering Gallery." *Hawthorne in His Own Time: A Biographical Chronicle of His Life, Drawn from Recollections, Interviews, and Memoirs by Family, Friends, and Associates*. Ed. Ronald A. Bosco and Jillmarie Murphy. Iowa City: U of Iowa P, 2007. 130–50. Print.

Fornieri, Joseph R. *Abraham Lincoln's Political Faith*. DeKalb: Northern Illinois UP, 2003. Print.

Franklin, John Hope. "The Use and Misuse of the Lincoln Legacy." *Chicago Tribune*, February 12, 1930, 32–33. Print.

Freehling, William W. *The Road to Disunion: Volume Two: Secessionists Triumphant 1854–1861*. Oxford: Oxford UP, 2007.

Gilmore, Michael T. *The War on Words: Slavery, Race, and Free Speech in American Literature*. Chicago: U of Chicago P, 2010. Print.

Goodwin, Doris Kearns. *Team of Rivals: The Political Genius of Abraham Lincoln*. New York: Simon and Schuster, 2005. Print.

Guelzo, Allen C. *Abraham Lincoln: Redeemer President*. Grand Rapids: Eerdmans, 2003. Print.

Hardinge, Emma. *The Great Funeral Oration on Abraham Lincoln*. New York, n.p., 1865. Print.

Hatch, Nathan. *Sacred Cause of Liberty*. New Haven: Yale UP, 1977. Print.

Hawthorne, Nathaniel. "Chiefly about War Matters." *Tales, Sketches, and Other Papers*. Boston: Houghton Mifflin, 1883. 299–345. Print.

Herndon, William Henry. *Lincoln's Philosophy of Life*. Los Angeles: privately printed by H. E. Barker, 1933. Print.

———, and Jesse W. Weik. *Herndon's Life of Lincoln: The History and Personal Recollections of Abraham Lincoln as Originally Written by William H. Herndon and Jesse W. Weik*. Ed. Paul M. Angle. 1930. New York: Da Capo, 1983. Print.

———, and Jesse W. Weik. *Herndon's Lincoln: The True Story of a Great Life*. 3 vols. Chicago: Belford, Clarke, 1889. Print.

Hertz, Emanuel, ed. *The Hidden Lincoln: From the Letters and Papers of William H. Herndon*. New York: Viking, 1938. Print.

Holzer, Harold, ed. *"Dear Mr. Lincoln: Letters to the President*. Reading, MA: Addison-Wesley, 1993. Print.

———. "William Osborn Stoddard." *American National Biography Online* (October 2008). Web.

———, Gabor S. Boritt and Mark E. Neely, Jr. *The Lincoln Image: Abraham Lincoln and the Popular Print*. Urbana: U of Illinois P, 2001. Print.

Howells, William Dean. *The Life of Abraham Lincoln*. 1860. Bloomington: Indiana UP, 1960. Print.

———. *Life of Abraham Lincoln; This Campaign Biography Corrected by the Hand of Abraham Lincoln in the Summer of 1860 Is Reproduced Here with Careful Attention to the Appearance of the Original Volume*. Springfield, IL: Abraham Lincoln Association, 1938. Print.

Ingersoll, Robert G. *The Works of Robert G. Ingersoll*. 12 vols. New York: Farrell, 1900. Print.

Jehlen, Myra. *American Incarnation: The Individual, the Nation, and the Continent*. Cambridge, MA: Harvard UP, 1986. Print.

Johannsen, Robert W. *Lincoln, the South and Slavery: The Political Dimension*. Baton Rouge: Louisiana State UP, 1991. Print.

Jones, Howard. *Abraham Lincoln and a New Birth of Freedom: The Union and Slavery in the Diplomacy of the Civil War*. Lincoln: U of Nebraska P, 1999. Print.

Kaplan, Fred. *Lincoln: The Biography of a Writer*. New York: Harper, 2008. Print.

Keckley, Elizabeth. *Behind the Scenes; Or, Thirty Years a Slave, and Four Years in the White House*. New York: G. W. Carleton, 1868. Print.

Kunhardt, Philip B., Jr., Philip B. Kunhardt III, and Peter W. Kunhardt. *Lincoln: An Illustrated Biography*. New York: Knopf, 1992. Print.

Kunhardt, Philip B., III, Peter W. Kunhardt, and Philip B. Kunhardt, Jr. *Looking for Lincoln: The Making of an American Icon*. New York: Knopf, 2008. Print.

Lamon, Dorothy, ed. *Recollections of Abraham Lincoln: 1847–1865*. Chicago: A. C. McLure, 1895. Print.

Lamon, Ward Hill. *The Life of Abraham Lincoln: From His Birth to His Inauguration as President*. 1872. Lincoln: U of Nebraska P, 1999. Print.

Limerick, Patricia. *Legacy of Conquest: The Unbroken Past of the American West*. New York: Norton, 1988. Print.

Lincoln and Cultural Value: A Forum. Special issue of *American Literary History* 21.4 (2009). Print.

Lind, Michael. *What Lincoln Believed: The Values and Convictions of America's Greatest President*. New York: Doubleday, 2005. Print.

Logan, Stephen T. *Memorials of the Life and Character of Stephen T. Logan*. Springfield, IL: H. W. Rokker, 1882. Print.

Lowell, James Russell. *The Writings of James Russell Lowell*. Vol. 5, *Political Essays*. Cambridge, MA: Riverside Press, 1890. Print.

Lucas, Stephen E. "Justifying America: The Declaration of Independence as a Rhetorical Document." *American Rhetoric: Context and Criticism*. Ed. Thomas W. Benson. Carbondale: Southern Illinois UP, 1989. 67–103. Print.

Luthin, Reinhard H. *The Real Abraham Lincoln: A Complete One Volume History of His Life and Times*. Englewood Cliffs, NJ: Prentice-Hall, 1960. Print.

Maier, Pauline. *American Scripture: Making the Declaration of Independence*. New York: Knopf, 1997. Print.

McPherson, James M. *Abraham Lincoln and the Second American Revolution*. Oxford: Oxford UP, 1990. Print.

———. *Battle Cry of Freedom: The Civil War Era*. Oxford: Oxford UP, 1988. Print.

Mead, Sidney. *The Nation with the Soul of a Church*. New York: Harper and Row, 1975. Print.

Mearns, David C., ed. *The Lincoln Papers*. 2 vols. Garden City, NY: Doubleday, 1948. Print.

Miers, Earl S., ed. *Lincoln Day by Day: A Chronology, 1809–1865*. 3 vols. Washington, DC: Lincoln Sesquicentennial Commission, 1960. Print.

Miller, William Lee. *Lincoln's Virtues: An Ethical Biography*. New York: Vintage, 2003. Print.

Morel, Lucas E. *Lincoln's Sacred Effort: Defining Religion's Role in American Self-Government*. Lanham, MD: Lexington Books, 2000. Print.

Morris, Jan. *Lincoln: A Foreigner's Quest*. New York: Simon and Schuster, 2000. Print.

Neely, Mark E., Jr. *The Abraham Lincoln Encyclopedia*. New York: Da Capo, 1982. Print.

———. *The Last Best Hope of Earth: Abraham Lincoln and the Promise of America*. Cambridge, MA: Harvard UP, 1993. Print.

Nevins, Allan. *The Emergence of Lincoln*. New York: Scribner, 1950. Print.

Nicolay, John G., and John Hay. *Abraham Lincoln: A History*. 10 vols. 1890. New York: Century Company, 1917. Print.

———. *Abraham Lincoln: A History*. Ed. and abridged by Paul M. Angle. Chicago: U of Chicago P, 1966. Print.

Oakes, James. *The Radical and the Republican: Frederick Douglass, Abraham Lincoln, and the Triumph of Antislavery Politics*. New York: Norton, 2007. Print.

Oates, Stephen B. *With Malice toward None: A Life of Abraham Lincoln*. New York: Harper Perennial, 1994. Print.

Paludan, Phillip Shaw. *The Presidency of Abraham Lincoln*. Lawrence: UP of Kansas, 1994. Print.

Percoco, James A. *Summers with Lincoln: Looking for the Man in the Monuments*. New York: Fordham UP, 2008. Print.

Peterson, Merrill D. *Lincoln in American Memory*. Oxford: Oxford UP, 1994. Print.

Pinsker, Matthew. "Lincoln Theme 2.0." *Journal of American History* 96.2 (2009): 417–40. Print.

Potter, David M. *The Impending Crisis: 1848–1861*. New York: Harper and Row, 1976. Print.

Quarles, Benjamin. *Lincoln and the Negro*. 1962. New York: Da Capo, 1991. Print.

Randall, J. G. "Has the Lincoln Theme Been Exhausted?" *American Historical Review* 41.2 (1936): 270–94.

Randall, Ruth Painter. *Mary Lincoln: Biography of a Marriage*. Boston: Little, Brown, 1953. Print.

Reed, James A. "The Later Life and Religious Sentiments of Abraham Lincoln." *Scribner's Monthly*, July 1873, 333–43.

Rohrbach, Augusta. *Truth Stranger than Fiction: Race, Realism, and the U.S. Literary Marketplace*. New York: Palgrave, 2002. Print.

Sandburg, Carl. *Abraham Lincoln: The War Years*. 4 vols. New York: Harcourt, 1939. Print.

Schwartz, Barry. *Abraham Lincoln and the Forge of National Memory*. Chicago: U of Chicago P, 2000. Print.

———. "Lincoln at the Millennium." *Journal of the Abraham Lincoln Association* 24.1 (2003): 1–31. Print.

Schwartz, Thomas F., ed. *For a Vast Future Also: Essays from the Journal of the Abraham Lincoln Association.* New York: Fordham UP, 1999. Print.

Segal, Charles M., ed. *Conversations with Lincoln.* New York: G. P. Putnam's Sons, 1961. Print.

Shenk, Joshua Wolf. "Eureka Dept.: The Suicide Poem." *New Yorker,* June 14, 2004. Print.

———. *Lincoln's Melancholy: How Depression Challenged a President and Fueled His Greatness.* Boston: Houghton Mifflin, 2005. Print.

Sorenson, Theodore C. "Abraham Lincoln: A Man of His Words." *Smithsonian* 39.7 (October 2008): 96–102. Print.

Speed, Joshua F. *Reminiscences of Abraham Lincoln and Notes of a Visit to California: Two Lectures.* Louisville, KY: John P. Morton, 1884. Print.

Stauffer, John. *Giants: The Parallel Lives of Frederick Douglass and Abraham Lincoln.* New York: Twelve Books, 2008. Print.

Stewart, Charles J. "The Pulpit and the Assassination of Lincoln." *Quarterly Journal of Speech* 50.3 (1964): 299–307. Print.

Stoddard, William O. *Lincoln's Third Secretary: The Memoirs of William O. Stoddard.* New York: Exposition Press, 1955. Print.

Stowe, Harriet Beecher. "Abraham Lincoln." *The Living Age,* February 6, 1864, 282–84. Print.

Sundquist, Eric J. *Empire and Slavery in American Literature, 1820–1865.* Jackson: UP of Mississippi, 2006. Print.

Thomas, Benjamin. *Abraham Lincoln: A Biography.* 1952. New York: Modern Library, 1968. Print.

Thomas, Brook. "Thomas Dixon's *A Man of the People*: How Lincoln Saved the Union by Cracking Down on Civil Liberties." *Law and Literature* 20.1 (2008): 21–46. Print.

Thomas, Christopher. *The Lincoln Memorial and American Life.* Princeton: Princeton UP, 2002. Print.

Thomas, John L., ed. *Abraham Lincoln and the American Political Tradition.* Amherst: U of Massachusetts P, 1986. Print.

Turner, Justin G., and Linda Levitt Turner. *Mary Todd Lincoln: Her Life and Letters.* New York: Knopf, 1972. Print.

Tuveson, Ernest. *Redeemer Nation.* Chicago: U of Chicago P, 1968. Print.

Twichell, Joseph H. "Army Memories of Lincoln: A Chaplain's Reminiscences." *Congregationalist and Christian World,* January 30, 1913. Print.

Ward, William Hayes, ed. *Abraham Lincoln: Tributes from His Associates.* New York: Thomas Crowell, 1885. Print.

Washington, Ernest Davidson, ed. *Selected Speeches of Booker T. Washington.* Garden City, NY: Doubleday, 1932. Print.

Washington, John E., ed. *They Knew Lincoln.* New York: E. P. Dutton, 1942. Print.

Weik, Jesse W. *The Real Lincoln: A Portrait.* Boston: Houghton Mifflin, 1922. Print.

White, Ronald C., Jr. *Lincoln's Greatest Speech: The Second Inaugural.* New York: Simon and Schuster, 2002. Print.

Whitman, Walt. *Complete Prose Works.* Philadelphia: David McKay, 1892. Print.

———. *Notebooks and Unpublished Prose Manuscripts.* Ed. Edward F. Grier. New York: New York UP, 1984. Print.

Wills, Garry. *Head and Heart: American Christianities.* New York: Penguin, 2007. Print.

———. *Inventing America: Jefferson's Declaration of Independence.* Garden City, NY: Doubleday, 1978. Print.

———. *Lincoln at Gettysburg: The Words That Remade America.* New York: Simon and Schuster, 1992. Print.

———. "Lincoln's Greatest Speech?" *Atlantic Monthly,* September 1999, 60–70. Print.

Wilson, Douglas L. *Honor's Voice: The Transformation of Abraham Lincoln.* New York: Knopf, 1998. Print.

———. *Lincoln's Sword: The Presidency and the Power of Words.* New York: Knopf, 2006. Print.

———, and Rodney O. Davis, eds. *Herndon's Informants: Letters, Interviews, and Statements about Abraham Lincoln.* Urbana: U of Illinois P, 1998. Print.

———, et al. "Reflections on Lincoln and English Studies." *College English* 72.2 (November 2009): 160–73.

Wilson, Rufus Rockwell. *Lincoln in Caricature.* New York: Horizon, 1953. Print.

Wolf, William J. *The Almost Chosen People: A Study of the Religion of Abraham Lincoln.* Garden City, NY: Doubleday, 1959. Print.

Zall, Paul M., ed. *Abe Lincoln Laughing: Humorous Anecdotes from Original Sources by and about Abraham Lincoln.* Knoxville: U of Tennessee P, 1995. Print.

———, ed. *Lincoln on Lincoln.* Lexington: U of Kentucky P, 1999. Print.

Zarefsky, David. *Lincoln, Douglas, and Slavery: In the Crucible of Public Debate.* Chicago: U of Chicago P, 1990. Print.

Index